P9-ECT-961

child of Satan, child of GOD

Susan Atkins
with Bob Slosser

LOGOS INTERNATIONAL
Plainfield, New Jersey

The excerpt from *Helter Skelter* by Vincent Bugliosi and Curt Gentry is © 1974 by Curt Gentry and Vincent Bugliosi. Used by permission of W.W. Norton & Company, Inc., the publishers. All rights reserved.

The excerpts from the Beatles' songs, "Helter Skelter," and "Sexy Sadie," by Lennon/McCartney are © 1968 Northern Songs, Ltd. All rights for the USA and Canada controlled by Maclen Music, Inc., % A.T.V. Music Group. Used by permission. All rights reserved.

CHILD OF SATAN—CHILD OF GOD
Copyright © 1977 by Logos International
All Rights Reserved
Printed in the United States of America
International Standard Book Number: 0-88270-229-7
Library of Congress Catalog Card Number: 77-81947
Logos International, Plainfield, New Jersey 07061

248.246
A53c

L. I. F. E Bible College
LIBRARY
1100 COVINA BLVD
SAN DIMAS, CA 91773

Then if any man shall say unto
you, Lo, here is Christ, or there;
believe it not.

For there shall arise false Christs,
and false prophets, and shall shew
great signs and wonders; insomuch that,
if it were possible, they shall deceive
the very elect.

Matthew 24:23-24

043409

ACKNOWLEDGMENTS

Without the vision and persistence of John Work and his wife, Sharon, this book would not have gone beyond the thought stage. As the president of the New Life Foundation, which provides the organizational support for Susan's ministry, John pushed, prodded, and pampered until the project was well on its way.

The authors also wish to thank Jamie Buckingham for his help and encouragement. And they are especially grateful to Frank Williams, Susan's correctional counselor at the California Institution for Women, whose faith in the project reduced many mountainous problems to molehills. Indeed, they are thankful for the help and courtesy extended by the entire staff at C.I.W.

v

The names of some of the peripheral characters
in this autobiography have been changed to protect them and others from harm that might result
from their identification. Names of all central
characters are actual.

Table of Contents

vii

1

MANSON

I gasped for breath and felt the dampness of perspiration across my lower back. Standing for a moment inside the door of the big brown house, I heard the pounding of my heart. There was a slight ringing in my ears. I was stoned.

The hallway was darkening in the late afternoon. No one was in sight. Faintly I heard music. "Someone's singing," I thought. I exhaled noisily, then stood still and listened. Somebody was singing upstairs. Delicate guitar patterns formed around the voice. I wondered. "No one here plays like that."

I waited, and my eyes adjusted to the dimming light. "Where is everyone?" I heard myself ask. My scalp suddenly tingled, and I felt goosebumps rise on my bare arms. Maybe the police had beaten me back to the house. They were really hot after Tom. I smiled. I had given them some chase.

Now what? I climbed the stairs slowly, my bare feet silent on the carpeting and my short skirt swishing barely audibly back and forth across my thighs. I turned to the left at the top of the stairs. The music came from the big living room. Passing through the massive, oak doubledoors, I was startled. My eyes landed instantly on a little man sitting on the wide couch in front of the bay windows. The fading sun's rays slanted through the partly opened curtains behind him, throwing his features into shadows. But I could see he was singing, his eyes seemingly closed. Without moving his head, he opened his eyes and stared directly into my face. I stared back.

A woman was seated on each side of him, and the rest of the girls in the house were ringed around him on the floor. Only two other men were in the room. A smoky haze deepened the tan aura of the wood-paneled room. The smell of marijuana was heavy, despite the sweetness of burning incense. Food and candy were piled high on the coffee table in front of the singer.

A slight smile flickered on and off the skinny little man's clean-shaven face. "The shadow of your smile when you are gone," he sang softly, seductively, "will color all my dreams and light the dawn." His voice was middle range and expressive. He played the guitar magnificently.

I stood for a moment longer at the doorway, fascinated by the scene before me. The women's faces were rapturous, uplifted toward the little man on the couch. Obviously most of them were stoned.

There was a space on the floor to the man's right. I tip-toed to it and eased myself cross-legged to the floor, my skirt rising nearly to my hips. He looked at me and smiled. I studied him, unsmiling. He had a tattoo on each forearm—the heads of women. He wore a white tee-shirt, blue jeans, and sandals, and several strands of multicolored beads hung from his neck almost to his waist. His small hands moved deftly upon the battered guitar. "He's like an angel." I don't think I spoke the thought aloud, but I was so loaded I couldn't be sure.

2

"I've got to dance—for him." The thoughts raced in and out of my mind. "He's playing pretty for us. I've got to show him what I can do. I've got to dance for him." But I was motionless on the floor. I watched the room deepen into brownness as the last sunbeams made little whirling figures in the smoke. I completely forgot my flight from the crazy cops. I was safe. Everything was beautiful.

I was aware that the man with the guitar had stopped singing. Voices and low laughter rose up and down almost lyrically. The little man's spell still prevailed.

He was talking quietly, and smiling. But he never looked at me. As my consciousness grasped that the music had stopped, I stared at the man's guitar. It seemed a thing of magic and wonder. "I'd like to play it," I thought. "I bet I can play it."

In a split second he turned his head slowly to look into my eyes. "Why don't you play it?" He started to move the instrument toward me. My mind swirled. Had I said that aloud? No. I had only thought it. How did he know it? "No, thanks," I said softly. "I can't play."

He smiled and looked, unblinking, into my eyes. It was as though something was sitting on his shoulder talking to something sitting on my shoulder. It was as though our minds were speaking.

In a second or two, he looked away and joined in conversation in the middle of the room.

"Who is this man?" I was shaken. "He's really strange."

Someone started the record player off to my left. It was The Doors—acid rock: "Break on Through to the Other Side." It was a driving beat, and my body began to move to it, even as I sat on the floor. The little man with the guitar was watching me again. I could feel it. "He's powerful," I thought. "He knows something. But he looks so ordinary."

3

His brown, rather wavy hair, fairly short, was combed straight back. He was just an unusual, little guy. "But I'm not sure I can handle him," I thought.

I got up and walked to the record player, flipping through the pile of records on the floor. The player was blasting out the driving, pounding music of The Jefferson Airplane—the White Rabbit album. I needed to dance. Some of the other kids had already begun. They were passing joints around, and the intensity in the room heightened. The thoughtful, melancholy mood established by the stranger burst into pulsating, stabbing emotion. I danced formlessly around the player as the record concluded. I stopped and dropped on another Doors record. It was alive, and furious.

I threw myself into the music and danced, lost within. "I'll dance for him." Within half a minute, the little man placed his guitar on the floor beside the couch and walked close to me. I sensed him more than I saw him. He began to dance behind me. The music was driving. I felt his hands on my hips, and he began to move my body. "What's he doing?" I thought in the storm of my mind. He was leading my body in movements I had never tried. Gently, with ever so little pressure, he guided my body in rhythmic, sensual variations. He moved very close to me, putting his arms around my waist from behind. He whispered into my left ear, "That's right. That's good. Yes. In reality—in your God-self—there's no repetition. No two moves, no two actions, are the same. Everything is new. Let it be new."

Our bodies moved together. Close. Then apart. We moved . . . he moved me. And we danced. It was all new. . . . It was all new. I was a good dancer, a professional dancer. I had done fantastic things with my long, slim body before the searching eyes of men. But I had never danced like this. I wasn't merely dancing. I *was* dance.

4

We swung to face one another, our bodies moving and jerking to the pounding drum beat. Suddenly, something happened that has no explanation. I experienced a moment unlike any other. This stranger and I, dancing, passed through one another. It was as though my body moved closer and closer to him and actually passed through him. I thought for a second that I would collapse. What had happened? Was I crazy? Had our physical bodies passed through one another? It was beyond human reality. As we turned to one another again, we mirrored each other perfectly. He moved as I moved. I moved as he moved. We were perfectly together—one. Something of him was in me. "That's it," he was saying. It seemed far away. "That's it. Everything is new." We danced savagely.

I don't know how much time passed. But, as though coming out of fleecy, white clouds, I became aware that the music had stopped. The stranger and I were standing face to face. He smiled. "You are beautiful," he said. "You are perfect. I've never seen anyone dance like you. It's wonderful. You must always be free."

For a few moments, I could only smile. I watched his face. Its features were slender, delicate, shifting into many expressions. His eyes were almost black, flat, hard. "Thank you," I finally said. I paused. "My name is Susan Atkins," I said. "Who are you?"

The eye contact was broken, and he lowered his head, brushing his hair with one hand. "Who? Me? Oh, I'm Charlie. Charlie Manson."

He turned toward the room. Most of the women were sitting on the floor again. He snapped his fingers once with a quick move of his left hand and said, "Let's go, girls."

Three of the women rose quickly and walked out behind him.

It was early afternoon two days later. The big brown house at Lyon and Oak Streets in Haight-Ashbury was quiet. The leaders, the men, were all in jail for selling drugs. What was to happen? Things were falling apart in our "family." I was fast falling into discouragement. We obviously couldn't survive without our men—Tom, the head of the commune; Bob, my man, who was second in command; and the others. I had been there several weeks and only occasionally felt the first tinges of acceptance. I could sense the smothering clouds of insecurity and dread rolling back in.

I walked into the second-floor hallway and there stood the strange little man, Charlie. He just stood there, empty-handed, slouched below his stretched-out, five-foot-seven height. "Hello," he said. Surprised to see him there, I said nothing for several moments.

"Hello," I finally said, unable to raise a smile.

"Where is everybody?" he asked.

"They were busted."

"Oh, no," he said softly. "I knew things were hot the other night, but I didn't know it happened."

I suspected he knew more than that. Somehow I thought he probably knew none of the men were there. But this only intensified the fascination he stirred in me. As we stood in the hallway, he seemed to change from a skinny, slouching little man in tee-shirt and jeans to a man with mysterious power. Suddenly, I was extremely vulnerable—but unafraid. I knew I had aroused interest in him. He was as attracted by the strong, willful spirit within me as I was by the powerful knowing spirit within him. I knew he was a challenge to me, and I suspected I was the same to him.

He watched me closely as we talked about the drug raid,

and I knew he was seeing inside me. I was tough, but still only eighteen. I felt my weaknesses—my fears—were being laid bare before his eyes.

"Why don't we go for a walk?" He said it matter-of-factly, simply. "You intrigue me. I'd like to talk to you about it."

We went out into the street and walked slowly, seemingly haphazardly, for several blocks. We ended up in front of a big, wooden apartment building, shabby and rundown.

"I'm staying here," he said. "Come on up and we'll talk some more." He said it so openly.

We stood in front of the mirror in the bedroom he had been given to use. It was a full-length mirror. He put his arms around me and we kissed, long and hard. Together we removed my clothes, and I stood naked before him. He looked at me in the mirror.

"Look," he said softly. "Look at yourself. You're beautiful."

Sex was nothing new to me. But his words still embarrassed me, and I was aware that the guy holding the apartment was just a few feet away in the living room. I looked at the two of us in the mirror. He was standing slightly behind me, holding my body.

"Don't be crazy," I said, half-giggling. "That's not beautiful."

He almost cut me off. "Yes. Yes! You are beautiful. You are perfect. You've got to see yourself as perfect—beautiful." His voice was low and soft. But even in its softness, it seemed to have an echo in it.

"You've got to love yourself," he said. As he talked, he kissed my shoulders and my neck. In the mirror, his eyes burned into mine. They never left my eyes.

"His eyes don't blink," I thought. I knew he saw inside of me.

Continuing softly, he said, "When you were a little girl, did you ever want to make love to your father?"

I was stunned. My mind went blank, and then raced swiftly over images of my dad. I'm afraid I giggled again. "Don't be silly," I said. "No."

"I know you have," he said. "You must be honest. Every girl at some time wants to make love to her father."

I was silent.

"You've got to be free of all your inhibitions and your fears. They're weighing you down. They're choking you. You've got to break free."

He moved his hands over my body, continuing to watch me in the mirror. "You've got to break free," he said again. My mind recalled the song by The Doors, "Break on Through to the Other Side."

"Make love with me." His voice was even lower. "Make love with me and imagine that you're making love to your father. You must break free from the past. You must live now. There is no past. The past is gone. There's no tomorrow. There is *now*. You've got to break free from your father. Now."

We made love in Charlie's bed. "How many others has he done this with right here?" The thought flashed into, and immediately out of, my mind. I tried to imagine that Charlie was my father. But my mind wouldn't hold that image either. It raced over and over Charlie's words. I knew he was right about the past. "I must live in the now," I thought. I was fully convinced.

It was late afternoon as we sat on a curb at the edge of the sidewalk. The streets were beginning to fill with people, the counter-culture people—"the hippies," the world called them. Haight-Ashbury in San Francisco was in full swing. I was well acquainted with it, having started with weekend flings into the life of a "flower girl" to escape the rushing, mindless, plastic world I had frequented as a topless go-go dancer.

Charlie seemed to talk in several directions at once, always driving in one way or another at escaping from the past and realizing the present. Sometimes it seemed that he babbled, but there was knowledge in it. There was power in his mind.

Suddenly he said, "Susan, if I postulate what I want, I'll get it, you know."

I didn't know what he was talking about. "What do you mean?"

"It's simple. If I think about a quarter, for instance—if I think about it, and see it, I'll get it."

I said nothing, watching the people go by. They were interesting—bearded, long-haired men in simple clothes; barefoot women, mostly young girls, in long dresses or faded jeans. Without warning, a young, brown-haired man turned around and walked up to Charlie. "Here, brother," he said, "I want to give you something." He put a quarter into Charlie's hand.

Charlie looked into my face. He said nothing. After a moment he got up and led me into a small fast-food shop and bought a cup of coffee with the quarter.

Back on the street, we walked along quietly. Rain was falling lightly, but it was warm. We started down an incline at a driveway and my bare feet slipped on the wet pavement. My body started backward. Suddenly Charlie grabbed my right arm and held me up. His face was close to mine. "I won't ever let you fall," he said softly. The words gripped me. *"I won't ever let you fall."* That's what I craved. I was a tough, streetwise, eighteen-year-old ready for a new world culture, but I needed someone who was stronger than I was. I needed someone who wouldn't fail me. I wanted Charlie to grab me and keep me from falling. He was short, skinny, almost emaciated, but he had strength. He had mind strength. I knew he would keep me from falling.

Even before he asked me, I knew I would leave the big brown house and go with him. He had other women with him; I knew that. But I wanted what he had.

"Come on," he said simply. "We're going to L.A."

The big, battered school bus had been remodeled inside as a camper. The seats had been replaced by a bed, sleeping bags, a sink, and odds and ends. I threw all my belongings into the back end, as did the five other women, and Charlie drove out to the highway and headed south. We were a strange-looking group—a skinny little man with a gang of girls yelling and laughing our way in an old, hollowed-out school bus.

It was late at night and we were somewhere between San Francisco and Los Angeles when Charlie pulled the bus off the road and stopped. We had picked up two guys and two girls who were hitchhiking south.

"Let's have a party," Charlie said, swinging out from the driver's seat. There were enough of us for that.

Each one of us dropped acid (LSD) immediately. And we all sat around on the floor of the bus. All but Charlie. He sat cross-legged on a huge pile of multicolored pillows, looking down on us. And he talked.

In minutes the scene was transformed. We all listened intently as Charlie talked. Suddenly my mind was paralyzed by the knowledge that I was going to die. I *was* dying. Through the paralysis came Charlie's words. "You are all going to die. You all must die."

It was the most frightening experience of my life. I looked at Charlie. His mouth was moving and his hands moved through the air, punctuating his words. But nothing was coming from his mouth. Yet I could hear his voice, eerie, echoing. I could hear his words plainly. "You are all going to die."

I turned my head. "My God!" I thought. "His words are coming out of the sink! He's speaking through the sink."

I looked up at him. He was still speaking, staring first straight ahead and then at one, and then another. "This is insane!" I screamed inside. But I kept my mouth closed.

"You must die to self," the voice said. "You must die. You must become one."

Suddenly the bus shook violently. It shook so hard that I nearly fell over. I looked at one of the guys leaning against the wall. I couldn't believe what I saw. He had turned to bones. He was all bones. A skeleton. He had no flesh or hair or clothes. Only bleached white bones. I couldn't believe it. The others watched him, too.

Then, just as quickly, his form, his flesh, returned, and he was the same young man. But his eyes were full of terror. Charlie slipped down from the pillows and yanked the boy to his feet. Like a flash of lightning he punched the boy in the mouth, knocking him to the floor. The force of the blow was superhuman. The youth screamed and cried, scrambling madly toward the front of the bus and the door. He tore it open and ran into the night.

Insane laughter filled the bus. It was Charlie's laughter—screeching, cackling, horrible laughter. It scraped nerves, grating, grinding. Charlie, standing in the

11

middle of the bus, had his head back and his mouth wide. But the laughter, the hideous noise, came from the sink. It boomed from the sink, filling the air.

I crawled on my hands and knees, dragging my drained, nearly paralyzed body across the hard floor, and clutched frantically at Charlie's leg. I grabbed it and held on. "Am I dying? Oh God, am I dying?" The words screamed in my head, but my mouth was tightly shut. I held onto his leg desperately. "I must hold on!"

Abruptly, everything became quiet. I was prostrate on the floor. Charlie went back to the pillows. The others sat or lay quietly. After several minutes, I was aware of people moving toward the door. All but our original seven left without saying anything. They disappeared into the darkness.

The bus was filled with fear. We were all afraid. I looked at Charlie, and his face was chalky white. He rubbed his hands back across his hair.

I walked over to him, and he looked up at me. "Did you see that?" His voice was almost a whisper, and it came from his mouth this time. He rubbed his head again. "My voice came out of the sink."

"Yes." That's all I could say. I didn't know what more to say. We had been out of control. We had been through something beyond this world.

2

JESUS

Someone spoke my name. It was a strong voice, a man's. "Susan Atkins." Mrs. Barstow—my Sunday school teacher—moved my arm toward the aisle, and with her other hand gave me a gentle shove forward. I looked at the front of the church sanctuary. Somebody, a man, was standing in front of the gigantic pulpit, and he was smiling at me, one of the smallest of the pre-school children. I was scared. But I walked toward the front, dressed in my finest white dress, black shiny shoes, and white stockings. People stretched and turned to see the tiny figure walking nervously down the aisle, the one who had received the greatest number of gold stars for her Sunday school lessons. I was not quite three years old on that Sunday morning in 1951.

I was aware of the man in the black robe in front of the pulpit, but all I really saw was the figure of a man hanging on a gigantic white cross, above and behind the black-robed man. I had never been in the sanctuary before. But I knew that the man on the cross was Jesus. I'm not sure how I knew. "Why is he hanging there?" I wondered as I walked slowly down the aisle. He was my friend. I had been taught that. He was gentle and good. And he loved little children. "Why does he have to hang on the cross?"

I reached the man in the robe, and he took my right hand, shaking it up and down. And then he handed me a Bible. I clutched it in both hands in front of me. It was white and beautiful, and my name was printed in gold letters on the front cover. I glanced swiftly up at the man on the cross. I hoped I had pleased him somehow. He loved little children, and I desperately wanted him to love me, too. People kept telling me he did, but I wanted to be sure. This was the first time I had seen him.

I turned and walked back up the aisle. I was still scared, but all the people were smiling at me. I looked down at the red carpeting on the aisle and went quickly to my seat. Mrs. Barstow guided me back into the pew.

It was a hot Sunday morning shortly after that first encounter with Jesus. I walked down the steps of our home in Milbrea, California, and saw my babysitter's dad standing in the driveway waiting to take all the kids to Sunday school. He had always taken us. Suddenly, he screamed and fell to the ground, clutching his head with both hands. He screamed louder. Everyone rushed to him. Neighbors ran to their front doors, and many went toward him. In a moment he was quiet. He died of a brain hemorrhage.

I stood in front of our house, terrified. I cried loudly and ran back toward the door. "Mama! Mama! What's the matter, mama? What's happening to him, mama?" I stood at the door and felt my body go rigid. I could hardly move. I could hear cannons exploding within my head, and red, white, and black flashes tore at my mind. I was horrified.

My babysitter, Shirley, was left without a father. I couldn't comprehend it. He was a wonderful man. I really loved him. And he was dead. How would I go to Sunday school now? "I won't go any more," I thought. "I'll never go again!"

The ambulance squad lifted the man onto the stretcher carefully and slid him into the back. I began to cry again. I knew I would never see him again. The jolly, kind, old man was dead.

I remembered Jesus hanging on the cross in the church. "Doesn't he love him just as much as the little children?" my frightened mind asked.

When my babysitter came the following Sunday, I refused to go with her. I would not go to church. My father became angry, but I wouldn't move. I stayed in my room.

Born May 7, 1948, I was five years old when we moved from Milbrea to San Jose. I didn't understand such things, but the Korean War had ended and everyone felt comfortable with General Eisenhower in the White House. But I wasn't all that comfortable. My mother had her third child, my little brother Steve, shortly after we moved. He demanded and received all her attention. I resented that, even though one part of me fully loved little Steve. And my father was always occupied with my older brother, Mike. They were forever doing things that looked like fun. I turned my love and attention to my Siamese cat, Pia. If I was going to be left out, I wasn't going to be alone.

It was nearing bedtime one night. Thunder was rolling across the sky, and lightning came faster and sharper. Soon the storm struck, and immediately the lights in our house went out. Mother quickly lighted two candles on the table and resumed rocking little Steve in her lap. Dad and Mike took a candle to the next room where they were playing a game.

The streaks and crashes came rapidly. Pia ran under the couch, and I was alone—and I was afraid. I sat for a moment and suddenly, with no apparent reason, I remembered the white Bible that had been given to me in Milbrea. I knew mother had packed it in one of the drawers in my room, but I hadn't touched it for two years. I ran to the room, and fumbling in the darkness found it, still clean and white.

Back in the living room, I went to one of the candles and started to thumb through the Bible. It contained color pictures of Jesus and other people. Some of the printed words were in red, too, amid the black lettering. I was deep in rapturous concentration and didn't comprehend my mother's excited words, "Something's burning." But I jumped when I heard my name, "Susan!" My mother's voice was almost yelling. "Susan! It's burning! Move! Quickly!"

I jerked backwards from my crouching position and fell over onto the floor, holding the Bible aloft. It was smoking. I dropped it to the rug, bottom side up, and, terrified, saw a black, ugly hole in the back cover. The flame from the candle had burned a hole in it. I slapped the spot over and over, and my mother grabbed it and riffled through the pages frantically to extinguish all the sparks. I was panic stricken. I had burned a hole in the Bible!

After a few hectic moments, I took it from mother and looked at the back. The beautiful, clean, white book was ugly—ruined. Tears flooded my eyes and I sobbed. Guilt swept over me and I couldn't control my tears even as mother stroked my head and told me it would be all right. I knew God would not forgive me for burning his book.

I thumbed through the Bible once more, slowly, and saw that the flame had burned right through the last section, the part I had trouble pronouncing—Revelation. I didn't understand all the words there, but the black hole burned into the pages frightened me.

I walked back into my bedroom and opened the bottom drawer of my chest, slipping the Bible back to the rear beneath a stack of sweaters and heavy clothes. I wanted it out of sight.

One day my father announced to us children that we were going to move to another section of town. Our opposition exploded. I wouldn't be able to leave my friends—we had lived there seven years—and my little brother sobbed in his despair. Mike didn't like the idea either, but he at least would be going into high school and would be with all his old friends. Our protests accomplished little, however, and we moved into a good-sized but modest home in the suburban community of Cambrian Park near the Blossom Hills.

One Sunday morning, our new next-door neighbors—a divorcee and her three children—asked me to go to Sunday school with them. I had been worse than irregular in going to church over the years, but the oldest daughter next door, Sherry, was fast becoming my best friend, and I thought it would be a good idea to go along with her. I sensed something special in Billy, the mother of the family, and I felt good going along with her.

Before long, I became a regular at the Cambrian Park Baptist Church. Each Sunday, the minister spoke about sin and people's need for salvation. His preaching struck terror into my twelve-year-old heart, and each time he invited people to go forward to the altar to repent, I was one of the first there. Each Sunday, week after week, I went forward and sobbed for the forgiveness of my sins. I knew I had many. The next day, or even the same afternoon, however, I put all that behind me and resumed my increasingly reckless life. But the next Sunday, there I was again, back at the altar rail. The minister never blinked an eye as this same girl kept showing up week after week to be prayed with. He preached on sin, and forward I went.

Over the next two and a half years, Sherry and I became intimate friends, but my heart grew warmest over her older brother, Albert. He hardly knew I was there. After strenuous days playing outdoors, Sherry and I would often allow our conversations to drift along serious, even solemn, paths during the summer evenings. We often talked about God. Sherry was convinced he was real; I, despite my weekly repentance, wasn't so sure.

"Okay, smart aleck," I said one sultry night. "What's he like if he's so real?"

"I don't know what he looks like," Sherry said quietly. "I just believe he's real. I know he's helped me and my mother a lot. And look at Lulu—she's only a kid, but she really loves God. Can't you see there's something different about her?"

I didn't say anything. But I remembered some of the times when little Lulu had pleaded with us not to do something mean or dangerous. She would always mention God.

"And what about my mother?" Sherry said, more vigorously. "She says Jesus is real and is with us all the time."

My love for Sherry's mother, Billy, rose in my throat. She was the kindest woman I knew. But I remained silent.

Sherry went on. "And I really think your mother believes in God. She acts like it to me." I wasn't so sure. I loved my parents, but I felt alone many times in my own family. I almost felt like an outsider when Mike and Stevie were around. And anger was beginning to smolder inside me because of something else I had recently detected. My mother and my father both drank a lot of liquor. I had become aware of it in my father several years before. I was certain he was an alcoholic—a word often used by other children about other people, but whose meaning was not quite clear in my mind. I knew that both my mother and my father were frequently drunk.

"Okay," I said. "Let's try something to see if God is real."

"What can we do?" Sherry agreed. We thought for several seconds in silence.

"I tell you what," I finally said. "Let's give God a present."

"What?" Sherry laughed. "How can we give him a present?"

"I don't know. There ought to be something. And if he takes it, he's real. If he doesn't, he's not."

We thought silently for several more seconds.

"I know," said Sherry. "Let's get a rose from your flower bed and put it outside. If it stays there, then he isn't real. If he takes it, then he's real."

"Okay," I said excitedly.

We got the rose, and stood in the middle of my backyard.

"Where can we put it?" I asked, holding the big pink rose carefully in two hands.

We looked around. "Let's put it in the center of that bush over there, way back inside where nobody can see it," Sherry exclaimed.

I agreed, and we carefully placed the rose back in among the branches of the six-foot-tall, heavily leafed bush. Then, standing shoulder to shoulder, facing the bush, we solemnly voiced a small prayer. "God," Sherry said softly, "if you are real, please take this gift from Susan and me. We both give it to you." Each of us said, "Amen."

Sherry went home and I went into the house.

I got up very early the next morning before anybody else was awake and went into the backyard. It was another sparkling, sunny day. Almost on tiptoe, I walked up to the bush. Lifting the branches, I stared at the center. All I saw was green branches.

"It's gone," I said inside. "It's gone!" I said aloud. "It's gone!" I shouted. The rose was gone. I got down on my hands and knees and scrambled around the bottom of the bush. Nothing was there except the bush. I looked all around the yard, but there was no rose. Then anger started rising in me. "I bet Mike and Steve took it," I said aloud. I raced into the house and into their room, but I knew from the surprise in their faces that they didn't know what I was talking about.

I raced next door to Sherry's. Her little sister was up, and let me in. I bounded down the hall and into Sherry's room. I was getting hysterical. "It's gone!" I cried. She looked at me in disbelief. "It's gone!" I shouted again. "He's real! He's real! God is really real!"

Sherry didn't believe me at first, but we ran together to my backyard and looked all around for the rose. I swore to her that I had not taken it, and I cried some more. We went back to her room and sat on the edge of her bed. First I would say it, and then she would echo, "He is real. God is real."

Later that summer, I was playing hopscotch on the sidewalk in front of our house as evening approached. I was the only one outside on the whole block, unusual for a summer evening in that suburban neighborhood. I smelled dinner cooking inside as I played by myself, determined to squeeze in as much time as I could before going in. The sun was getting low and its rays were intense in the pale blue sky.

Our community sat right at the foot of the Blossom Hills, a part of the Los Gatos range. And our home was only about three and a half blocks away from those hills, rising gently to the east and covered with fruit trees and grape vines. As I hopped on one foot, fully absorbed, I felt an unbelievably strong urge to turn around. Without much thought about it, I turned and looked at the hills. My feet froze on the sidewalk, and I became perfectly still. Fear pushed outward against my chest. Right before my eyes, just a few hundred yards away, was a huge burning cross. It covered half the hill—at least a hundred feet wide and a hundred feet long. I stared at it for several moments, but it was so bright it actually caused a slight pain in my eyes.

After several seconds I ran into the house, yelling, "The hill's on fire! The hill's on fire. It's burning like a big cross. It's on fire!"

My father looked up from his chair and said, "Take it easy, Susan. Calm down. What's the matter?"

"It's a fire, dad," I said, half-screaming. "Come and look. It's on the hill."

"I don't smell any smoke," he said, smiling up from the newspaper.

"But it's burning!" I exclaimed. "Come and look."

"Now, Susan," he said, "go back out there and take another look. I'm sure your eyes are playing tricks on you."

I was angry because he didn't believe me. But I turned and raced back out the front door and down into the yard. I looked up at the hills. My heart sank. The cross was gone. There was no fire. The beautiful trees and hills were just as they had always been. All I could see was a man carrying a

21

ladder toward a shed on the side of the hill.

I cried. I didn't let anyone see me, but I cried. I was angry and bitter and confused. The cross was gone. But I had seen it. It had been real.

I sat on the front porch step and cried. "That was God," I sobbed softly. "I know that was God. But nobody believes me."

3
DEATH

Karen and I stood on the sidewalk in front of the variety store, spellbound by the women's clothes. Eventually we worked our way to the lingerie display and stopped, staring in wonder at the flimsy articles.

"I've got to get a bra," Karen said out of the blue. I looked at her. "Mom won't get me one," she went on. "She says I'm too young." She paused. We were both twelve. "But I really need one." She blushed ever so slightly, and giggled. I giggled, too, because I certainly didn't need one.

"Let's go get one," I said with a toss of the head. I grabbed her hand and led her to the swinging door. The women's things were in the back and to the right.

"You wait here," I said to her. She knew my reputation. "I'll be back in a minute."

I went nonchalantly to the lingerie counter, stopping now and then to look at something in the glass case. I reached a rack holding brassieres of all shapes and sizes, from misses to matrons. I spotted the smallest one there. It was at the end. With a quick look around, I took it off the rack, examined it for several seconds, looked around again, and slipped it under my jacket. I started toward the front, not rushing so as to attract attention, and could see Karen on the other side, fidgeting quite noticeably. She had watched the whole thing.

So had someone else. One of the clerks. She cut me off as I turned to the door. "Just a minute, young lady." Panic filled my throat, and I thought I was going to be sick. I had been caught.

"Let me see what you have under your jacket."

There was nothing to do but hand it over. The lady called the store manager, who took me to his office and sent for the police. The manager pressed me to identify my accomplice, recognizing immediately that the bra was not for me. But Karen had stayed in the background and was undetected. I was handed over to a policeman. We rode in silence to my home as my mind whirred over my prospects. Could I jump out of the car and run? No. I'd get killed. Could I make up a story that would convince my mother? No. The police are always right. What could I do? Nothing.

We stood just inside the front door as the young officer, who didn't crack a smile throughout it all, told my mother what had happened. He spoke of my being sent to Juvenile Hall if I were caught again. Mom began to cry, jerking both hands to her face momentarily and then to her chest. I started to cry. The tears were real, but they were angry. For the first time, the policeman betrayed emotion and, embarrassed, quietly backed out the door.

My tears increased and I rubbed my eyes with clinched fists. I clinched them tighter. "They'll never catch me again," I thought. "I'll never get caught again."

I immediately remembered a similar vow nearly nine years earlier when I was between three and four years old. "I'll never get caught stealing again," I had sobbed after being soundly spanked by my father.

I was caught on my first venture as a thief. It was Christmas time, and we were at grandmother's house. We called her "Momo." Without announcement I walked to the corner store with nothing more than curiosity on my mind. It was a fascinating place. I walked in, unintentionally quiet and unnoticed. In fact, nobody seemed to be around. And there was the candy counter, with every kind of gum and penny candy imaginable lying right out in front. Again with little forethought, I reached up and helped myself to four penny Tootsie Rolls and strolled back out, still unnoticed.

Back at grandmother's house, I opened one of the Tootsie Rolls and bit joyfully into it. My dad watched me open the wrapper and wolf down the first piece before asking me, "Susan, where did you get the candy?"

A chill gripped me. "At the store," I said. "I found four pennies on the ground and bought the candy with those."

My father didn't accept the story, and I eventually acknowledged that I had stolen the candy. He took me by the hand and rather roughly walked me back to the store. Inside, he said to the elderly storeowner, "My daughter here took four pieces of candy from your store a few minutes ago. Now, she wants to return three of the pieces, and here's a penny for the fourth."

The old man looked at me. He had a white, bushy moustache and very soft, brown eyes. He didn't smile, but his eyes twinkled. Anger showed in my father's face and voice. "What do you say, Susan?" he asked.

"I'm sorry I took your candy without paying." I looked at his neck rather than his eyes. I was humiliated.

By the time I reached the third grade I was the best shoplifter in my neighborhood. I had a strong reputation

25

among all the kids, and that put me at the center of our loosely structured gang. If anyone needed clothes for her dolls, I could get them for nothing at the five and ten cent store. And I moved on to small items of clothing and accessories. But I left the gum, candy, and sodapop for the boys in the gang. They took care of the heavier things for our after-school parties.

I maintained mostly A's in school until the fifth grade, and then my downhill slide began. Up to that point, I mixed a number of wholesome activities with my escapades and presented at least a facade of respectability. There were Brownie meetings when I was younger, and then came Girl Scouts as I reached out more and more for a sense of belonging. One of my favorite times came during walks through the vineyard on the way to the old mission house where we held our scout meetings. I walked as though in a trance through the rows upon rows of vines, approaching the big old house at the center of the vineyard. I was in a fairy tale, warm and secure, on my way to my friends.

And then came boys and parties, more fun and freedom. But school was suffocating me. My first male teacher was a pushover, a soft touch. I had him around my finger. Why work? So my A average faded, and then evaporated, in the fifth grade. Finally, the assistant school principal called me to his office one day. "Susan," he said, his prominent jaw sticking out even farther in his close-mouthed firmness, "you've completely fallen apart. You're failing just about everything in sight."

If he wasn't going to smile, neither was I. I stared into his eyes, but he outlasted me. "I'm trying as hard as I can," I lied. "I try to do all the work, but I just seem to be having a bad time."

He interrupted. "It's so bad that you're not going to pass.

You're not going to make it into the sixth grade. You're going to have to repeat the fifth grade."

I was stunned, and my tough look crumbled. Tears filled my eyes, but I was determined not to cry. I didn't succeed. Tears slipped from my straining eyes as the news sank in. I would not move on with my friends. I'd be left behind. I was humiliated again in front of everybody.

The second year of the fifth grade was no better from my point of view and not much better from the school's. I passed, but my enthusiasm reached bottom. Boys and physical education—they were okay, in that order. English, arithmetic, geography—ugh.

My second brush with death began when I was fourteen years old.

My father did not look into my face. Twisting his hands together, he then stiffened them, and let them go limp. I knew what was coming. Mother had been in the hospital too long. There had been too many wrong diagnoses.

"Mom's got cancer," he said finally, simply. "They say it's terminal—she's not going to make it."

Panic surged into my throat; a bitter taste rose into my mouth. He continued to talk, but I didn't know what he was saying. My whole body shook, starting from my legs and then up into my torso and then my arms. I was very cold.

"What about Stevie and me?" I thought, trying to hold my hands still; they quivered perceptibly. Mike had enlisted in the navy as it became obvious American involvement in Southeast Asia was not decreasing, but Steve and I were still there. "What will we do?" I said to myself, knowing dad couldn't cope with us.

Our house grew quiet in those autumn days of 1963. It was quiet and gray, especially before mom was finally brought home and everything was left to her pain pills. I scrambled around the kitchen in the mornings and the evenings, trying to cook, to wash clothes, to cheer up Steve—trying to squeeze my way into the in-crowd at school but never making it—trying to find out what God was doing to me.

By mid-fall, I was exhausted, and my school work plummeted into nothingness. I was standing by the stove in the early evening as the outside darkness enveloped and then penetrated our house. I was tired and angry. In a flash, I understood my anger. I was mad at my mother for being sick, I was mad at my father because I didn't think he understood what a load I was carrying, I was mad at Steve because he needed so much help, I was mad at myself because of my resentment toward my own dying mother. "She's just let go," I thought. "She's just dying. I don't understand why. Why does she have to die?" I'd only seen one person die, and that had taken place quickly. Mom was dying right before my eyes, a bit each day. "She was beautiful," I thought. "But now she's ugly." I didn't like what I was thinking. I didn't like the flames of resentment consuming me within. I didn't like myself at all.

During this period of bitterness and regret, Sargent Wright, the pastor of the Cambrian Park Methodist Church, began to stop by our house regularly. Dad knew him from the time he had led the Boy Scout troop at the church.

"Why don't you come to church, Susan?" he asked me once. I didn't know how to handle his bluntness, so I said I would go. Week after week I went, hoping it might do something to change things. I even joined the choir and often volunteered as a babysitter for the nursery during church services.

One afternoon I walked into the house after school and saw Mr. Wright standing alongside mom in her bed in a room at the rear of the house. His head was bowed. Mom's eyes were closed. I couldn't hear what they were saying, but I assumed they were praying. When Mr. Wright left, he took my hand and held it for a moment, then smiled and walked out.

That night mom seemed to be smiling all the time. She even laughed out loud when she and dad were talking alone. It seemed that her room had gone from gray to bright blue and yellow and pink and even orange.

It was the third week in December when the young people in the choir met at the church to go caroling. I was happy when I joined them, ready to go to the houses of the old people and entertain them with carols. We piled into three cars and set off in the cold, biting air. There was no snow, but it was cold.

The kids said very little as we drove along until we reached my school. They saw me look at it, and traces of smiles began to show on their faces, but they were secretive. We turned the corner onto my street and I knew where we were going. Instantly my eyes filled with tears and I was unable to see. The cars stopped in front of my house, and the kids put their fingers to their lips and said, "Be quiet, now. We want to surprise her."

They had come to sing for my dying mother. I was crying openly as I rushed into the house and told mom to look out the window onto the patio. There they were, fourteen teenagers, boys and girls, forming a semicircle outside the window. We turned on the outside light, and they began to sing—"Silent Night."

Tears streamed down my mother's face. Dad was crying, too. I grabbed Steve's hand and squeezed it tight. We all joined hands and laughed and cried and laughed and applauded as they sang six of the prettiest Christmas carols

29

I had ever heard.

The kids left without me, and I stayed with mom for several minutes. She was smiling and happy, but she was quiet. She took my hand and drew me to her.

"Dear little Susan," she said softly. "Dear little Susan, it's been so hard on you." She looked at me silently for a moment. "I've asked God to let me stay with you until the New Year."

I was suddenly stone cold.

"I'm sure he will," she smiled. "He's been so good to us tonight. I'm sure he'll let us have the holidays together."

My mother died on January 9, 1964.

4

SLIDE

"It's a regular Peyton Place," I thought. And it was. Everyone in Los Banos, California—population considerably under ten thousand—knew everyone else. And everyone knew what everyone else was doing. In a high school of six hundred ninety students, that meant everyone knew who was joy-riding and having sex with whom. Those were the main preoccupations for the majority. I was in the majority.

Jeff was good looking, a football player, and he had a car. He was persuasive. "Susan, you're crazy. This is a whole different time. Things have changed." His left hand caressed my neck and shoulders; his right hand tightened around my waist. "You can't stay pure all your life."

I laughed within. "Pure! Who's he kidding?" But aloud I said, "Well, I can try can't I? What's wrong with wanting to save yourself for the right guy—for your husband?"

"Aw, come on," he chuckled. "You sound like my mother. That's for their generation. If you lose your virginity, who's ever going to know it? You might as well enjoy it now. Everybody else is."

I lost my virginity that night to Jeff during a party at an older bachelor friend's apartment. I was quite drunk.

My sexual purity was about the only thing I had held onto after my mother's death. At her graveside that day nearly two years earlier, with absolutely dry eyes and stony face, I turned loose of everything that I had clutched to my being. "I will not cry," I said inaudibly. "It won't bring anything back. They can all go to hell. All of them. All of humanity can go to hell. God can get lost."

I was cold. And alone.

Our move to Los Banos—with my dad and my brother Steve—was just one more step into bitterness and loneliness. I had resisted because of my friends in San Jose—and a boy friend, too—but dad was having trouble holding jobs, it seemed. I had no other options—for the moment.

Dad, Steve, and I moved into an apartment complex and I drifted drearily into a life of loathsome schoolwork, cooking, cleaning—and moral chaos. Guilt stabbed at me because of my inability, my unwillingness, to handle responsibility. "It's not fair that I have to do all this," I said aloud one night as I wiped crumbs from the tiny table that Steve and I had eaten our supper from. "Why do I have to do it? Why can't *he* do some?" *He* was my father. As on so many nights, he had not come home. He was drinking somewhere, trying to wipe away the memory of my mother's death.

I finished the dishes, looked at Steve in front of the television set, and went out into the darkness. "If he can drink all night, I can, too," I muttered angrily.

On the sidewalk in front of the A&W root beer stand, three of the guys and two girls were ready to go—anywhere. So off we went. After a while of purposeless driving, I asked to be let off on the outskirts of town, where the bars were.

For the next several hours I hopped from one bar to another, anywhere I could charm the bartenders into serving me. Dad never went to the outskirts. He would never catch me. I hated liquor, but I learned to force it down for the sake of a good time—sweet drinks when possible, grasshoppers, screwdrivers, stingers. It was better than being alone.

I had gotten my first strong taste of the lush life even before that, the summer after my mother died. Bitter, angry, and rude, I had agreed to go to stay with Aunt Ethel and Uncle Bob down in Whittier in the hope that I might find a new spark of life. Kindness flowed in Aunt Ethel's home, but I twisted it into opportunities for wild parties and the first steps toward alcoholism, which seemed to plague my family. The famous Southern California beaches weren't far away, and they were loaded with boys and girls. The bartenders were easy prey for my conning talents and ability to look older than I was.

It was my junior year in high school. Things seemed out of control. I had taken a job at the International House of Pancakes in Los Banos—good work, one of the best jobs available to women in that town at that time. It helped fend off the deterioration at home but added another strain to my overstretched life.

My homeroom teacher handed me a note one day. It was an instruction to see the dean of women that afternoon.

"Susan," Mrs. Edgeworth said, "I want to talk to you about your future."

I sat stonily, unblinking.

"We have spoken to you about your schoolwork. It's getting worse and worse."

I maintained silence, looking just below her eyes to make

her think I was staring her down.

"And now," she went on, "it looks as though you'll have to repeat your junior year next year."

"What else is new?" I heard my voice speaking inside of me. "You're nuts if you think I'm coming back here." But aloud, I said, "Quite frankly, Mrs. Edgeworth, I don't plan to be back next year."

She raised her eyebrows and pursed her lips.

I went on. "You see, I'll be eighteen before school starts next fall, and I'm going to leave school to take a job."

It was her turn to be stony. Several seconds passed in silence. "You're making a serious mistake, Susan. You'll regret it all your life."

For the first time I smiled, bitterly, arrogantly.

"I know things have been hard for you this year," she continued. "I know you've been under a heavy load. But to quit now is all wrong. You have a good mind, and you can build a good future. You can start by turning things around next fall."

The smile—bitter victory—stretched my face. I shook my head, slowly, back and forth. "Thank you, Mrs. Edgeworth, but I've already made up my mind. I'm leaving." I rose from the chair. "But who knows? I may try it again sometime."

"The next move," I thought as I walked out the door into the hallway, "is to get free at home. I've got to get out of this. I've got to get out on my own."

In the hallway, I was cold, even in the spring warmth. I was cold, and lonely.

I ran as hard as I could, but my feet were heavy. They hardly moved as I tugged and strained to get them off the ground. As I dreamed, I saw doors everywhere, dozens of them. All white doors. I couldn't see behind me clearly. Much of the place—the wide, sandy desert, or wilderness—was dark, cloudy. But a huge black sheet billowed and flapped noisily behind me, like the sound of bats in the night. It was close to me as I fled from door to door. I knew it would smother me. But I couldn't get into any of the doors. Their golden handles did not turn in my hand. Groaning, I tried to turn the handles, but my hands were weighted and numb. I couldn't clinch them tight enough to turn the handles.

Each of the doors remained shut as I raced up and down the shrinking area in front of them. I pulled and scratched with my finger nails on their shiny surfaces, but they wouldn't move. The flapping grew closer and louder. I tried to scream, but nothing would come out of my opened mouth. I suddenly heard Steve calling to me. He seemed to be behind me, but I couldn't see him. Then I heard a sobbing sound—long, deep sobs. It was my father. Where was he? He was behind me, too, but I couldn't see him. "I must find them." I could hear my voice. "But if I turn back, I will die." The billowing sheet was behind and above me. It was closer. "I'm going to die," my voice said. I could feel the billowing sheet.

I swung quickly to look at it. Who was waving it? "Somebody's there!" But it was a gray mass, a form, shapeless. "Who is it? Who are you?" I tried to scream again, but nothing came out of my mouth.

"The doors! I must get into the doors. It will be safe there." I threw myself against one, but it was like concrete. I crumpled to the ground, and the monstrous black sheet closed over me. "I'm dying! I'm dying! Steve! Daddy!" I stopped breathing.

I lay awake in the single bed in my tiny room. I yanked the

cool, white sheet off my face and breathed deeply. My heart pounded wildly, and I was drenched in perspiration. But my entire body, stiff in the bed, was freezing. I was all alone.

Late in the summer, I moved out of the apartment and into a room in the home of a little old lady. The rent was cheap and close to my work at the pancake house. In three weeks I turned eighteen, quit my job, and headed for San Jose. Back to the city and freedom. Steve would be okay for the time being. Dad could drink all he wanted, too, and who cared? So could I, and who cared?

5

SAN FRANCISCO

Night after night, for seven weeks, I returned to the tiny apartment. Most of my conversation was with the two gay men who operated the building. Sam was nice—good looking—but conversation was all he was interested in. I couldn't entice him. Joel was just too effeminate.

The other girls in the office seemed to disappear into the San Francisco evenings, and I returned to the one and a half rooms on upper Market Street that were described as a studio apartment—but without windows. Short, fat, bald Mr. Pritchard, the president of the company, had never followed through after his initial advances. Dollar signs were all over him and his green silk suit as he leered at me through his horn-rimmed glasses that first day.

"I can do great things for you," he had said, unabashedly surveying my lean figure, theatrically heavy makeup, and short, bleached hair. "I'm going to put you into the field as a follow-up girl." His company was in the magazine subscription business, and I had been hired as a telephone surveyor through a newspaper ad and interview in San Jose with young, ambitious Jim, my supervisor.

But the talk had been bigger than the payoff. I hadn't even received any money yet. Just an apartment and a blue Rambler station wagon. It seemed I was being kept—but with no money—and my skimpy savings from my waitress work were just about gone. And neither Mr. Pritchard nor Jim had followed through on their obviously intrigued first glances. I wasn't sure what was going on.

It was Thursday night. And I was alone. With a hard snap, I turned off the television set and threw myself face down onto the bed. I sobbed and cursed deep in my throat, pounding the pillow with my right hand. "I won't go back!" I cried aloud. "I'll die back there." I wanted to call home. My mind swirled madly—black and white streaks spinning round and round, first like a cylinder, then like a wheel. "But I won't call them. I hate them. To hell with them!" I pounded the pillow viciously.

Suddenly I saw a printing machine—a teletype machine. It silently spelled out words in my mind. "Your pills. Codeine pills." I knew instantly what they were. After a trampoline accident the year before, I had been given a bottle of codeine pills for pain in my sprained knee. I had never taken any of them.

Pushing myself up from the bed, I went to the tiny bathroom. There they were, in the medicine cabinet, untouched. I took the bottle—there were at least a dozen pills in it—and went back to the bed. I could still see the teletypewriter. "Slender Thread," it wrote. I said it aloud, "Slender Thread?" I smiled. *Slender Thread* was a Sidney Poitier movie I had seen late one night.

I rose again, went back into the bathroom, ran water into a glass, and swallowed all the codeine pills, three and four at a time. The teletypewriter continued to pound out words—like a script.

Returning to the bed, I grabbed the telephone book from the night table and found the listing for hospitals. "Emergency room." That's what I wanted. I placed the telephone on the floor beside the bed, dialed the number, and lay back on the bed.

A woman answered. "Emergency room."

"Hello. I want to talk to somebody."

"What about?" The woman's voice was level, but rushed.

"I'm not going to be here long," I said solemnly. "I'm going to be with my mother."

The voice tightened slightly. "Where?"

I paused for two or three seconds. "In heaven."

"Oh, I see." The voice became softer, confidential. "I hope you haven't done something foolish." I detected a muffled sound, then the voice continued. "Why don't you tell me what the problem is? Let's talk about it."

I smiled. She was stalling for time—just as I had known she would.

"Oh, you'll see pretty soon," I said, quite cheerily in fact.

The woman, obviously a nurse, talked on swiftly, but gently, without panic.

I saw the teletypewriter. "Give her just enough time," it spelled out a letter at a time. Several minutes went by.

"I have to go now," I said abruptly. "Thanks for talking with me."

I put the receiver down, pushed the button, but then left the receiver off the cradle.

Forcing myself up from the bed with some difficulty, I fastened the chain lock on the door, but left the door ajar. The chain could be snapped. I smiled at the deadly melodrama I was playing out.

I rummaged through my chest of drawers and pulled out the old, white Bible. It was scuffed and turning gray. The hole through Revelation was as ugly as ever. I withdrew the picture of my mother that was tucked inside and returned to the bed, sprawling face up. My arms and legs felt removed, no longer part of me. My head seemed hollow. I put the Bible under one arm and the picture under the other and closed my eyes. The teletypewriter was gone.

"What if they don't come?" I thought frantically. I tried to sit up but was unable to move. "My God! I hope someone finds me!"

Then in the distance I heard sirens. I smiled.

Soon I heard a buzzer. It was so far away; it must have been the basement flat. Then there were excited voices, shouts. A fireman burst into the room. I forced my eyes open momentarily.

"My God!" a man shouted. "It's just a kid!"

Everything became jumbled. Somebody yanked on my arms, pulling me to a sitting position. Then he put his arms around my waist and jerked me to my feet. His face was close to mine. Then he reached up and slapped me. It hurt. He slapped me again. "Come on, walk," he said. "You can walk, young lady. Now walk!"

He dragged me across the floor. "Walk, damn it!" Back and forth we went. "Walk. That's it. Keep moving your feet."

Several men were in the room. Some were policemen, I thought.

We walked and walked, back and forth, without stopping. Several minutes went by. Suddenly someone took hold of my chin and held my head up. "This is coffee, now," he said. "Drink it."

It was scalding. "I know it's hot," he said. "But drink it. Don't horse around." He spilled as much down my chin and the front of my sweater as went into my mouth. I wanted to smile, but I couldn't.

There was a guy on each side of me then, walking, walking, walking. They were firm, rough.

I didn't remember the ride in the ambulance, but I soon found myself sitting on a table. One of the firemen was there—the head one—and he was angry. "It beats me why they do something like this."

A nurse put a plastic cup in my hand. "Drink it," she said.

"No more coffee," I mumbled—my first words since arriving.

"No, it's not coffee," she said. "Drink it, and do it quickly. All of it." She shoved it against my lips.

Before I knew it, I was vomiting—over and over. I had never vomited so much. My stomach ached. A nurse led me to a stretcher pad on the floor in the hall and told me to lie there. I learned later that a nurses' strike had left the hospital understaffed and overworked. They just didn't have enough time to give to someone like me.

Three hours later I was taken back into the emergency room, where I overheard one of the supervisors ask, "Should we put her in ninety-day observation?" I couldn't make out the muffled answer, but in less than a minute, a man in a gray suit walked up to me and sat on one of the tall, four-legged stools in the room. "I'm here to talk to you about what you did. I'm Dr. Stone."

Fully aware of my surroundings, but sick to my stomach and aching all over, I was instantly angry. Everything was rotten. "Get the - - - - out of here," I shrilled. "I don't need any - - - - - - - psychiatrist to tell me what's wrong. I just want to go home."

He left. And ten minutes later a nurse supervisor, a gentle woman, came up to me. "Who can we call to help you?"

"Call my boss," I said. "He'll come and get me."

Back at the apartment, Jim, my supervisor, was making scraping noises in the tiny alcove that was called a kitchen. He turned around with a smile on his face and moved like a tightrope walker toward me with a bowl of steaming chicken soup. I lay on the bed with both pillows piled behind me and slowly spooned the soup into my mouth. He sat in a chair three feet from me and periodically reached toward me with a paper napkin. The soup kept dripping onto my chin. I was like a little kid to him, I was sure.

Finally, he asked the question he'd been wanting to ask. "Why did you do it?"

There was a long silence as I pressed the napkin to my lips. "I was lonely, I guess. This apartment is a box. I feel all cut off."

"Well, we can fix that," he said. "We'll get you something else."

In a few minutes he left, standing at the door and looking pitifully toward me. I was a mess. "If you need anything, call me. And don't go anywhere tonight."

The next morning Jim took me to a second-floor apartment in a building next to our office building. I stood in the door and looked at the big living room. It was fine—spacious and loaded with windows. But it had no furniture. All I had were my clothes and a mattress. "Well," I said with a shrug, "I can always use boxes. At least it's not a chicken coop like the other one."

Late that afternoon, after having wrestled the big mattress out of the first-floor apartment and into the back of the Rambler wagon, I stood on the sidewalk in front of my new building. "I can't get that mattress up two flights of stairs," I said to myself.

I stood on the curb and looked to the right and to the left. Two doors to the left was a bar. "Maybe there's some help in there," I smiled. I went into the dark, long room, stopping just inside the door as my eyes adjusted to the change in the light. A half-dozen men were seated on barstools. I put my hand on the doorjamb and leaned rather dramatically against it. "Is there a man here who'd like to help me carry my mattress upstairs?"

Everyone swung around to look at me. A smile was on each face, and some began to laugh aloud. I refused to let it faze me and maintained a big, knowing smile for several seconds.

Two men—one a big, blond guy—got up and said, "Sure, we'll help you. Where is it?"

I led them to the car and they easily carried the three-quarter mattress up to the empty apartment, flopping it onto the floor and turning to me.

I gave them my biggest smile. "Thanks."

"Is that all?" the smaller one said with a leer.

I stared right back at him. "Yes, that's all." My voice was even, but sharp. "Thanks."

They both laughed and went out.

When I went down to the street to get my clothes—a suitcase and a medium-sized cardboard box—the big, blond guy was standing by the car. "Hello again," he said. "I'm Bill. Can I help you with the other things?" He seemed genuinely interested in helping me, and he was good looking.

"Sure," I said, and he carried the box as I walked ahead with the suitcase.

"Since you're new around here," he said easily, "why don't I take you out to dinner tonight and show you around?"

"Sounds like a good idea to me," I said. "There's not much here but four bare walls right now."

We ended up in his apartment. His gentleness and easy strength were just what I needed. We made love that night.

We spent many evenings together in the next three weeks, mostly in bars or his apartment. With him, I seemed to be able at least to get my head above water. But twice during that period I fell back into great loneliness and depression, and had to be taken home by two considerate bartenders. I became so drunk that I couldn't walk. At other times, I boarded a streetcar and rode up and down the streets of the city, watching the people and fantasizing about their worlds.

One night, I sat at the bar near my apartment and saw Bill's friend—the one who had helped with the mattress—stagger through the door. He stood weaving for several seconds and came over to me. He was very drunk.

"Hi, Tony. Where's Bill?"

He looked at me, and then at the floor. "He's dead."

I knew he was serious. The muscles in my face froze. "What do you mean?" How can he be dead? I was just with him night before last."

Despite his drunkenness, Tony spoke clearly but slowly. "He went up into the mountains with two other guys—climbing."

My hands shook, and I was suddenly very cold.

"Bill fell, and was killed." He started to sob softly.

My body was rigid; my jaw muscles were tight. "Crying's not going to bring back the dead, Tony. I know."

I got very drunk that night. I don't know how I got home.

My next affair began with an automobile accident. The Rambler wagon stalled on the streetcar tracks in heavy traffic and before I could get out it was struck on the driver's side by a streetcar and pushed seventy-five feet along the street. The impact knocked the passenger door open and threw me halfway out of it. I was dazed.

A police car and an ambulance quickly arrived and people were running around in several directions. I sat half in and half out of the car, my dress riding high on my thighs. I didn't bother to lower it. "Let them look," I thought.

The ambulance medic obviously looked, and helped me out of the car. I seemed okay, but he said, "You'd better get checked out at the hospital. There might be something wrong that you don't know about."

So, for the second time in less than a month, I was on my way to an emergency room—this one in a small clinic. An intern pulled and poked for a couple of minutes and pronounced me unhurt.

As I left the room, the young medic was waiting. "Let me take you home," he said.

"Okay," I responded, "if you're sure you want to."

Among other things, I convinced him as we drove to my place that I was twenty-two years old and quite sophisticated. Meanwhile, I was nervous about the company car. "My boss will kill me," I said.

"He doesn't have anything to blame you for," the medic said. He turned out to be right. The transit department accepted responsibility and made a settlement for the car. But I was determined to leave the company anyway. I still hadn't been paid anything. Jim, the supervisor, kept telling me I was on commission and would get my money in one sum.

"To hell with that," I said. "I'm quitting and taking a job that will pay money."

The medic, who was growing romantically serious about me, introduced me to a friend who recommended me for a waitress' job at a corner coffee shop. Things were complicated with the medic—he was too straight, too clean, for my tastes—but he opened the way for me to support myself. Tips were good for a girl who knew how to smile and walk right.

I had to move out of the apartment and into a seedy, old hotel that had all the earmarks of skid row. "But at last I'm supporting myself," I said, "even though this really isn't up to what I expected."

The room, at fourteen dollars a week, was on the third floor of the three-story building. The wallpaper was filthy gray, with faded burgundy-and-olive-green flowers, which were bleached out almost into nonexistence. I could almost feel the grit in the ancient carpet, deep burgundy with a dirty cream design. I was glad to have windows, even if they were so streaked and dirty that the sun could hardly penetrate them. The drapes, ceiling to floor, were just as dirty as the windows. For furniture there was a wrought-iron, sagging bed that squeaked, an overstuffed, worn-out chair, an old dresser with a huge mirror, a wardrobe, a little coffee table in a musty bay window area, and an old metal pitcher, a wash basin, and a towel rack on the wall. The bathroom was at the end of the hall, to be shared with the old women and men living out their lives, often in drunkenness. I seemed to fit in well with them.

One night, about 7:30, there was a knock at my door. I opened it and a huge, burly man in a gray suit was standing there. His neck bulged over his shirt collar and his tie was pulled into a tight knot like a piece of string. He was a private detective.

"Your brother Michael has hired me to track you down, Miss Atkins. He wants me to bring you home."

Fear caused my skin to tighten. "My family has found me!"

I shrieked to myself. Aloud, I said calmly, squinting my eyes into hardness, "Tell him to go to hell."

I started to shut the door, but the man showed no sign of moving. I opened it wide again, and looked him straight in the eyes. "And you get the hell out of here, too, or I'll call the cops and have your - - - locked in jail. Get lost!"

I closed the door, turned the key loudly, and went to the middle of the room, clasping my hands around myself. I was cold and shivering.

I walked down the grim, smelly hallway, tired and ready for bed. Suddenly my eyes felt as though they would pop out of my head. My door was ajar an inch or two.

I was terrified, but I knew I had to go in. I grabbed the knob and flung the door wide open. I couldn't believe it. My father was slumped into the overstuffed chair, half-conscious. It took about a second and a half to see that he was hopelessly drunk. He opened his eyes and looked at me. Tears slipped over onto his cheeks.

"What are *you* doing here?" I screamed, planting both feet firmly in front of him and letting my rage roll out.

"Hello, Susan." He tried to continue talking, but sobs tore at his throat. He cried for several minutes. I just stood there, determined to say nothing. But my insides were pushing down on my bones and muscles like great weights. From my chest to my groin was one solid concrete block. I was afraid I would collapse.

"Can I stay, Susan?" he sobbed. "I don't have any place to go."

"What do you mean—stay *here*? In this lousy one room? Where do you think I'm going to stay?"

"I'll just stay right here in the chair," he sobbed.

I turned silent, refusing to talk to him the rest of the night. I immediately changed into my pajamas behind the wardrobe and went directly to bed.

The next morning began where we had left off.

"Susan, why don't you come back with me and Steve?"

"Are you kidding?" I smiled sarcastically. "Back with you and that life? I've had it with you."

He was unable to argue as tears once again overcame him. "Why don't you be a man and take hold of me and make me go back?" The thought startled me. I was sure I hadn't said it out loud. Instead, I said, "Yes, I've had it. I'm out on my own, and it's going to stay that way. And I don't want you and that stinking detective bothering me any more. Do you understand?"

I was amazed at my viciousness. I repaid in full for old injuries, for old resentments, for drunkenness, for mother's death.

My father cried as he left. I could feel the cold concrete block in my chest.

6

CRIME

It was the night shift. The boss was upset about something, but at first I didn't pay much attention. Then I understood what was bothering him. "If those guys don't clear out of the back alley in five minutes, I'm calling the cops," he said through clinched teeth.

"What's going on, Max?" I asked.

"I don't know except those guys are laughing and talking out there, and they're up to no good; I can see that."

"What are they doing?" I persisted.

"I can't tell for sure. They just seem to be drinking beer and shooting the breeze."

When Max wasn't looking I opened the door to the alley and stuck my head out. There *were* four guys—men—just outside the door. "Hey, you guys," I whispered as loudly as I dared. "You'd better get going. My boss is going to call the heat on you."

I went back into the coffee shop. Things were slow.

Five minutes later, the four guys walked in the front door. They seemed to be in their early or mid-twenties. They didn't look as though they had enough between them for a cup of coffee, let alone for the fifty-cent-a-person minimum charge for the booth they crowded into. They didn't sit in my area, but I decided I should wait on them just the same. They might get into more trouble. Besides, the tall blond was really handsome.

"What'll you have, fellows?"

As I suspected, they didn't have enough for the minimum.

"Don't worry about it," I said. And I brought each of them a piece of pie and a cup of coffee, paying for it out of my tips. "I'm dead if Max catches me," I thought, but I was curious about the foursome and interested in the blond.

"When do you get off work?" he asked as I brought the pie.

"Why?" I asked.

He smiled. His teeth were beautifully white. "Just curious."

"At eleven." It was eight-thirty.

They returned a few minutes after ten, going to the same booth. They had more coffee.

I walked out the front door with a smile in their direction. They got up and followed me out. I started up the street toward my hotel. I could hear footsteps behind me. It was just one person. I managed a sidelong glance behind me. The good-looking blond was about fifty feet away. My heart began to pound, and I was excited. My latest attachment, Bob, was just too dull. He loved me, and wanted to marry me, but I needed more excitement than he could generate. The man behind me was exciting. I sensed it.

The faster I walked, the faster he walked. When I slowed, he slowed. Finally, I stopped and he came up to me, smiling that full, handsome smile. "I just wanted to thank you for saving our skins tonight. We shouldn't have been making so much noise. We could have gotten busted over nothing."

"That was nothing," I said. "Max was just jumpy."

"Well, thanks for helping us, and thanks for the pie, too."

We stood on the sidewalk looking at each other. "Can I walk you home?" he asked, finally.

"Sure, if you want to," I said, as nonchalantly as I could.

We reached my fleabag of a hotel and before I was even aware of it, I had asked if he wanted to come up.

"Sure," he said, "if you would like to talk awhile."

"Talk?" I thought.

But that's what we did. I was astounded. That mysterious young man—he told me his name was Al—merely sat and talked to me, about everything under the stars, until the sky began to lighten. He made no passes at me. We didn't even kiss. He was too occupied with his dreams of getting together enough money to go to Oregon, buy a place, and settle down. It was fascinating. But I wasn't sure I believed it all. He was too much of a man to be vanishing off into the woods somewhere.

When the sun finally appeared over the building tops, he asked me if I wanted to go for a motorcycle ride with him through the San Francisco hills in the early morning.

"Why not? I'm not sleepy."

I changed clothes and away we went. At his place I was surprised to find six men living together in one large room. They seemed rough, but they were certainly polite enough to me, and they seemed to hold Al in especially high regard. They made me uneasy, but that all vanished as we roared off on his bike.

It was near noon when he stopped. Al turned to me abruptly and said point blank, 'I'm going up to Oregon to take care of some things that have to be done, and I'd like for you to come along with me. I want you as part of my life. And when things get straightened out, and we can settle down, I'd like you to be my wife."

I immediately knew I would go with him. "If you're sure you want me along, then I believe I'd like to go."

"That's good," he said. "Cliff—he's one of the guys back at the house—he'll be going with us."

My face showed my disappointment.

"But you won't mind him," Al pressed on quickly. "He'll just be with us for a while. You and I will be together."

I had faith in Al. I knew he could take care of me. He was big, beautiful—and mysterious. I was in love with him and with the mystery of him. Even if he wasn't precise about what was ahead, I still trusted him.

"Okay," I said. "If that's what you want."

The brand new Buick Riviera was smooth and quietly powerful. All my belongings were packed neatly in the trunk, and my job, my hotel, my dear, dull boyfriend, Bob, were all far behind. Stockton, California, was not far ahead.

Clifton was a surly, unlikeable fellow. He and Al talked softly and sporadically as I slouched between them, sometimes dozing, sometimes staring into the star-filled night. The radio played good music—the Beatles were sweeping the country. It soon became clear to me that the motives for their trip north were not especially honorable. They apparently had robbery in mind. Both were ex-convicts. My big, handsome, mysterious Al had spent a lot of time in prison, it seemed, and was then on the run from his parole agent. Clifton declined to tell me what he had been in prison for, but the look on his face frightened me, even without words. He, too, was on the run. And the rented car was by then a stolen car. I was glad to feel Al close beside me. I leaned into his warmth.

"I'm involved with criminals." The thought finally

penetrated my consciousness. "The kid from the green country is running with two cons." I didn't know if I should laugh or cry. An inward chuckle finally prevailed. "Just like the movies. It sure beats rotting away in that hotel. And my old man can't bug me any more."

I began to piece together the immediate plans. Way back behind my suitcases in the trunk was a high-powered rifle. It would serve to get more guns, which would open the way for a big heist. "Then," Al said over and over, "we'll have enough money to get married, buy a home in Oregon, and go straight."

My faith in him was so great that I believed him.

In three or four days, we abandoned the Buick, guessing that an alarm for it was out by then. Using money stolen late at night from a gas station, we acquired what seemed to be the perfect car for us, a well worn, nondescript Rambler sedan, just right for young people doing some camping in the beautiful Oregon countryside.

Equipment was easy to steal from the local stores, and we had everything we needed for camping in the woods near a river. Our chosen site was actually property owned by relatives of Clifton. My main concern was their reaction to the noise of our target practicing with the rifle and the two handguns acquired by Al and Cliff. They were turning me into a sharpshooter.

One late afternoon we prepared to go to town for supplies, but the Rambler's battery was dead. "What do we do now?" asked Cliff.

"Let's go up to your cousin's and see if he'll drive us into town to get a new one," replied Al calmly.

"It's worth a try," said Cliff, "but don't be surprised if he says no. I'm not his favorite cousin, you know." Cliff smiled, evilly, I thought.

We were camped more than half a mile from the cousin's mobile home. As we approached it, we saw two Highway Patrol cars in the driveway.

"Hold it," Al said quickly. The next thing I knew I was rolling side over side with another body down a scratchy, rocky ravine. The other body was Cliff's. He had his right hand clamped tightly over my mouth. My hands and wrists were scraped and scratched by the small, wiry bushes. They stung, and I sat upright, brushing the dirt away from them.

"Be quiet." It was Cliff. Al was nowhere in sight.

Before I could ask, Cliff said, "Al's gone around back to see what's going on."

"Just like the movies," I thought. But I didn't smile inside. I was scared and confused. Cliff had a revolver in his hand, and the sight of it brought back his words in the car one night, "When you see cops, shoot first. Don't play around."

Lying at the bottom of the ravine, he whispered to me, "I told you you were in this with us, but I don't think you believed me. Maybe you should have split when you had the chance. It's too late now. You're part of the stolen car and now you're running with us." His smile was almost a sneer. I still didn't like him. And my fear was deepening.

In a few minutes, we heard Al's birdcall whistle and he slid quietly down the ravine to my side. The fear eased. "We've got to go," he said in a whisper. "They're after us."

For a day and a half we walked north, staying several feet off the road and running for the woods when we heard anything approaching. Our progress was slow during the daytime and we sat out a lot of the daylight hours. The first night, a strong wind and rain storm drenched us, but we kept moving in the dark. I was ready to give up.

"You guys had better go on without me," I said desperately. "I'm holding you up. You're just going to get busted. I can go up to a farmhouse and give them a sob story. They'll take me in."

Al shook his head. "Absolutely not," he said. "We're not leaving you behind. You and I are together."

And Cliff wasn't about to go without Al. He, too, saw him as a protector.

"I'll tell you what, though," Al said. "We're not getting anywhere with all this running and hiding. We haven't seen a cop car in hours. So let's stop hitting the dirt every time we hear something coming."

Cliff wasn't happy with that proposal. "They'll bag us for sure."

"Maybe not." Al was aggressively positive. "We'll get out of here faster. They've probably given up on this road anyhow."

That seemed to settle it. Cliff was obviously against it. But I wanted only to be close to Al.

Ten or fifteen minutes passed. Then we heard a car coming. Cliff and I both looked at Al. He kept walking.

It was a Highway Patrol van.

The next thing I knew I was lying face down on the concrete highway, with a booted foot pressed into the small of my back. A shotgun was aimed at my head. "Don't make one false move or you're dead," said a voice above me.

We were searched head to foot, then handcuffed behind our backs. With my head resting on the pavement, I looked solemnly at Al. I could feel a tear running across my nose.

One of the two patrolmen spoke enthusiastically to the other. "It's a good thing we got that alert down the road there. We might never have spotted them."

Just three miles up the road, they had received a radio description of two men and a woman, armed and dangerous, wanted on suspicion of robbery and parole violation.

Al managed a smile at me. "We almost made it, kiddo."

Three months later—three months among hardened prisoners in Rock Butte county jail—I arrived back in San Jose, free on a suspended sentence and two years' probation. My father and Aunt Joy met me. I was stone cold inside. I could not smile, even as I embraced each of them. This was not my family, although I agreed to stay with my aunt. The warmth had long ago dissipated. Life was somewhere else.

And then, there was Al. His parting words echoed in my head: "Don't get lost, Sue." I would probably never see him again. The one I had chosen as my refuge was locked securely in prison.

7

BREAK

"Just like the movies." The thought stuck with me.

Dan the sailor was absorbed in rolling a cigarette—a joint. He held the small pouch of marijuana between his legs and carefully rolled a cigarette, then a second, then several. Dan was a nice guy, medium height, with black, wavy hair. "You'll really like it," he had said in the cheap lunch room-pool hall where we'd met just two hours before. "It beats booze."

That was a welcome thought. Liquor seemed to do very little for me anymore except leave me with a hangover. I was drunk a lot, but enjoying it less. I wanted something different.

I watched him intently. He was still young but seemed to know what he was doing. The idea of the movies filled my mind. It was just like the film they had shown us in high school about drugs. "Don't abuse them," it had said. And it had shown a scene of two kids in a cheap flophouse, just like the one we were in. One buck per room. A chair and a bed—dark, damp, and smelly. Dan sat on the edge of the bed, and I sat in the rickety, straightback chair. The scene was right out of that movie. It gave me the creeps, but I sat still and watched.

He lit one of the joints and handed it to me. Then he lit one for himself. We said little and did little, except inhale deeply and let the smoke swirl around us. Not much happened. But then we smoked two more, and the movie scene seemed more far-fetched. It felt really good. I was happy and relaxed.

"They didn't know what they were talking about in that movie," I said aloud.

"What's that?" said Dan dreamily.

"That movie I saw in high school about dope. They didn't know what they were talking about. This stuff is good. How can anything this pleasant be all that bad?"

Dan smiled. "Yeah. It's the same old crap. Don't do this. Don't do that. Don't even live." He laughed. "You're right. They don't know what they're talking about."

We spent the whole night in the flophouse. But we only smoked and talked and dozed. Dan didn't try to get me into bed. He liked me just for myself, he said. I wasn't used to that sort of attitude in the bars I had been hanging out in. I'd been sleeping with one guy after another ever since landing in San Francisco for the second time.

Four months had passed since my arrival back in San Jose, my head hanging and my lover, Al, locked up in the Oregon penitentiary. I had lasted less than a month with my aunt, then took off once again for San Francisco. Max had given me my job back at the coffee shop, I had moved into a two-dollar-a-day hotel on Market Street, Bob had forgiven me for my "little fling" but he was duller than ever, I had reported regularly to my probation officer, and I had hopped from bar to bar night after night. I needed excitement.

"Maybe grass is the answer," I said aloud, dragging on

another joint and watching Dan's head sink lower onto his chest.

The early evening was quiet as I stretched full length in the overstuffed chair by the cloudy window in my little room. "You're eighteen, and what have you done?" I thought. "What are you *going* to do?" The room was quiet. Once again, the full, choking feeling of loneliness swept over me. I was cold.

"You've been in jail, you've deserted your family, you're an alcoholic, and you're no better than a tramp with the neighborhood men. How much lower can you get?"

My cheeks were wet. I was crying without knowing it. "I can go a lot lower," I said audibly. A sour taste flooded my loneliness. "I'll show them how low I can get. They think I'm in the gutter now. They haven't seen anything."

I got up, the tears still streaming over my cheeks, and changed clothes, putting on a mohair suit and high heels. "Everybody's talking about drugs—this LSD stuff—let's see what they're talking about." The thoughts raced quickly through my mind. "They were full of crap about grass. Let's see what they know about LSD." I didn't have the slightest idea where I was going, but I was going.

It was nine o'clock when I walked onto the street. I took a streetcar toward the Tenderloin area of Market Street. I knew the long-haired people—"the hippies," the papers called them—had taken over a three-block area. *They* were different. *I* was different. "Let's see what it's all about," I said, my eyes dry by then, and my face in control.

The area was filled with discount stores, a few coffee shops, and some declining restaurants. A group of the long-haired people sat on the steps to the entrance of one of the discount stores. They looked friendly enough, but I was scared. I stopped in front of them and picked out one person to speak to. He was the strangest-looking guy I had ever seen—long red hair and a bushy beard that was even redder than his hair. He was large, and the beard and hair made him seem even larger.

"May I speak to you for a moment?" The question hung in the air. The redhead looked at me with a placid, wide-open face. Then he looked at his friends, and suspicion crept across his eyes. My high heels and fitted clothes were definitely not in keeping with the surroundings.

"Sure, lady." He shrugged and rose. He was at least six-foot-four, bigger than I had expected. But he was lean and gangling when standing erect. He obviously thought I was a cop, but he stepped away from his friends. "What can I do for you?"

I was embarrassed and nervous, but I pushed ahead. "Do you know where I can get some of that LSD stuff?"

Silence. He lowered his head slightly and stared into my face. Then he stood erect again. "What do you want LSD for?" His voice contained a smile, but his face was sober.

"Well, that's all I've been reading and hearing about for weeks, and I've decided I want to try some to see what it does. I've done just about everything else, and I want to try this."

Apparently my answer was so naive and my manner so awkward that his eyes and then his lips crinkled into a smile. But he didn't laugh at me. He just smiled, and let several seconds pass.

"Well, it takes money, my friend," he said.

I started for my purse—it didn't contain much money—but he pretended not to notice. "But that's no problem," he went on. "We always panhandle it and then it's easy from there."

"What do you mean *panhandle?*" I asked, even dumber-sounding than I actually was.

He laughed loudly, throwing his head back. The others on the steps stopped talking for a moment, and looked at us. Then they resumed.

"Come on, little girl, I'll teach you."

After less than two hours of conning and begging people for money on one of the busier streets, he took me by the arm and walked up to a flower vendor. He talked quietly to the man and in two minutes we were walking back down the street. He handed me a tablet and said, "Here, swallow it." He popped one into his mouth, and I swallowed mine. We headed in the direction of my hotel.

As we walked, the buildings and lights began to change shapes and colors. Within a few blocks, everything was changing. We managed finally to get to my dingy hotel room where I fell over backwards onto the bed and stared around me at the weird things that were happening.

I was immobile. All sounds were alive—noises from surrounding rooms, noises from the street, the flushing of the toilets in nearby rooms—all were vibrant, living sounds. The redhead—his hair aflame—bent over me and stroked my hair.

"Who am I?" I asked.

"You're Susan. You're Susan," a message he was to repeat frequently in the next twelve hours as I slipped from fear to hilarity, and back to fear. My brain was on a roller-coaster, with dizzying rushes upward and down.

"Oh," I moaned. My eyes nearly burst as I watched grotesque, living beings come out of the walls and the ceiling. They were monsters, every color from yellow to black. Some crawled; others crept. Some twisted and slithered; others moved in massive blocks.

I remained silent as the flowers in the faded, worn-out wallpaper came to life. They bloomed and withered away to stubs, and flourished back to blossoms, an endless array of speeded nature. "It's just like time-lapse photography," I said, or thought, or dreamed.

My bearded friend stroked me and kissed me and talked to me. "You're Susan. You're you. You're all right."

"No, I'm lost," I moaned. "It's all so bright, and so fierce . . . I'm not coming back . . . I will stay . . . I'm on the other side . . . and I'm above, and behind . . . Oh . . . I don't know myself . . . I can see myself . . . but I can't remember. . . ."

"You're Susan," he said softly, far away. "You're Susan Atkins."

The clock said 2:25. The sunlight glared against the dirty window. I was in bed with no clothes on, and I was alone. The room was just as it had been. The walls and the ceiling were the same. My clothes were strewn on the floor.

"That was insane," I thought. "I've never done anything like that before."

The hallucinations. "What were they? Everything became life. There were things I didn't know were there. Where did they come from?"

I shuddered, and pulled the covers close around me.

"I saw new things." My thoughts were smooth, not erratic. "Those were . . . things. They had beautiful colors. But they were scary."

I squeezed my arms across my breasts. I smiled.

"It was dangerous . . . but it was exciting. It was an adventure. It was what I've been looking for. There *is* something there."

I looked at the glaring window.

"Maybe it's God."

I jumped out of bed and went into the bathroom. I had to work that night.

"But there'll be other times."

It was shortly after the first of the year in 1967. The country was churning with discontent. Race riots and antiwar protests were rampant. In my discontent, I was moving more and more away from liquor and into drugs. But that night, in that North Beach nightclub, it was strictly booze. With Bob far behind me, I was with one of a long list of nameless, faceless guys—good guys, but mostly the same, mostly like me, thriving on sex and the best highs available.

About every hour, the lead guitar player in the musical group would say something about "our big amateur topless contest tonight—the night when you can fulfill your dream and make it as a dancer."

"Hey, that's for you," my faceless friend said. "The way you dance, there'll be no contest."

I was drunk, but I was in control enough to know what kind of dancing they were talking about. "You expect me to get up there naked in front of everybody?" I laughed.

"Why not, Susan? It'll be no contest in that department either."

An hour later, the guitar player announced "the final call for the dancing contest."

"You know something?" I said, interrupting my companion in mid sentence, "I think I'll do it. I think I'll enter this contest. It'll liven things up."

I danced well. I had done it all my life. My ability may have been linked with my fondness for physical education. I was coordinated, and could flow with every rhythm conceivable. I didn't have to think about it. It happened. It was part of me—within me.

Fortunately I didn't have to stand motionless before the staring men and women. I entered dancing and soon became oblivious to the fact that I was naked from the waist up, covered only by my half-slip, which was rolled high up onto my thighs. I yielded my soul to the dance and felt warm, straining pleasure from my body's movements. I knew they were nearly perfect.

When the number ended, the applause was loud and wild. Male shouts rose all over the room. The band—behind me—shouted its approval.

I won the contest, and became the youngest go-go dancer on the North Beach strip. My biggest problem—and my bosses'—was staying ahead of the vice squad, which regularly checked I.D.s among the younger customers and would have loved to have grabbed me. Alertness and an alias—"Sharon King"—kept me out of trouble with the law. When the heat showed up, I'd be sent out for a walk.

The pay was good, and so were the drugs. The apartments were better than dingy flophouses, and the men were just as ravenous as anywhere else.

I began work at four in the afternoon, dancing half-hour sets, with fifteen-minute breaks, until two in the morning. This was usually followed by a visit to some other club to dance for nothing until daybreak, hoping continually to be "discovered" by a talent agent. It was a plastic world of booze, drugs, sex, flashy clothes, and big-time as well as small-time hoods. Money bought anything.

It was a slow afternoon, and I considered my first thirty-minute routine as merely a warm-up for the wilder things to come with nightfall. I was just finishing when Mr. Garnet, the owner, walked in with a man I had not seen before. The room was quite dark but the afternoon sunlight splashed through the swinging door behind them. The man seemed to be dressed entirely in black. His face and the top of his bald head were extraordinarily pale—white.

Garnet and the stranger walked toward me. "Sharon," my boss said as I reached for a wrap and moved toward the side of the stage. "Sharon, I'd like for you to dance one more number."

"But I've just finished, Mr. Garnet."

"I know, sweetheart," he smiled, "but I'd like for you to do one more number for Mr. LaVey here. This is Mr. Anton LaVey."

I smiled at the man. His gaze was as intense as any I'd ever seen, even though his mouth was smiling. His eyes seemed to be black—and glistening.

"It's important, Sharon," Garnet said. "You can stretch your break a bit afterward."

"Okay." I walked over to Tommy the bartender and told him to put on my favorite record. "I might as well give him the works," I mumbled to Tommy.

The intensity in the stranger's black eyes deepened as he watched my movements. A smile curled about his lips. I slipped into one of my fantasies about Sharon King the dancer, the sensuous, long-legged, full-breasted movie starlet, the Broadway queen. The music penetrated the lower depths of my abdomen and up into my chest cavity. It possessed me.

Garnet motioned me to the small table where he and Mr. LaVey were seated. "She is one of my best girls, Mr. LaVey.

Do you think there's a part for her in your production?"

"Hello, Sharon." LaVey's voice sounded as though it were in an echo chamber. "That was very good."

He turned to Garnet. "Yes. Yes. She would be very good for the vampire role."

"Vampire role?" I asked, silently.

Garnet turned to me. "You see, Sharon, Mr. LaVey has agreed to stage one of his productions here at the club—a witches' sabbath."

"Yes, Sharon," LaVey smiled, his face paler than ever. "I'm going to produce and direct for your Mr. Garnet a genuine witches' sabbath—topless and all—and I think it could be fun for you if you're interested."

"What's a witches' sabbath?" I asked, looking first at Mr. Garnet and then back at the bald-headed man.

LaVey threw his head back and gave a barking sort of laugh. "It's a time, my dear, when the witches worship their leader—Satan. It's a marvelous ceremony and will be very colorful for your club. It's a bit out of the ordinary."

I shrugged. "It sounds it." I thought it was weird, but it might be the trick to launch my career. "Sure, if Mr. Garnet wants me in it, he's the boss."

"Good. Good." LaVey rubbed his palms together.

"But what about costumes and all that, Mr. Garnet?" I asked, trying to understand the thing better.

"Don't you worry about those details," LaVey interrupted. "You won't need much to wear. Besides, we will be having a meeting at my house to discuss these matters. It will all work out."

He turned to Garnet. "I think she will be excellent. And she will also be good for the witch in the torture scene."

"*Torture* scene?" Again I spoke only to myself.

"It has been nice meeting you, Sharon," LaVey said to me,

turning to walk away. "I know you will find this most interesting."

I was near exhaustion the next night. The men in the crowd demanded more of me than I was able to perform. They seemed to want explicit sex acts, not merely free dancing by a nearly naked young woman. They equated dancers with hookers. I welcomed Garnet's high sign to cut my last number short and come to his table.

"Sharon," he said, "I know tomorrow is your day off, but I would like to have you join the other selected girls and me in going to Mr. LaVey's house. He wants to fill us in on the witches' sabbath and black magic. We've got to start preparing."

"Why his house?" I was still uneasy about LaVey.

"It's all part of a Satan worship routine. You know anything about that?"

My silence spoke for itself.

"Everyone has his own hustle going," Garnet said. "LaVey's is this Satan thing. He calls himself the high priest of Satan. He's a full-fledged honcho in that stuff. His wife is a full-fledged witch. They have a Satan church in their home. It's a big thing around here."

"You're kidding. You mean they *really* worship Satan? It's not just for show?"

"Hell no. They really mean business. Of course," he grinned, "they put on a pretty good show, too. It's good show business. And that's what I need right now—something to get us out in front of the other clubs. We can be the hottest thing on the strip."

He paused, looking first at the drink in his hand and then into my face. His mouth was set. "So I need you to come with us tomorrow. We'll leave from here at three o'clock."

"All right, Mr. Garnet. But only because I need the job. I don't go for this Satan stuff."

He laughed. "Neither do I, but business is business."

We turned the corner and there was no mistaking LaVey's house. It sat in the middle of the block, with empty lots on each side. The house was wholly black. Not one bit of white or other color showed. Even the curtains were black.

"Wow!" one of the girls wheezed softly.

"This is weird," I said.

"Look at the lawn," Garnet said. "It's all weeds and dirt."

He was right. Nothing of any beauty seemed to be growing around the two-story black monster.

"What a place for halloween!" one of the girls said. We all laughed, a bit too loudly.

When I stepped out of the car, I was actually shaking. "Mr. Garnet," I asked weakly, "are we really going into that house?"

"Aw, come on, Sharon. If you don't believe in black magic, nothing can hurt you. Don't be afraid."

I wasn't convinced. I don't believe the other girls were either.

Garnet reached for the doorbell. I expected a gong, or a howl, or something. It was an ordinary "ding dong."

The door opened, and there stood LaVey, all in black, his powdery white skin glowing. I felt sick at my stomach as I walked past him. His smile was sickly, I thought. Then I froze in my steps. Straight ahead at the far end of the entrance hall was a human skeleton in a glass case. It seemed to have the same sickly smile as LaVey.

"This is all the horror movies rolled into one," I thought.

"What am I doing here? I wonder if I'll get out of here in one piece."

"Please come right into the living room," LaVey said, with refined politeness. His manners were exaggeratedly excellent.

My stomach sickness immediately deepened. The first object to attract my eyes in the living room was a huge, black grand piano. That was okay. But right beside it stood a stuffed, full-grown wolf, and atop the piano itself was a stuffed raven. The fireplace mantle held a large stuffed owl.

LaVey and Garnet launched immediately into discussion of the witches' sabbath. But I had trouble maintaining concentration. The decor of the house was beyond my imagination. I examined the stuffed animals and found myself shivering. Their eyes seemed alive.

"The May Pole ritual is a fertility dance." LaVey's voice penetrated my consciousness for a moment.

I smiled and felt a giggle inside. "I played that all the time when I was a kid," I thought. "How come I'm not pregnant?"

The giggle choked inside me as I caught a glimpse out of the corner of my eye of someone descending the staircase in the hallway. It was a woman with the longest hair I'd ever seen. It was as black as it could possibly be and hung at least three feet below her shoulders, full and thick. At first I thought it must be a wig, but it was real.

"Ah, my wife," said LaVey, rising.

"Hello, everybody," the woman said, softly and seductively. Her manners were as impeccable as her husband's. She stood for a minute, smiling warmly at everyone, and then said, "Would you girls like to come into the kitchen with me? I'm going to prepare some coffee."

"Yes, ladies, why don't you go with Mrs. LaVey while we finish up these details? But we'll be finished soon, and I do want you to stay for our evening services. Things will come a lot clearer to you when you see it first hand."

We all looked quickly at one another.

I spoke first, and my voice was not particularly steady. "I'm afraid I won't be able to stay, Mr. LaVey. I hope you won't be offended, but I don't believe in the devil, and. . . ."

LaVey interrupted me with a wave of the hand and a wide smile across his white face. "But, Sharon, we don't believe in God either, but that doesn't mean he isn't real."

I only shook my head and followed the others into the kitchen. His remark left me speechless, but my first sight upon walking into the large, quite ordinary kitchen changed that. Through a full-glass back wall I could see a real lion in the yard. He was huge, and rather mangy-looking, but he gave a loud roar as he saw us enter the room.

"That's too much," I said, only barely audibly. "What kind of place is this?" I added under my breath.

I backed out of the kitchen and retreated to the living room.

"Mr. LaVey," I interrupted. "I'd like for you to excuse me, please. I'm not feeling too well." I turned to Garnet. "Mr. Garnet, I think I'd better leave now. I'll be your vampire and witch, but I must be going now."

"Sharon," LaVey's voice was gentle, but his smile was still strange. "You've only just arrived. Won't you please stay? I'm holding services this evening—there will be special secret rites—and I'm sure you would enjoy it. It isn't often that I invite an outside guest to these rites."

I looked right into his eyes momentarily, but I couldn't withstand his gaze. "No thank you, Mr. LaVey. I hope you won't be offended, but I was raised to worship God, not the devil. I must leave now."

Garnet apparently recognized the urgency and decided

70

against getting tough with me. "Okay, Sharon, you take the car and we'll get a cab later on."

He walked me to the door and out to the car. "Will you be all right?"

"Yes." I stopped beside the car. "I'm sorry, Mr. Garnet, but my imagination must have been working overtime. I had visions of somehow being sacrificed and all that. Besides, I'm tired and need to go to bed early tonight." Looking back at the scary, black house, I wasn't sure I'd be able to go through with LaVey's plans, but then again, what other course did I have?

I looked at my two-inch-long false fingernails, painted brilliant red. And my face was something special, as I looked up into the mirror. It was eerie—milky white, broken by bright red lips that matched the color of the fingernails and by seemingly sunken blue-black eyes expertly twisted upward at the outside corners—grotesquely exaggerated cat eyes. Jet black hair framed it all. I was the perfect, sexy vampire, ready for my casket lying at the center of the stage.

Using care because of my fingernails, I reached into my big, black handbag and fished out a pill. Rehearsals had gone well—we were ready for the weirdest show on the strip, but I knew I'd never be able to get into that casket for real without being stoned. I popped the acid tab into my mouth, carefully avoiding any lipstick smears.

As the end of the production neared, I lay inside the casket. I remembered very little of the show. I had shaken several people with the reality of my performance when I had risen from the casket and pointed a long, blood-red fingernail at the audience and marked them as my next victims. Gasps, from both males and females, had sounded all around the club. But as I lay there, I fancied the idea of being dead and still hearing all the sounds around me. I heard everything—the footsteps, the breathing, the sighs in the audience. "But I'm dead," I thought. "It's so pleasant . . . I'm outside my dead body . . . I'm a spirit . . . I can see and hear everything . . . I'm dead . . . But I'm really alive. . . ."

I lay in the casket so long that I missed the curtain call by five minutes. I just didn't want to get out of it.

The audience went wild over the performance. Garnet had himself a hit. I was convinced he had a whole lot more than he realized.

But the night's success spelled trouble later. Gary, my current lover of about three weeks' standing, lay quietly in bed as I entered the room. I was still stretched tight from my acid trip and sat down next to him.

"You're awfully quiet, Gary. Is something the matter?"

"I don't like what's happening to you, Sharon," he blurted out. "This whole thing you're into at the club is crazy. It's changed you. All through the rehearsals I've watched you change."

"I don't understand," I said softly, not wanting to get into a hassle. "I haven't changed."

"Yes, you have," he said sharply. "It's hard to describe. But something's happened to you. When you play your autoharp, for instance, it's creepy. There's a strange sound to it, and when you sing with it, it's like something far out, from somewhere else."

I persisted with my soft approach. "Aw, come on, Gary, you're imagining things. This is just a job. There's nothing to that black magic stuff if you don't believe in it. Relax, babe."

"Please, Sharon, baby, get out of this show. You don't

need the money. We can live dealing dope. You don't need this stuff."

Gary was getting to me. And the room started to close in.

"I'm going out for a while, Gary. I'm really wired from the acid I dropped tonight. You go to sleep. I'll be back."

I picked up my harp and walked out onto the street, throwing a gray cape over my shoulder. The night was foggy. I walked along quietly for several minutes and then began to strum the harp softly. I tripped out again—and was a little fairy playing my music. I sat down under a window and played softly for the whole neighborhood. Strangely, no one bothered me.

It was dawn when I walked back into the apartment and found a note from Gary. I saw immediately that his things were gone. "Sharon," the note read, "I love you too much to sit and watch you lose yourself to LaVey. Goodbye."

I sat quietly and sadly, strumming my harp and humming.

The show was a smash hit along the strip. Garnet had scored big. But the witches' sabbath, and my total sellout to LSD, marijuana, and hashish, and to sex with virtually any attractive man, landed me in the hospital in four months. I was half dead from gonorrhea and had a complete physical breakdown.

COUNTER-CULTURE

My job was gone, but I was glad. The plastic world was not for me. The only people I'd found who seemed to understand and welcome me, as me, were those in Haight-Ashbury, those of the new culture, the counter-culture. They had found the world crooked and perverted and had dropped out of it except for their protests against the Vietnam War and pollution. "Make love, not war," they shouted. That sounded good to me and I found myself more and more into the Haight, more and more into the new culture, the drug culture; more and more into the new morality.

One girl friend continually counseled me, "Quit playing games. Come on over to the other side."

My first step to the other side came when I met Michael. He spent a lot of time in the Haight but lived in a big house overlooking Muir Beach a few miles north of the Golden Gate. "I need a housekeeper," he said to me one night with a grin. "Why don't you come with me? It's a free area. You'll like it."

I moved in with him and immediately set off on a big trip, nature and drugs. It was all there—earth, sky, and sea, plus lots of dope. Everybody in sight was a dopehead. The house sat on one of the cliffs framing the beach. Down below were little cottages sitting close to the beach itself.

Michael was fine—for a while. But we eventually grew tired of one another and I moved in with a guy at the other end of the beach. But I didn't confine my favors to one man. I had by then decided that no one man could keep me happy, either with sex or with other mental and physical stimulation. I kept looking for that *one place*, but nothing lasted.

I ended my Muir Beach stay with John, a carpenter. He fell in love with me and was rather pitiful about it. He asked me to marry him, but I knew he wasn't for me.

One night we experimented with a heavy hallucinogenic drug that was new to me—STP. It took me beyond anything I had known. I lay on the floor and, as though I could see inside myself, I surveyed a massive battleground right within my chest and stomach. I couldn't distinguish one from another, but spirits or some such force battled and clawed and screeched within me. Before long, the increasing numbers of spirits spilled over to my exterior and battled and raged all about me and upon my skin.

I screamed, "John! John! Oh, God, help me! It's good and evil. They're battling in me. Help me! Please! There's the good! And there's the evil! Oh, John, help me! They're killing me!"

John stroked my forehead and kissed me all about the face. "It's all right, Susan," he said softly. The screaming eased into moans and groans, but my body twisted and squirmed. John fondled me all over, seeking some way to bring me through this terrible turmoil. He gently removed my clothes and began to make love to me. I finally quieted and the hour of horror passed.

Again, John asked me to marry him. I lied and told him I had to go ask my father. Instead I went straight to Haight-Ashbury in search of a life I could lead.

"Hey, Susan!"

Standing alone in front of the Drug Store, one of the Haight's better known hangouts, I turned in the direction of the voice. It was an old friend from Los Banos.

"Barbara, what are you doing here?" I said. It was exciting to see a familiar face. Barbara was a good-looking brunette, about my age, but not the kind I'd expected to find in the Haight. I remembered her as a straight kid, right off a Los Banos farm.

"I've been here quite awhile," she said. "Everything else was a drag, but things are happening here."

"I know," I said. "It's one of the few places where I feel comfortable."

"Me too. And I've got a great new family here. You'll have to come over and see them."

"What do you mean, 'family'? You're not married, are you?"

"Heck no. This is another kind of family—a real one. We all live together and take care of one another. I've got an old man, and he watches out for me."

"How many of you?"

"Eleven right now," she said. "Some come and go after a while. We figure a dozen is about right—six couples."

"Someone's missing?"

"That's right," Barbara smiled. "Bob needs a woman. He's my man's partner. That's Tom, the head of the family."

"I see."

There was a pause as we watched the people go by. "Why don't you come on home with me?" Barbara asked. "I want you to meet everyone and see our house. It's great."

"Sure, if you think it's all right."

"No problem," Barbara said. "We have a lot of visitors."

The family's home was a big, two-story brown house at the corner of Oak and Lyon Streets. It was an impressive old home in the midst of several impressive ones. The area had passed its prime but still maintained a certain elegance.

"Janis Joplin lives over there," Barbara said, pointing to the house next door. "There are a lot of great people around here."

We entered the brown house and Barbara took me up one flight of stairs to the big room, the living room where I was to have my first encounter with Charlie Manson.

Dominating the room was one guy who turned out to be Tom, Barbara's man. He was the head of the family. I stood in front of him and he smiled at me. He was sitting in front of a huge hookah pipe, dragging periodically from the long flexible tube that passed through water.

"The best Acapulco Gold in town," he said as I stared at the contraption, which was right out of an old Errol Flynn movie about the desert sheiks.

I smiled. "It looks good."

It was a strange scene. Rock music was playing in the background—the Jefferson Airplane. Every man seemed to have a woman—except for one. "That must be Bob," I thought. He smiled at me.

We spent the next two hours talking and smoking grass—it *was* as good as any I'd tasted. Before long I was talking exclusively to Bob. He told me a lot about the family. Each man in the group was a dope dealer, moving some of the highest quality drugs in the country out into the streets of Haight-Ashbury. The girls were often used to go out into the streets and hand out samples of the latest batches as advertising.

Of course, he explained, they used a lot of the drugs themselves. They shared everything in common—except for the girls. In sleeping partners, they were monogamous, following the developing hippy life style.

Bob eventually asked me to accompany him to his room. We made love there, and from then on I was *his* woman.

For three weeks I was constantly loaded on hashish, marijuana, or acid. I was fulfilled for the first time in my craving for dope. There seemed to be an endless supply. One of my favorite pastimes was sitting, stoned, on the front balcony and listening to Janis Joplin playing, singing, and boozing.

Other times I would just sit watching the trees and the birds and then the steadily increasing numbers of young people finding their way to Haight-Ashbury. There even came the time when we picked up word that the FBI was watching the house. Not only were we heavy into drugs, but we also were militantly active in the peace movement sweeping across the youth of the land. Once we knew, the agents were easy to spot. Many times I sat on the balcony listening to the radio, waving at them from time to time. That seemed to panic them.

But there was one sunny afternoon when I, again, was stoned on hash and my serenity failed to hold steady. I had many moments like that, but that afternoon was especially difficult. Despite the excitement around me, the apparent love, the sex, the drugs—despite my "family," I was lonely. The afternoon was warm, but the old familiar chill of loneliness moved up and down my body. It was far deeper than tears—a fullness in the throat and the chest.

"I'm still an outsider." The thought rushed across my mind over and over. "Bob likes me for sex, and the others put up with me because of him. But they don't like me. I'm too weird. I'm not like them. Barbara and Ella accept me. But that's all."

I listened to the street sounds for several seconds. "What's wrong with me? Won't I ever belong? First my own family; then Al, and all the others; and now here. Can't I find a place anywhere?"

Things suddenly slipped out of control when the police and the federal authorities intensified their pressure on us. My man, Bob, was arrested for selling drugs. Tom was immediately obsessed with the desire to free his partner. And that required considerable money for lawyers, fines, and related activities.

It was early afternoon when Tom and I went out onto the street. We immediately knew we were being followed. We crossed the Golden Gate Panhandle and, when the way seemed momentarily clear, we separated and I began a big circular swing back toward the house. Tom was to keep moving and hide out for a day or two. I would be in a position to come with help if he was caught.

I was breathless as I shut the door of the old brown house behind me and stood for several minutes listening to the music—a man's voice—coming from the big room upstairs. I climbed the stairs slowly and stepped into the dusky room. Seated on the couch in front of the bay window was Charlie Manson, playing a beat-up, old guitar remarkably well and singing in a clear, but soft voice, "The shadow of your smile when you are gone will color all my dreams and light the dawn."

After listening to Charlie sing and talk, after dancing with him and making love, after sensing and seeing the power of his mind, I knew I would go with him if he asked me. I felt fully responsible for my actions, but at the same time I knew there was something inside me that was attracted to something inside him. I knew I had never encountered this before, and I knew I had to have what he had.

I was eighteen, but older inside. I was free. My father, brothers, and I were irreparably torn apart, it seemed. I had come close, but so far had found no substitute. Charlie had instantly seemed more of a father to me than my own father. It was obvious from the way those three girls—Lynn, Pat, and Mary—followed him that he could lead. He could make things happen.

If he were the head of a family like Tom, there would be no falling apart. He would know how to keep it together. He could make one-for-all-and-all-for-one work. He not only preached love, he had power. What he wanted he could get. He often sounded like God.

When Charlie said, "Come on; we're going to L.A.," I was prepared. It didn't take much to talk Barbara and Ella into going with us.

9

ON THE MOVE

By the time I joined him, Charlie Manson had spent more than half of his life—seventeen of thirty-two years—in institutions. Although I knew virtually nothing of his background, he had only recently been released, on March 21, 1967, from federal prison. Over the previous seventeen years, he had served time as burglar, car thief, forger, and pimp.

According to Deputy District Attorney Vincent Bugliosi, Manson had begged the authorities to let him stay in prison even on the day of his release. It had become his home, he told them. He didn't think he could adjust to the outside world.

His request was denied. He was released at 8:15 A.M. on March 21, 1967, and given transportation to Los Angeles. That same day he requested and received permission to go to San Francisco. "It was there, in the Haight-Ashbury section, that spring, that the Family was born" (Bugliosi and Gentry, *Helter Skelter*, p. 146).

By "the Family," Bugliosi was referring to that steadily enlarging group of young men and women which began to gather around Charlie, starting with Lynn, Pat, Mary, Barbara, Ella, and me.

Charlie was born "no name Maddox" on November 12, 1934, in Cincinnati, the illegitimate son of sixteen-year-old Kathleen Maddox. The only possible identity available for his father is "Colonel Scott" of Ashland, Kentucky, the target of a bastardy suit filed by Kathleen in 1936 in Boyd County, Kentucky. The court awarded her a judgment of twenty-five dollars, plus five dollars a month for the support of "Charles Milles Manson." Later court actions indicate that Kathleen had trouble collecting.

Following is an excerpt from Bugliosi's findings regarding Charlie's very early life:

> According to her own relatives, Kathleen would leave the child with obliging neighbors for an hour, then disappear for days or weeks. Usually his grandmother or maternal aunt would have to claim him. Most of his early years were spent with one or the other, in West Virginia, Kentucky, or Ohio.
>
> In 1939, Kathleen and her brother Luther robbed a Charleston, West Virginia, service station, knocking out the attendant with Coke bottles. They were sentenced to five years in the state penitentiary for armed robbery. While his mother was in prison, Manson lived with his aunt and uncle in McMechen, West Virginia. Manson would later tell his counselor at the National Training School for Boys that his uncle and aunt had "some marital difficulty until they became interested in religion and became very extreme."
>
> A very strict aunt, who thought all pleasures sinful but who gave him love. A promiscuous mother, who let him do anything he wanted, just so

long as he didn't bother her. The youth was caught in a tug-of-war between the two.

Paroled in 1942, Kathleen reclaimed Charles, then eight. The next several years were a blur of run-down hotel rooms and newly introduced "uncles," most of whom, like his mother, drank heavily. In 1947 she tried to have him put in a foster home, but, none being available, the court sent him to the Gibault School for Boys, a caretaking institution in Terre Haute, Indiana. He was twelve years old. (*HS*, p. 137)

Along the way, Charlie landed at Father Flanagan's Boys Town after it was erroneously reported that he was a Roman Catholic. He stayed only four days, breaking out with another boy and finally committing his first armed robbery at the age of thirteen. From there on, it was in and out of one institution after another, all across the United States.

Reports on him over the next nineteen years painted a picture of a young man with a "marked degree of rejection, instability, and psychic trauma," heightened by a sense of inferiority in connection with his mother, by his small physical stature, and by his lack of parental love. Others found him to have "homosexual and assaultive tendencies" . . . "safe only under supervision" . . . "criminally sophisticated". . . headed for "serious difficulty soon". . . "young, small, baby-faced, and unable to control himself" . . . "an almost classic textbook case of the correctional institutional inmate" . . . one who "hides his loneliness, resentment, and hostility behind a face of superficial ingratiation" . . . "an energetic, young-appearing person whose verbalization flows quite easily," who "gestures profusely and can dramatize situations to hold the listener's attention."

The records showed that Charlie had married at least two women and had fathered at least two boys before I met him. They also showed a deep, but temporary involvement with a number of religious sects, including Scientology, Buddhism, and many Eastern religions. He was described as knowledgeable about certain portions of the Bible and Christianity.

And it was in prison that Charlie developed his musical ability—the guitar playing, the singing, and the song writing. He took himself so seriously as a musician that he was described as jealous of the monumental fame that flowed to the Beatles in the mid-sixties. It was this Charlie—the balladeer, the self-made philosopher—that I was learning to know as we wound our way toward Los Angeles in 1967.

We picked up a hitchhiker, Scotty, as we approached the Los Angeles area, and he invited us to his place in Malibu, on Topanga Canyon Lane. We pulled the big bus up in front of his house, which we very quickly named "The Spiral Staircase House" because of its stairway.

Topanga Canyon, a surprisingly steep and rugged area above Santa Monica on the coast, just off Santa Monica Bay, was fast becoming a hippy haven, at least in its southern portion. Large numbers had established communal living in the houses on both sides of the canyon winding south to the ocean. Topanga Canyon Boulevard was the main thoroughfare running north and south. Topanga Canyon Lane, where Scotty took us, was a little, curving road at the southern end of the canyon leading down to a cluster of small beach houses. Scotty's house was midway along this lane, with houses on each side and across the street.

We had no sooner arrived at Scotty's than a spontaneous

gathering developed, with about forty or fifty people, including us, and a big acid party was underway. It came right on the heels of our bus experience with Charlie.

People were all over the house—on couches, chairs, the floors, upstairs, downstairs. Records were playing one after another—The Doors, Jefferson Airplane, Dylan—and lights of every color tinted the walls, ceilings, and floors. Someone even presented a light show on one bare wall.

Again, I was in my customary position during the heavy stages of a trip, prostrated on the floor. My arms were stretched out, and I sensed I was on a cross. "I have to die for all these people," I thought. "They don't know it. They don't know I'm dying for them."

People were everywhere, doing everything imaginable, and I was inside them. I was one with every person there. "I love them," I said inside myself. "I love them so much that I want to die for them. But they will not know it. It doesn't matter. I love them."

As this sense slipped away and I was aware of myself on the floor, I yearned to see Charlie. I wanted him to share this experience. But I couldn't see him as I wandered from room to room. Everyone was tripping in a dozen different ways.

I eventually wandered out to the bus. Charlie was there, alone. He was dressed in a long white robe. I immediately knew that he might be God himself; if not, he was close to him. He held a pan of water in his hands, resting on his lap as he sat on a pile of pillows.

"Susan . . . love . . . I'm going to wash your feet."

"No, Charlie, you can't do that," I said softly, yielding fully to the realization that this was a deep spiritual moment. "I'm not worth it."

"Susan, you are beautiful. You are perfect. You are one with God. We're all one with him. I must wash your feet. I must show the way."

I sat on the floor of the bus and he rolled over onto his hands and knees and washed my feet. Right in the middle of the washing, a tall, rugged, auburn-haired guy came into the bus and watched.

Charlie looked into my face and said, "Now you must wash this brother's feet."

Without hesitation I moved to my hands and knees and washed the feet of this giant of a man whom I didn't know. He merely stood, looking down at me, unsmiling, completely solemn. He looked as though he might weep.

Others began to arrive in the bus, men and women, perhaps a dozen or fifteen. The next thing I knew people were making love all over the bus in every possible way and position. Bare bodies were everywhere, some pale and soft, others hairy, bony, and tan. It was a full-fledged orgy of the kind I had heard about but had never witnessed or participated in.

I made love with the big, auburn-haired fellow, but as I did so I was, in a flash of light, aware that I was once again inside all those people. I was inside them—even inside the auburn-haired guy.

"My God!" I screamed inside myself. "I'm making love to myself."

All consciousness and awareness of my individual self slipped away. I had no idea who I was—only that I was in total oneness with everyone in that bus, indeed everyone in the whole world.

"Who am I?" The voice yelled deep inside my bowels. "I don't know who I am."

Then a voice said, "You're everyone. You're with everyone. You're in everyone."

All sense of being slipped away as I abandoned myself to

the man whose feet I had washed.

LSD and marijuana were the center of our lives at Topanga Canyon Lane. I was losing my individuality—my identity—more completely as each day passed. It was an evolution that I welcomed as I sensed a oneness, a togetherness, with others. But with this loss of individuality came what seemed to be an increasing contradiction—a craving for attention from others, especially Charlie. And he did not give me attention to the degree I was begging for. There was a hug here, a smile there, with no dependable pattern. But he had me hooked.

Several times he took me aside during my petulant moods and repeated his earliest line with me, "You are beautiful and perfect. You must accept yourself. You must love yourself."

Somehow he knew of the insecurities within me. I had terrifying moments of feeling very ugly inside. He knew this. And during those frightening moments, he was there.

In my manic moments, he shot needles at me over my desire for the spotlight. "You just want to be the queen bee," he said.

Both forces, seemingly opposites, played within me, and he watched them keenly, as he did with the peculiarities of all "his girls."

We were in Scotty's house in late afternoon a few days after arriving. Charlie took the floor, as usual. "The thing we must understand," he said softly, pacing the floor, "is that the past is over. There is no past. It is dead—severed. In fact, there is no time. Get rid of your watches. You don't need them. There *is* no time."

The room was silent. Mary, Ella, Pat, and I, with some new girls and guys, watched every move Charlie made. He had talked a lot since we had left San Francisco, but this was on a new level of intensity. He was serious, and we knew it.

"Now listen to me," he said, raising his voice and slapping his palms together. "Yesterday is dead. Tomorrow never gets here."

He looked around the room. His eyes were on fire.

"Do you understand that? Yesterday is dead. Tomorrow never gets here. We live in the eternal now."

He stopped walking and stood in the center of the room.

"All your roots are cut," he said, lowering his voice again. "You are freed from your families and all their old hangups. You are cut loose into the *now*. You are free. And because we are free, we can become one. The Bible says we must die to self, and that's exactly true. We must die to self so we can be at one with all people. That is love."

We all felt we understood that, and several heads nodded enthusiastically in agreement. Smiles were on several faces.

Out of those lectures by Charlie came constant actions aimed at ridding us of our inhibitions. One of the most-used techniques was the one he had used on me about making love to my father. "Don't be afraid of that," he said. "Pretend you're making love to your father, and get rid of the inhibition."

Another technique growing out of that was the use of orgies to break down inhibitions. If we were hung up on any aspect of sex, he would lead us into group activities aimed at shattering those hangups. In fact, it seemed to many of us that Charlie pushed the orgy concept too far. Quite a number had come out of the hippy lifestyle where monogamy was far more prevalent in sexual relationships.

Most of the men were growing beards and long hair, and several of them were quite attractive. The women were young, also growing long hair—in fact, giving up even the shaving of underarms and legs. Natural, free—those were the bywords.

Clothing trended toward blue jeans or work pants, tee-shirts, and other inexpensive, earthy attire. The women were more varied. Sometimes we wore blue jeans; other times, extremely short miniskirts; still other times, long, old-fashioned dresses and skirts. It wasn't long before we began to share clothing communally on a first-come, first-served basis. Everything was washed together, and we each took what we wanted for the day.

It was obvious to all that one of Charlie's plans was to use his attractive young women to lure men to the group. We weren't talking about "family" at that time, but that was the direction. Hundreds of young people were on the move throughout California, and the promise of lots of sex and dope was enticing.

One of the most attractive men to show up during this period was one who gave Charlie a run as a leader. He was Bobby, an outstanding guitar player with an unusual ability to motivate young people, especially women. He arrived on the Topanga Canyon scene one day with his own following of girls. He didn't tie up with Charlie permanently then, but came and went throughout the whole period, with his stays increasing in duration.

Music was important to Charlie, and so was Bobby's talent. In fact, Charlie often used music as a device to break down our lingering inhibitions.

"Come on," he said. "You can do anything you want to. You can sing. Shake all the past and throw yourself into it."

We did become more than moderately accomplished, most of it singing behind Charlie, who was obsessed with the belief that his music could change the world.

From Scotty's house we moved into a rented house farther up into Topanga Canyon. Several people were coming and going from the group and our numbers were increasing, but the core consisted of Charlie, Mary, Lynn, Pat, Ella, myself, and three or four others. Pat and I were quite close during this period, and I even adopted part of her name, to become known as "Patty Sue." She, in turn, became "Katie," a name that was to stick with her.

One night in the rented house, we were high on grass, and for some reason the women and the men were momentarily separated. In a stoned condition, I looked at Charlie across the room. The men were clustered around him. I counted; there were twelve. In his lengthening hair and beard, his eyes staring intently from face to face, he looked like Jesus talking to his twelve apostles. The thought simultaneously startled and thrilled me. I felt he might be Christ.

Highly mobile at that time, we traveled all over Southern California in Charlie's school bus, which we had by that time painted black. We stayed in the bus, or with people we'd strike up friendships with, or in the woods, and we soon made our first trip out into the desert, Death Valley. Charlie seemed fascinated by it.

"This is part of our return to the land," he said. "We've got to get back to the land. We must learn how to live off the land."

Hardly impressed by the endless wasteland, I merely shrugged my shoulders. "It's okay to live off the land, Charlie," I said to myself. "But the *desert?*"

Then, with no clear explanation—we had no explanations for the things we did in those days—we agreed we should go to Florida for the approaching winter. Charlie wanted to go, and we were with him. So off we headed toward the southeast.

We got as far as Texas. There Charlie's teeth began to

bother him. He was in great pain, both from receding gums and deterioration from the use of drugs and lack of proper care.

"I've got to get help," he declared, grabbing his face with both hands.

We went in at the first hospital sign in a little Texas town and drove to the emergency entrance. A doctor said it seemed to him the only solution was to have Charlie's teeth pulled. Charlie was like a little child. "You can't pull them," he whined. "I'm a singer—a performer—and I've got to have my teeth."

He prevailed and the doctor shrugged his shoulders, giving him some medicine for the pain.

That was the end of the trip to Florida. We turned back and roamed around New Mexico for several weeks, stopping off in a little college town and attracting considerable unpopularity. We were a weird gang, in an even weirder black school bus.

In Arizona we were caught in a snowstorm, forced to halt for several hours and then to move slowly and wearily westward. Charlie, hurting from his teeth, went into a deep depression that no amount of care and concern from us girls was able to lift. The next morning, he announced to all that he was leaving the bus to hitchhike back to Topanga Canyon. "I can't take this any more," he said. "The rest of you stick with the bus and come on back as quickly as you can."

The next day, we were still getting practically nowhere. I was fed up, too, and I talked one of the guys, New Bruce—as distinguished from Old Bruce, an earlier family associate—into hitchhiking back to California with me. When we arrived back at the house, Charlie flew into a rage, swearing and yelling at me and coming very close to striking me, for having left the others.

"Don't you have any loyalty?" he screamed. "What about the others? You just left them out there alone, maybe to die? Who in the hell do you think you are? I told you to stay there."

I tried to hold my ground, but I was too frightened to say what I was thinking. "- - - - you, Charlie!" I roared inside. "You can go jump off the cliff. You left, didn't you? You're no better than the rest of us. So I left. What difference does it make?"

Things were cool for several days between Charlie and me. But it passed after the others made it back with the bus.

So life resumed in Topanga Canyon for "Crazy Charlie and his girls." We were increasingly unpopular with the hippies because we lacked any sort of code at all, especially sexually. They saw Charlie as a strange little guy who was exploiting a gang of attractive, wild, young girls to feather his own nest.

Even in Topanga Canyon days, most of us had been busted by the police several times and were on parole. We were always in danger of being picked up for anything from vagrancy to drug possession—and more.

"We need new I.D.s," Charlie said, and before long who should arrive, fresh from prison, but Randy, a master counterfeiter. Seeing our problem, he agreed to make new driver's licenses for everyone.

When he got to me, he asked what name I wanted on it.

"I don't know," I said. "But don't make it Sharon. I've worn that one out."

Suddenly Charlie said, "She's Sadie Mae."

"*Sadie Mae?*" I exclaimed.

"That's right," he said persuasively. "That's the perfect name for you."

"Sadie Mae what?" I pressed on.

But Charlie was silent. After a moment, Randy said, "Glutz."

He and Charlie roared with laughter.

"That's it," Charlie said excitedly, still laughing. "Sadie Mae Glutz."

"What are you guys laughing about? What is Glutz?"

After a pause, Randy explained. "It's a prison term, Susan. You know, Joe Glutz, like Joe Smith. We used to call the guards 'Glutz'."

So there was born Sadie Mae Glutz, a name that I could rattle off in perfect Arkansas accents when questioned by the police. "I'm Sadie Mae Glutz from Arkansas, and I'm just thrilled with your California." Strangely, it seemed to work.

Other names awarded at that time were "Hymie Hobsnopper" (Charlie), "Katie B. Everglad" (Pat), "Ella Beth Cinder" (Ella), and someone even reached so low as to take "Ima Fibbin." Some avoided bad puns, adopting names that were to stick in many cases—"Squeaky," "Gypsy," "Ouisch" (oo-WEESH), "Little Patty," "Sandy."

One day a group of us were picked up for vagrancy by the police outside Los Angeles. We were sitting in the courtroom when the bailiff began to read off the names. The judge, a woman, started laughing. "This is like a fairy tale," she said. The cases were dismissed.

It was just after our move into a second rented house in Topanga Canyon that I discovered I was pregnant. Conception apparently occurred during a trip to Phoenix by New Bruce, Mike, and me to visit Mike's parents, who were wealthy and socially active. They put us up in the city's leading hotel and for several days we engaged in a luxurious, high-society binge of fancy clothes, the latest hair fashions, the best food available, and one party after another. My lover on that trip was New Bruce.

Charlie flew into another rage over how we had backslidden into the world's way when he saw us with good clothes and groomed hair.

"Can't you guys get it through your heads? You've got to break—once and for all—with that plastic world. It's doomed."

I was the second woman in the group to become pregnant. Mary gave birth to a boy, Pooh-Bear, in Topanga Canyon, which delighted Charlie more than any single thing in that period. He was radiant over the fact that I was going to have a baby.

"We want lots of babies," he said. "They're the kings of this world—completely uninhibited and free from all the garbage of society. We can let them grow up free—free from the plastic world. They won't even have to go to school. They'll learn in their own freedom—even how to talk."

His eyes sparkled and his smile grew wider and wider as he watched Mary's baby.

10

THE RANCH

I walked out of the supermarket and headed across the shopping center parking lot. The walk from our Topanga Canyon house had not been bad, but two shopping bags full of groceries made the return walk look difficult. I reached the road and turned to see two fellows in an old car slowing down as they approached. They were smiling.

"You're headed back down the canyon, aren't you?" the driver asked. "Hop in."

"Yeah, I sure am," I said, reaching for the door. I had seen them before, but didn't know them.

As the opening conversation lulled, I asked, "Hey, you two guys don't know a place where about twenty people can live, do you?"

The one on the passenger side said, "You're with Charlie Manson, aren't you?"

"Yeah," I replied, "and we need a place to live. We're being kicked out of our house. It's gotten too small anyway."

"Well, there is a place," the passenger said. "I'm not sure you can get in there, but it's perfect for you guys."

I was excited. "Where is it?"

"Well, it's the old Spahn Ranch, an old rundown place that was used for cowboy movies. I think the old Gene Autry and Roy Rogers movies were made there. It has a complete western town movie set right there."

"But who's there now?" I asked.

"It's not used for much of anything now. Old man Spahn—George—lives there with a few cowhands, and they keep some horses for people to rent and ride. It's kind of a mess, but there's a lot of room, several houses and barns and other buildings. I think a few of the people from Topanga Canyon may be living in some of the buildings out back."

"Where is this place?" I asked.

"It's not too far, up at Chatsworth, up by Santa Suzanna Pass."

When we got to the house, I took them in to meet Charlie. He was extraordinarily friendly and asked them several more questions.

"Sounds great, you guys," he said. "Maybe something will work out for us. We'll check it out."

The two agreed to take me up to Chatsworth, north of the canyon, to look at the place. They were right. It was perfect. It had some wide open fields, lots of trees, and all kinds of gulches and hills—some rough and craggy just like the wild west movies, some gentle. It *was* perfect. It was real nature, at last.

The buildings were for the most part run down, in fact dilapidated in some cases. The main building, the owner's house, was right in front. Behind it was another house and some outbuildings. To the left was the movie set—a western street, a saloon, several stores. To the side and behind the street were a big corral and two barns.

Farther back behind the buildings was a cliff, running down to a creek that crossed the property. Even farther back, a perfect setting for the little western town were rough terrain and woods, then the mountains. It was rugged land.

To the right, some distance from the main buildings were a sizable house and some shacks. Hippies had moved into them, apparently with Spahn's permission.

After my enthusiastic report, Charlie went to see Spahn and apparently did a masterful job of conning and manipulating the old man, who was nearly blind, into letting us live on the property. He convinced him that we would fix the place up in return for his letting us stay. And never missing an opportunity for enticement, Charlie told George about his young girls, about how nice it would be to have such pretty young women looking after him and meeting his every desire.

When we showed up, Charlie drove the bus way out back behind the hippies' house, out into the fields, virtually out of sight. We camped there for some time as Charlie steadily ingratiated himself into Spahn's favor, convinced him the hippies were giving the place a bad name, and finally drove them out. It wasn't long until we—a group ranging from fifteen to twenty—had taken over the entire ranch, with the exception of George's house. And even there, several of the girls moved in to take care of the old man and keep him convinced we had his best interest at heart.

Part of the movie set, including the big saloon, was turned into a main hangout for us. We set up a kitchen and used the saloon for our meals, parties, and other family events. We slept all over the place, in beds, sleeping bags, and whatever else would suffice.

It was a perfect place for us. We got along well with the cowhands and managed not to interfere with the horse-riding business. In fact, we used the horses a lot ourselves.

All seemed to be going well until, after several weeks, Charlie, for reasons that were never clear to me, decided we should split up. I never understood Charlie's reasoning in this. I knew only that he had fallen into one of his erratic, dark moods. He seemed to feel that the family concept would never work, that we were getting on each other's nerves, or that we just needed a change of scene. It could have been simply another of his calculated maneuvers to keep us shaken up, confused, and utlimately subservient to him.

At any rate, under his direction, Mary, Pat, Ella, Stephanie, and I headed north in the old black schoolbus. We rented a house in the little town of Philo and launched a female duplicate of life at Spahn's. It seemed that I was in charge—although others may have disputed this—and it was astounding even to me how I could control people just as Charlie had. I was able to mimic him perfectly. I could walk like him, talk like him, to the amazement of all who knew Charlie.

The spookiest thing about it, however, was that I seemed to have the same sort of mind control over some of the girls that Charlie had over his followers. I found that I could actually read people's thoughts, just as Charlie could. I knew what the other girls were thinking and was able to manipulate and control them. I seemed to draw from them the same sort of loyalty that Charlie, as mean as he sometimes was, drew from us.

Even some of Charlie's musical talent rubbed off on me. Just as he frequently did, I found myself composing and singing songs that were uncannily applicable to whatever situation we were in. The words and music just flowed into my mind.

We were using drugs just as much as we had been at

Spahn's, perhaps even more so, and my similarities to Charlie were powerfully revealed to me during one acid trip. It was late at night. Everyone was tripping. As I sat watching the other girls, I was aware of other persons within me. I had often sensed that I was in other people, but at that moment I actually saw the dark, indistinct shapes within me. They were alive, moving, talking, laughing. I immediately recognized them as the same beings I had sensed in Charlie. My imitation of Charlie was perfect because we had the same things inside us.

One day I drove into San Francisco to replenish our LSD supply. While I was away, a gang of high school boys from Philo raided our house and with threats and sheer strength forced the girls to have sex with them. It was rape.

When I returned, the gang of seven or eight boys was still there. They were threatening the girls further. But my roughness and confidence intimidated them and I was able to entice them to stop by offering them acid. It was an unwise move. They went wild, turning their energy and wrath on the house and the bus. They literally tore up the bus, ripping out the insides, and rendering it unusable. I was afraid they might kill us, but the rampage attracted attention and before long the police arrived. They arrested the girls and me on charges of drug possession and contributing to the delinquency of minors. The boys were freed, but we were sentenced to three months in the Mendocino County Jail, finally getting that reduced to time already served while awaiting trial, plus probation.

Similar experiences for the other members of Charlie's group brought us all back to Spahn's Ranch. None of us could make it for long out in the world. It was a dangerous place.

Child of Satan—Child of God

Life at Spahn, although intentionally unorganized, developed patterns. There were certain chores that had to be done, and most of the people accepted them without grumbling. Not me. I was a constant complainer—just plain mean. The assignments, of course, were ultimately dictated through subtle manipulation by Charlie, but usually most individuals took certain kinds of work on themselves without duress.

Some of the women cooked for the men, including George Spahn and the cowboys. Some made beds, some washed dishes, others did laundry. All clothes were washed in buckets and hung out to dry. Very seldom were they ironed.

Some were assigned the jobs of finding ways to get things we needed, usually in the early days by panhandling, using a parent's credit card, and stealing. We Manson girls were noted, for example, for our junkets to shopping centers where we raided the garbage cans for discarded food that was still edible. Most of us carry traces of acne and other problems resulting from eating things that were less than wholesome.

Often the afternoons were quiet and slow, devoted to sleeping and lying around. Of course, sex was a major preoccupation and love-making was apt to occur at almost any time of the day or night. During more leisurely times, games of every kind—checkers, chess, cards, and many varieties of word and number games—might break out.

And, despite our professed corner on the world market of genuine love, much time was consumed in arguments and squabbles and, frequently, petty gossiping and back-stabbing. If they got out of hand, however, Charlie would always move in and "suggest" solutions, which was tantamount to dictating them.

Dinner was an important time for us—the time when we

102

overtly drew together as a community or family. We all gathered in the movie set saloon, sitting on the floor, the stage, chairs—some merely standing—and ate our evening meal out of the same pot. Because of our numbers and the fact that so much depended on our scrounging for food, our main meals usually took shape as stews, rice dishes, bread, and coffee. Brown rice was such a main staple that we bought it in bags of fifty or more pounds.

After dinner, we almost always smoked dope of some kind, getting high, singing a lot, dancing, and making love, usually in couples, but frequently in groups if Charlie could talk us into it.

During this period, my hair was returning to its natural dark-brown color following the San Francisco bleached and frosted days, and it was growing long. Standing nearly five-foot-five and weighing one hundred fifteen pounds, I followed the fashion trend of mostly jeans and shirts, with an occasional turn in a long granny dress or sometimes a short-short skirt with a tight top. None of us wore shoes ninety-five per cent of the time, and no makeup, but we were heavy into beads and jewelry.

We had reached the point of sharing everything, even underwear, although none of us wore bras. Sometimes girls would stash things they particularly liked— one girl was always trying to do this with underwear— but we would be discovered after a few days.

Then, given a chance, I always preferred the sexier clothes. I wore pants as tight as possible and, in other things, I strove for the clingy look.

We women made many of our clothes, following the lead of a new girl, Nancy, who was an excellent seamstress. We could scrounge material and she could do wonders with it. One thing we girls made that was special at that time was a multicolored vest for Charlie. It was begun by Lynn, and then Nancy joined in. One by one, all the girls made a contribution to it, except for me. I felt totally inadequate in the embroidery department at that time, and thought the whole thing was rather foolish besides. But I eventually felt guilty about it and made a tiny patch, which someone later covered up anyhow. The unspoken idea was that your contribution represented how much you loved Charlie. As the last touch, we used our own hair and wove a hair lining and hair tassels for it. It actually was beautiful.

Typical of the jealousy and rivalries among us, each of the guys decided he wanted a vest like that, too, and picked out a girl to get it started. For nonconformists, we conformed a lot.

We had just finished our evening meal, and joints were being passed around. It was a relaxed time. Charlie was seated in a chair somewhere near the middle of the saloon. I watched him for a minute as he began to warm up for one of his "preaching" sessions. Then my eyes wandered over the group, picking out the new faces. There was Tex, a quiet, rather clean-cut guy of about twenty-one. His hair was getting long, but he still looked like the college student he had been before he dropped out with just a year or so to go. He was good-looking, and I immediately liked him.

And there was Bobby. It appeared that he had decided to throw in with us and stop trying to go his separate way with his own family. He was still very good-looking, although a bit scraggly right at that moment.

There was Leslie. At eighteen or nineteen, she had considerable mental and emotional strength. She was smart, more than able at that early stage to hold her own with anyone, except perhaps Charlie.

There were many more, Catherine, Clem, Linda, Old Bruce.

Charlie was talking. He was sold on the idea of reincarnation. "We are ageless," he said. "We will never die. But nothing else is secure because time is running out for the world. The end of the world is coming. Society is killing the planet. Vietnam is just a part of it. And pollution, too. Society is evil. Big business is evil. The establishment is evil. Time is running out and we've got to get out into the country, into the desert, to live off the land."

It seemed to make so much sense. There was hardly a head in the room that didn't nod in concurrence, although later conversation convinced me that when Charlie talked like that, we all heard different things. He spieled generalities and we supplied the details individually.

"But despite this," he was saying, "we have to continue to live one day at a time. You should have all thrown away your clocks and watches. That's a must. There *is* no time. We're ageless. There *is* no time. Everthing is now."

Being stoned helped us to maintain this consciousness.

"Love is free," he went on. "Love just loves . . . We are all one . . . God is everywhere and everyone is God . . . Nothing makes sense . . . There is no such thing as no such thing. . . ."

The sentences all ran together, and my mind seemed torn and twisted as it tried to wrestle with them, but to the twenty or more dropouts in that little parcel of Southern California in the late summer of 1968, the year of the assassinations of Robert F. Kennedy and Martin Luther King Jr., they sounded like the greatest words of wisdom ever uttered.

In fact, many of the girls wept quietly as Charlie discussed the source of his understanding. "This is not something I've wanted," he said. "It happened one day in prison. The Infinite One just came into my cell and opened up my head. He showed me the truth. But I didn't want it. I cried and yelled at him, 'No. No. Not me.' But he showed me the truth."

It was an October evening, and I was more than seven months pregnant. Nearly a dozen of us were gathered in the back house at Spahn's, getting ready for a party with our supply of liquid acid. But Charlie and two of the girls were giving me a hard time about taking acid since my pregnancy was so far along.

"Come on, Sadie," Charlie said. "Children are precious and you've got to take care of yourself for your own sake as well as for the kid's."

But I wasn't convinced. I felt the warnings about drugs had for the most part been lies.

"Nothing's going to happen to me, you guys," I said, laughing it off. "You've been giving me the best food for months and taking good care of me. Everything's going to be all right."

Selfishness was in high gear within me. I wasn't going to miss out on some fun just because I was pregnant. So I prevailed and joined in the acid party.

Little of a supernatural nature seemed to occur to me, but I did watch the baby's form within my belly drop drastically. There was no particular sensation, but the baby dropped.

Giving it little thought, I joined in the party, except for the love-making, and we stayed up until dawn. I slept the whole day, waking in the evening with considerable discomfort in my lower back. I got out of bed, but was unable to stand for long. Finally I gave up and went back to bed after refusing to eat the lunch one of the girls had brought me. I didn't feel like eating. All night I tossed and moaned, waking early the next morning exhausted and certain that my insides were coming apart.

I couldn't sit, and I couldn't stand. So I decided to walk, and for the whole day I walked from the back ranch house up to the front of the ranch, back and forth so many times I lost count. Some of the men saw me on the road and offered me rides as they made their daily runs into town, but I couldn't bear to sit. So I walked—and smoked marijuana almost constantly, trying to alleviate the pain.

At one time, when I was near the front of the ranch, I asked one of the girls, Sherry, to saddle an old mare for me, so I could sit on her. As crazy as it seemed, I thought that straddling a horse might prove a way for me to sit down. But the pain was intense. "Surely I can't go another two months like this," I sobbed.

As evening came, I walked back to the ranch house and lay on the couch in the big room, placing pillows under the small of my back. The women were preparing dinner, and it smelled good for a while, but then I knew I wouldn't be able to hold anything down. I was hungry and nauseous at the same time.

About seven o'clock, one of the men started a fire in the fireplace. It was cheery, and everyone was in a good mood. Soon another party had evolved, but I was really out of it, although I did manage to get a toke on every joint that was passed around. I was desperate to overcome the pain, which by then was coming from contractions, although I didn't know what was going on.

There were about twenty people in the room, the music was getting better but louder, and the smell of marijuana blanketed everything. I couldn't take it any longer and slipped almost unnoticed into an adjoining room. The wall was paper thin, but I was away from the crowd. I soon was in deep labor and my groans become louder.

Some minutes later, I was aware of someone beside the bed. It was T.J., one of the guys. He was kneeling beside me. "The baby's coming, isn't it?" he asked softly.

I began to cry. "Yes—and quick."

For at least twenty minutes he knelt beside me, holding my hands during the contractions and then giving me a toke off his joint.

But Charlie interrupted this scene. He seemed angry as he entered, and told T.J. to leave.

"What in the world are you doing?" he said, turning to face me. His voice was sharp.

I looked at him, almost in panic. "I'm going to have the baby real soon."

He burst out laughing. "Aw come on, Sadie. You're not due for two or three months."

"You're wrong, Charlie," I said in desperation. "It's coming now."

The anger returned to his face. "You're imagining things. Now knock it off, and stop worrying about the baby. I need to shave. Will you boil me some water?"

We didn't have a hot water tap in the back house, so I got out of bed, went to the kitchen and began to boil some water. "He's never lied to me before," I thought. "Maybe he's right. Maybe I *am* foolish."

But as I stood in the kitchen for at least twenty minutes—our old stove didn't put out much heat—the contractions came faster and faster. I managed to pour the water into a wooden bowl, got a fresh towel, and set up a mirror for him in the bathroom, and then, almost out of my mind, sat on the toilet. As I relieved myself, I saw I had passed a lot of blood. I staggered to my feet and into the bedroom.

"I don't care what you say, Charlie, the baby's coming

now!"

I gasped for breath. "Charlie! T.J.! Mary!" I seemed to cave in.

Everything else came to a halt in the house. In my delirious state, it seemed people were running in every direction. Someone yelled, "Play music for the baby," and the guitars and singing started up again. I yelled for them to stop, and there was silence, then a rising and falling hubbub.

The girls were all around me. Someone stroked my head with a damp cloth, two held my hands during the contractions. They whispered softly to me from time to time. At one point of great pain, I yelled for Mary.

"Thanks a lot," Charlie said sarcastically. Despite the agony, I heard him clearly. He seemed to think he was the father and should be called first. He was not the father.

At two o'clock in the morning, October 7, 1968, my baby was born—tiny, weak, and transparent looking. His cry was a mere squeak. He was, in fact, the smallest baby I'd seen, two months premature, but alive and well.

I heard one of the men—I'm not sure it was Charlie—tell one of the women to bite the umbilical cord. "That's the way primeval man did it," he said. "Besides, we don't have any clean razor blades."

The women took charge, however, and the cord was tied off with a violin G-string, the only cat gut available.

Nancy took charge of cleaning up the child as others tended to me. I was totally exhausted, but aware of a feeling I had never experienced. I felt I had transferred all my life into the child's—and somehow it seemed a holy glow engulfed me. I felt someone else present. It might have been the result of the large quantities of drugs I had been taking for days, but my awareness and perception were sharp, not drugged.

The baby and I were both treated to clean, fresh clothes and sheets. We had all panhandled for money to buy the things that would be needed for this special event. Tired, clean, and warm, my son and I went smoothly to sleep on a bed placed near the fireplace just for us.

The next day, one of the girls called a doctor she had known, and he came to check the baby and me. He said my son weighed only two pounds, yet every organ was perfect. He instructed me to use a doll's baby bottle to feed the child from my own milk.

Five days later, the women arranged for me to move with the baby to a nearby religious mission and retreat house called the Fountain, where some of the girls had stayed occasionally, hoping to obtain it someday for the use of the people at Spahn's. I was granted permission to stay there as long as I would help with the work.

So then the family had two children of its own—Mary's and mine. We eventually named my son Ze Zo Ze Cee Zadfrack for no other reason than that at the torn and twisted time it seemed like a good name. His name later became Paul.

11

HELTER SKELTER

When I get to the bottom I go back to the top
  of the slide,
Where I stop and I turn and I go for a ride
Till I get to the bottom and I see you again.

Do you, don't you want me to love you?
I'm coming down fast but I'm miles above you.
Tell me, tell me, tell me, come on, tell me
  the answer;
You may be a lover but you ain't no dancer.

Helter skelter helter skelter
Helter skelter.

Will you, won't you want me to make you?
I'm coming down fast but don't let me break you;
Tell me, tell me, tell me the answer;
You may be a lover but you ain't no dancer.

Look out helter skelter helter skelter

helter skelter.
Look out, 'cause here she comes.

When I get to the bottom I go back to the
    top of the slide,
And I stop and I turn and I go for a ride,
And I get to the bottom and I see you again.

Well do you, don't you want me to make you?
I'm coming down fast but don't let me break you;
Tell me, tell me, tell me the answer;
You may be a lover but you ain't no dancer.

Look out helter skelter helter skelter
    helter skelter;
Look out helter skelter;
She's coming down fast;
    Yes she is,
    Yes she is.
                        "Helter Skelter"
                        Lennon/McCartney
                        The Beatles, 1968

Charlie obtained The Beatles' so-called White Album in late 1968. It had a tremendous impact on our lives, especially Charlie's. One night when many of us were playing records and listening to the album, Charlie said, "They're speaking to me." He was convinced that he had some sort of apocalyptic connection with The Beatles. I never fully understood it, but I knew Charlie, our unchallenged leader, was deeply affected. And I and most of the others believed that, in some way, "helter skelter"—the end of the world—was "coming down fast."

But, as always, our pattern was inconsistent. We were running helter skelter ourselves. For example, during this time we struck up a relationship with Dennis Wilson of the famous Beach Boys. I was never sure how Charlie got to know him. It undoubtedly had something to do with Charlie's own musical aspirations, plus our constant need for money. But at any rate, we spent a lot of time at Dennis' house on Sunset Boulevard. Large numbers of us lived there for irregular, but sometimes lengthy, periods. At one time, nearly a dozen of us stayed there, and at Dennis' expense, had thousands of dollars' worth of dental work done. Because of heavy drug use and neglect, our teeth were in constant disrepair.

I was never sure whether Dennis tolerated us because he liked us, or Charlie, or because he feared us. But through him and others, we were often in contact with well-known, respected people within the Los Angeles-Hollywood-Beverly Hills community. We were great at crashing parties.

Charlie was preaching constantly about the end of the world and the need to flee into the country, specifically into the desert. "We have to find a place to live," he said. And he was convinced that the desert was the place. None of us disagreed. We felt an intense pressure mounting on us, a pressure from society, especially the police. We were a strange gang, and the police watched us constantly. They knew Charlie was on parole, as were several others. They also knew, but had trouble proving, that we were heavy into dope, both using and, before long, dealing. They followed our bus frequently. The least little safety violation—a burned-out light, for instance—brought them down on us.

Large numbers of runaway kids were also showing up at Spahn's, looking for a place to stay or hide out. They were from all over the country—New England, the South, the Southwest, and up and down the West Coast. We felt an intense pressure to help them lie low until the heat was off.

But most deeply, we felt that society was destroying itself but that we were immune because we were in "the Thought." The early Christians had referred to themselves as being in "the Way"; we were in "the Thought." We were tuned into God—at least Charlie was, and the rest of us through him. But we believed we had to fight to survive. "We have to survive above all things," Charlie said over and over.

We thus made many trips to the desert, taking the bus as far as it would go, and walking even farther. We explored places all over Death Valley. I had not known an area as desolate or impenetrable before. We had to have a way to travel. Then we came upon the idea of dune buggies. They were to be our solution.

We had a place in the desert to go finally. One of the girls, Cathy, was the granddaughter of a woman who owned a place deep in the desert—Myers Ranch. Not too far away, less than half a mile, was another place we believed we could move into—Barker Ranch. But we needed transportation—dune buggies.

We launched an all-out program to get them. And this led us into serious crime, which became like quicksand. We dealt dope actively to get money for the buggies. Tex, during this time, became one of our main dealers. We agreed on a plan to build buggies, using Volkswagen bodies but engines and parts from other vehicles. This meant stealing cars, which we entered into on a fairly modest scale. The parts we didn't use—a whole chassis, for example—were buried out back at the ranch. We were very expert, and many of the men who had either joined us or hung around a lot, were excellent mechanics.

As our desperation mounted, we began using shifts and working around the clock on the buggies. The rest of the world didn't understand, but we were serious.

My loyalty to Charlie continued through all this, and probably heightened, although there were moments when I wanted to leave. In fact, I did leave several times, staying with some hippie friends in the canyon or others in L.A., but I always returned. Several of the other people did the same thing, but most of us, at least the core group, came back. We were hooked, even on the hysteria.

Since the birth of my baby, Charlie had an additional grip on me to go along with my addiction to his internal power, which I thought was from God. If I got out of line, Charlie would subtly maneuver me to the children and go to work on me about their security and future. He frequently became cruel, manifest most horribly when he would take my baby by the feet and swing him around and around high over his head and then down to within an inch of the rocky ground. He was crazy at those moments. But a split-second later he would seem to be full of love for the children, which he continued to think of as gods or kings.

Despite his control over me, Charlie kept criticizing me for being too independent and disobedient. He played me like a yo-yo, first hugging and praising me, then demeaning me in some way.

One night in the desert, we were walking some distance away from the others. He was dressed in a black cape and was rather subdued, moody. He abruptly swung the cape around him and turned to me. "Sadie," he said softly, evilly, "the trouble with you is you don't fear me enough."

He was wrong. I feared him deeply. But I was at the same time thoroughly committed to him and desired probably more than anything in the world to please him. My desire for his attention was an obsession. I was constantly torn up with the thought that he didn't like me very much, which he kept churning up within me by reminding me that I didn't like myself enough.

The ugliest turn in our course to that point came when Charlie thought he had killed a black man. This sent a fresh wave of paranoia that gave us a vision of all-out war between blacks and whites that was to usher in helter skelter, the end.

Few of us knew any details, but we were told that Tex had been "burned" by a black man in a dope deal. The black man—Bernard (Lotsapoppa) Crowe—was said to have cheated Tex. I frankly assumed that Tex had ripped off the dope, but regardless, Charlie ended up going to Crowe and ultimately shooting him, leaving him for dead. In fact, Crowe was severely injured, with a bullet lodged next to his spine, and was on the hospital critical list for eighteen days.

Meantime, Charlie thought Crowe was a Black Panther and was dead. He was terrified, figuring that the Panthers would come after us. To begin with, Charlie hated blacks, and this only intensified his fear. He often said that all the black men wanted was to get "the little white girls," while he, Charlie, wanted to keep the race pure.

I believe most of the analysts of the Manson family and its crimes failed to appreciate the impact the shooting of the black man had on future events. Vincent Bugliosi, the deputy district attorney who later prosecuted several of us, in my view gave Charlie more credit for criminal intelligence than he deserved. Bugliosi seemed convinced that Charlie was leading some grandiose plot against the world, when from where I was, Charlie was merely reacting for the most

116

part to a situation that flew out of control. Initially, he was reacting to the supposed killing of the black man. He already felt a black-white "armageddon" was coming and then feared that the Crowe case might trigger it. Charlie was not, in my opinion, trying to initiate the black-white showdown, but was merely reacting to it.

To us, helter skelter was real. To the Beatles, their song was a takeoff on the use of a slippery slide in a children's park, to which they added some suggestive, primarily sexual, connotations. To us, it meant things were going out of control in the world, and the end was coming. But we were reacting to it; it was running parallel to our crazy circumstances. We were not starting it. But we knew we had to survive it—out in the desert, for example, where Charlie believed there was a "bottomless pit" in which we could escape the apocalypse and perhaps return to show the way to a new world. This was all very fuzzy, very tentative, very mixed up. But I am convinced that none of us believed helter skelter was something we were going to direct.

I, for one, was somehow aware in my subconscious that things had slipped out of control with us, but I did nothing about it. The feeling broke over me when Charlie called us together one day. "You all know that they're after us. The cops, the niggers, the establishment—they're all after us. And they'll be cracking down harder and harder."

Everyone was grim-faced as we watched him. "I'm going to start carrying a knife. Each of you might want to get one." That was always his way—a hint, a suggestion, never a direct order to do something. "This Buck knife here—that's a good one."

We watched him hold it aloft. "It's not too big, but it can do the job. You might get yourself one and get it sharp. Keep it with you. We'll probably be getting some guns, too, and we'll have to learn how to handle them."

"And another thing," he said, taking a few steps across the floor, "we ought to establish a guard here. We need to put guards on top of our buildings twenty-four hours a day. We can't afford to let them sneak in on us when we're not expecting it."

I shook my head. "What is this?" I thought. "Twenty-four-hour-a-day guards; twenty-four-hour-a-day shifts on the buggies; knives, guns?"

But that wasn't all. We needed more money. So we started stealing more. We stole credit cards, especially gasoline company credit cards to meet our soaring need for gasoline and mechanical parts for the dune buggies. I went "creepy-crawling" with Linda into homes and garages—an expression that came from me as we practiced and mastered silent entry into places, armed with our knives, and moved about the occupied houses without being detected. Barefoot, in old, dark clothes, deadly earnest, we became expert in burglarizing right under the noses of the occupants.

The fear and thrill were exhilarating. I had always liked danger, although it kept me close to hysteria and panic. Furthermore, I felt we were perfectly justified in what we were doing. We were "in the Thought" . . . "in the now" . . . "free from thought" . . . "escaping from a doomed society. . . ."

Darting in and about the dark recesses of my mind was a thought that I had trouble articulating, however. It flitted in between thoughts of knives, creepy-crawling, stealing. It was a genuine awareness that something was happening to the ingredient we had once talked about so much—love. "What's happening to our love for one another and for other people?" I thought one night in one of my more lucid moments, which were less and less frequent. I felt a similar concern in a number of the other girls, but none of us put our thoughts together.

Our thinking had turned to something like this: "We have real love—the kind Charlie talks about. And we have to protect this precious love. We have to protect it from the policemen. They are our arch enemies. Society is blind to the fact that it is under the control of those same enemies. Society is in fact one big prison yard, and the policemen are the guards. The policemen are getting worse. We have to retaliate. We have to attack before we are attacked. We need money to do this, but the money is ours. Everything in the world is ours—the homes, the cars, the credit cards. People only *think* these things are theirs. But nothing is real."

The Beatles' White Album—which, it must be understood, we were being immersed in, along with consuming unimaginable quantities of drugs—had a song that summed up much of our thinking. It was entitled "Piggies" and seemed to liken the straight people of the world to pigs. It spoke of little piggies crawling in the dirt, and bigger piggies in starched white shirts stirring up the dirt. It criticized the unconcern of all the piggies about what was going on around them and said they needed a "damn good whacking." And the final verse told of the piggies and their piggy wives out for dinner, "clutching forks and knives to eat their bacon."

We had a friend over in Topanga Canyon, on Old Topanga Canyon Road, who had been kind to us in the last year. He had helped Mary with food and other things for her baby. His name was Gary Hinman. He was in his early thirties, big, husky, six-foot-two, with thinning, short-cropped hair, and a very gentle spirit, a kind man, who practiced transcendental meditation. A music teacher, he was a homosexual who was attracted to Charlie and Bobby.

One afternoon, Charlie came up to me as I was perched on a huge rock on the street near the movie set saloon. No one else was within earshot.

"Sadie," he said, "you're not a front-line person. You're a behind-the-scenes person. Why are you always trying to get in the living room? You belong in the kitchen."

He paused. "If you want to do something important, why don't you kill Gary and get his money?"

His eyes stared hard into my face. The tension between us was palpable. But within me, I could hear the words, "I'll show him. I'll show him I can be just as tough as he can."

The discussion ended abruptly for the moment. But two nights later Charlie told three or four of us that the need for money was great. I wasn't sure exactly what the money was needed for, except for dune buggies. But Charlie told us that Gary had inherited $21,000.

"I want you guys to go get it from him." He spoke directly to Bobby, Mary, and me. "He'll give it to you, I'm sure, but I want you to get it."

His earlier words drove into my chest. "Why don't you kill Gary. . . ." My body was frozen. I knew I wasn't rational. "I'll show him," I had said. I was out of control. I was a scared young woman. But somehow I sensed Charlie was just a scared little man.

> Sexy Sadie, what have you done?
> You made a fool of everyone;
> You made a fool of everyone.
> Sexy Sadie, oh what have you done?
>
> Sexy Sadie, you broke the rules.
> You laid it down for all to see;

You laid it down for all to see.
Sexy Sadie, oh you broke the rules.

One sunny day the world was waiting for a lover.
She came along to turn on everyone;
Sexy Sadie, the greatest of them all.

Sexy Sadie, how did you know
The world was waiting just for you?
The world was waiting just for you;
Sexy Sadie, oh how did you know?

Sexy Sadie, you'll get yours yet.
However big you think you are;
However big you think you are.
Sexy Sadie, oh you'll get yours yet.

We gave her everything we owned just to sit
    at her table;
Just a smile would lighten everything.
Sexy Sadie, she's the latest and the
    greatest of them all.

She made a fool of everyone,
Sexy Sadie.

However big you think you are,
Sexy Sadie.

"Sexy Sadie"
Lennon/McCartney
The Beatles, 1968

12

MURDER

Old Bruce let Bobby, Mary, and me out of the car and drove away. I looked up at Gary's place. It was a two-story wooden house on the side of a hill, set back off Old Topanga Canyon Road. Because of the hillside the first-floor living quarters seemed to be on the second story, with a long row of stairs leading up to it.

The three of us began to climb the stairs. I was scared. The summer sky seemed very blue, and the hills were magnificent as my eyes swept across the landscape. Sadness mingled with my fear. I was heavy and sad that late July day in 1969.

Bobby seemed nervous but his natural arrogance compensated for it, and he was as cocky and confident as ever. I thought of his competitiveness, especially with Charlie. He was gripped with the need to prove that he could do anything Charlie could do. He seemed to need to prove it to himself, to Charlie, and to all of us. I knew he would kill to prove it.

Mary was quiet and brooding. I can only surmise that she felt much as I did—afraid and sad. Gary had helped her retain her baby when authorities had threatened to take him.

Bobby knocked on the door. After several seconds, Gary opened it and grinned broadly at the three of us. I knew he felt more than friendship for Bobby, but he had been a genuine friend to all of us.

We said, "Hi!" almost in concert. "Can we come in?" Bobby asked.

"Sure," Gary said. "Please do." He led us directly into the kitchen. "Sit down," he said, motioning to the chairs around a kitchen table pushed close to the wall in a little alcove, with just room enough for a chair on each side. Bobby took the place next to the wall. Mary and I were on one side, and Gary sat opposite us, cater-corner to Bobby.

Small talk continued for a minute or two, and then Bobby looked into Gary's face. "We need money, Gary. Would you give us the money you have in the bank—and your cars?" Gary owned a van and a car.

Gary's face clouded, but the smile remained. "I don't have any money in the bank, or anywhere else," he said. "I'll give you all that I have, but it's only ten or fifteen dollars."

Bobby's face was starkly emotionless, without a hint of a smile. "We know you have a lot of money, Gary," he said huskily and barely audibly.

Gary stared back into Bobby's eyes for several seconds and moved as though to rise from the table, but remained seated. "I think you'd better leave now."

Bobby reached quickly under his shirt and pulled out a gun—a .22-caliber revolver. "You don't understand. We want your money!"

Gary stood up and in a flash Bobby reached across the table and hit him flush on the mouth with his fist, knocking him to the floor. Gary spit out a piece of tooth and rose slowly to his feet. Bobby scrambled from behind the table and they began to fight. Bobby fired the gun once, and the slug splintered the wooden cabinets on the opposite wall. He then handed the gun to me and said to Gary, "I'm going to teach you a lesson."

They battled furiously, slugging and wrestling and kicking, all over the kitchen, down onto the floor and then up again. Without thinking, I put the gun on the table, and Gary immediately lunged for it, getting it ahead of Bobby as they struggled. Gary broke clear and held the gun on Bobby and on Mary and me. We stood absolutely motionless. The only sound was the gasping, desperate breathing of Bobby and Gary.

Bobby began cursing me. "You dumb bitch!" he screamed. "Why did you let him get the gun?" He blistered me, and I wilted close to tears, but held them back, determined not to let my weakness show.

We stood there for several minutes. Gary obviously didn't know what to do. There he was, threatened right within his own home. He had no place else to go. His gentleness and sensitivity began to show on his face. He was a pacifist in the truest sense, and clearly had no stomach for the madness of that moment.

With tears in his eyes, he handed the gun back to Bobby. "I just don't believe in violence," he said. "Here. You take the gun. I don't want it. Why don't you just go? Just leave me alone."

Bobby took the gun and with it motioned Gary up one step into the living room. Turning to Mary and me, he said, "You clean the room up and then fix some coffee. We'll be in here."

I could hear Bobby trying to persuade Gary to give him the money. His voice was low and gentle, then sharp and harsh. Gary insisted over and over that he had no money.

Finally he said, "I'm tired, and I want to go to sleep." He lay on a couch in the living room.

Bobby stuck his head into the kitchen and told me to go watch Gary. "I'm going to call Charlie," he said.

It seemed less than an hour before Charlie arrived, accompanied by Old Bruce. Gary was awake. He began yelling at Charlie, "I thought you were my friend!"

Charlie had a twenty-inch, razor-sharp sword buckled to his waist. I had seen it before at the ranch. He pulled it from its metal scabbard and, without warning, slashed the whole right side of Gary's face, from ear to chin. It was a ghastly cut and blood spurted all over the room. Gary screamed and fell back onto the couch, grabbing his slashed right ear. He was in terrible pain. Mary ran to get a towel for him to hold over his face. The blood was spattering everywhere.

Mary and I went back into the kitchen and Charlie followed us. I was shaking all over and was terrified. "Take care of his wounds," Charlie said to both of us. "Make him comfortable."

Then Charlie and Old Bruce abruptly left. I had no idea what was going to happen. I'm sure none of us did.

Gary fell onto the floor and went to sleep, holding the towel against his face. He frequently moaned, and occasionally deep sobs came from his throat.

Throughout that night, Bobby, Mary, and I took speed. One of us always kept close to Gary, while the other two talked and dozed and listened to the radio.

Late in the morning the next day, I walked to the Topanga Canyon shopping center to get supplies. I was in a stupor and hardly remembered going and coming. I ran into some friends from the canyon, I remember, and they all said I looked terrible. Fortunately, they couldn't see inside me.

I bought food, bandages, hydrogen peroxide, and dental

floss. We had decided to try to sew up Gary's face and ear with dental floss, although this never materialized.

Back at the house, Mary tended to Gary's wounds, trying to clean them, but infection had already set in. I prepared chicken and rice soup for him and spoon fed it to him on the floor.

"Don't talk now," I said. "Just eat this so you'll get better." I continued feeding him. He was unable to smile, but his eyes were filled with tenderness and affection.

"Please give us the money, Gary," I said softly. "Then everything will be all right."

He didn't say anything, continuing to accept the soup from my hand. He looked directly into my eyes. "Sadie, you're an angel."

I couldn't take it any more. I finished giving him the soup and left the room. I was on the verge of vomiting.

Several jumbled hours of indecision followed. I don't believe anybody knew what was going to happen next. Bobby, Mary, and I tried to persuade Gary to give us the ownership-registration papers for his cars. He wouldn't tell us where they were.

Then we asked him again for the money. He persisted with his denials that he had any. Then came more hours of indecision and waiting.

Late in the day—the second day—Bobby fell asleep and Gary made an attempt to escape. But Bobby awoke as he neared the door and beat him horribly.

The second night was long. The three of us slept in shifts, and the confusion and desperation deepened. Everything was unreal, surrealistic, in slow motion.

By early morning of the third day, we were convinced that Gary had no large sum of money. We figured it was impossible to hold out as long as he had in his condition if he was lying. But we continued to badger him for the car papers. Finally, he told us where they were and, under Bobby's threats, signed them over to him.

It was late in the afternoon of the third day. Mary and I were in the kitchen. Bobby walked in and said quietly, "You two stay in here. I'm going to have to kill him."

I stood facing away from the living room. I knew Mary was in the kitchen, but I felt alone—alone and cold. I shivered.

From the living room, I heard Gary's voice, "No, Bobby! My God!"

I couldn't stop myself. I ran into the room. Gary was standing, holding his stomach, and Bobby clutched a knife. Gary lurched toward the bathroom off the living room. He stayed only a few seconds and came back into the room. I couldn't believe what I was seeing. Gary was obviously mortally wounded, but we were all standing or moving around. Reality had vanished. A dark brown color had settled over everything. We all seemed transparent.

Gary eased himself down onto the floor and lay on his side with his legs pulled up, still holding his stomach, moaning and sobbing. Bobby went to him and stabbed him again.

Turning to us abruptly, with absolute blankness in his eyes, he swept his arm across the room. "Get a sponge and go through and wipe everything clean," he said. "Don't miss anything."

I looked out of the corner of my eye at Gary. He was dying.

Mary and I did as we had been told and then began packing everything we had brought—food, first-aid supplies—into a big brown paper bag. Suddenly we were moving quickly, scrambling. The slow motion had turned to double time, like an old Charlie Chaplin movie.

We decided on a plan to throw confusion into any police

investigation by making the murder look like the work of revolutionaries. Bobby used a glove to write "political piggy" in Gary's blood on a wall of the living room. Then we checked everything over one last time and went out the door, locking it from the inside. As we turned to start down the steps, we heard a noise from inside. It was Gary. He was still clinging to life.

"We can't leave him like that," Bobby said. The panic in his voice clutched at my throat. He then went to a side window that had been left unlocked and went back into the house. He was inside several minutes, and the hysteria grew. Mary appeared to be near to collapsing. I feared I might begin screaming.

Bobby stepped back onto the small porch. "I had to smother him with a pillow."

We took one of Gary's cars and drove away in silence. Bobby said he'd return for the other one. It struck me that that didn't make sense. We should have taken both cars, or left both of them. But they were in Bobby's name then. Chaos overpowered any rational thinking and we sped away.

In Chatsworth we stopped at a small restaurant where we removed all clothing that showed bloodstains and dumped it in a large outside trash receptacle, along with the supplies we had taken.

Then, fighting desperately to control ourselves, we went into the restaurant and ordered coffee and pie. Bobby's eyes were steel blue once again as he turned to me midway through the pie and said flatly, "I should have killed you too, Sadie, for letting him get the gun."

It was nighttime when we arrived back at Spahn's Ranch.

I went immediately to the back ranch house where everyone seemed to be asleep. I crawled in alongside Ella and Sandra, whispering to Ella as I lay my head on the pillow, "Gary is dead."

The next morning, Ella and her man, Bill, disappeared, taking a truck and some camping equipment. Things had apparently got too far out of hand for them. They were not the only ones to leave during those crazy days. We had grown to about twenty-five steady people, with a core or inner group of fifteen, and many were not prepared for the sort of violence that was unfolding. Even a handful from the core group decided to leave.

Through all this uncertainty, Charlie continued to use "his girls" to attract male followers. He made extra efforts, some successful, to attract motorcycle gang members. They were free and tough, and Charlie both admired and feared them. But not many wanted any part in what we seemed to be driven to.

We took Gary's van way out back at the ranch so it wouldn't be seen. But Bobby felt it was not good for him to hang around Spahn's, so taking Gary's other car he left to let things cool down.

I was scared to death at this time. Mary and I decided we should stay in hiding during the daytime and only move around and mix with the others during the night. I was beset with the fear that I would tell everything if I was caught by the police. All of us were thoroughly programmed not to talk if caught, but I had an overwhelming tendency to blurt things out under pressure.

Even then, I knew the cause of this weakness. Part of it was fear and part was pride—the desire to prove myself to be something special, a bigshot. Throughout all those days, I was consumed more than ever with the desire to "belong." I was becoming more and more possessed with the fear that I was not accepted. In fact, however, it seemed that the others saw me as strong and tough. When the others were practicing with the guns we were acquiring, for instance, Charlie said I didn't need to practice. "You're strong enough to take care of yourself," he said.

Despite my huge fears and weaknesses, I was being perceived as strong because of a power within me that was not mine. Charlie recognized this power and, even though I was sure he didn't really like me, he admired this strength because it was just like his. Over and over, he told me, "You have power, Sadie. You're strong, tough. You're a leader. You know what to do." But he only told me this when we were alone. In front of others, he degraded me. I know now that his motive was to lift the other girls up by putting me, a strong one, down. He played yo-yo with all of us.

During this period of chaos and confusion, especially after Gary's death, we underwent hours and hours, nights and nights, of lecturing and indoctrination by Charlie. He was more intense than I had ever seen him.

"Helter skelter is coming down faster and faster. . . ." The veins stood out on his neck as he declared this time after time. "We must survive. We have to kill or be killed. . . ."

And he spoke repeatedly about the need to escape to the desert.

"Those people out there in the world—they are so busy running for the almighty dollar, they don't have time to just sit and be with themselves to get in tune with the One. They are like robots programmed to work those eight hours a day, all caught up in their little worlds, like living in little boxes, waiting to die, every one of them racing along those freeways to their doom. Even if they could stop and take a look at themselves, they wouldn't be able to accept what they see because of the guilt they carry around. They eat cows and animals and tear down trees and all the things this planet gives us, and don't put nothing back into it—selfish and greedy robots.

"With their bombs they think they're going to blow it up one day. Not as long as I'm around, they'll never blow it up; they'll never blow it up. . . ."

He stopped and then broke into one of his songs, and we picked up the chant with him, "Garbage dump, my garbage dump, the world is my garbage dump, the world is my garbage dump. Garbage dump, oh garbage dump, that sums it up in one big lump. You could feed the world with my garbage dump, you could feed the world with my garbage dump, that sums it up in one big lump."

We all laughed and passed joints around. That seemed to be the only way we would get a handle on what Charlie was telling us. But, before our attention wandered, he took the floor once again and pressed on with his monologue.

"Guilt. Look at guilt. What is guilt anyway? It is just something mommy and daddy put in you to control you to do what they wanted you to do. If you didn't do what they said, you felt guilty about it. Well, listen, I've told you this over and over, right from the beginning, there is no such thing as guilt. You don't got to do what mommy and daddy say to do any more. You are your own person, and you just do what you want to do. Do what you do, and don't think about it. *There is no guilt!*" He shouted it. "Guilt is all in your head. It is an illusion. It isn't real. Everything you see is an illusion, a figment of your imagination. You create the world you live in. You are what you see. Get outside yourself and look back at yourself, and you will see that even you are an illusion. There is only One, and we are all part of that One."

I watched Charlie carefully. We all did, hanging on his

132

every word. "But does it make sense?" I asked myself, taking a toke on a joint. "Sometimes it doesn't seem to make sense." But then I laughed. Charlie had the answer for that, too. He was forever saying, "No sense makes sense."

On August 6, a couple of days after Bobby had left, we received word that he had been arrested and was in the Los Angeles County Jail. His knife had been found in the trunk of Gary's car that he was driving.

Instantly the atmosphere at Spahn's tightened even more. We figured it would be only hours before the police came down on us. But, additionally, we all were affected by Charlie's obsession with getting Bobby out of jail. Bobby had been driven by a need to prove himself as tough as Charlie, and now Charlie was possessed with the need to prove his loyalty to his "brother," to die for him if necessary.

"He's our brother," Charlie almost shouted to a small gathering of the core group. "Our enemy has him in its territory and we have to get him out!"

I had never seen him more determined. His eyes seemed to burn. I, meanwhile, sensed doom. I felt a great cloud—a huge, gray blanket—beginning to fall over me. But Charlie's loyalty touched a similar spark in me, and I forced myself to join in the round-the-clock sessions to find a way to free Bobby.

Out of all the confusion and the mass of words, the constant use of drugs, came a vague sort of scheme to try to convince the police that Bobby could not have done the Hinman killing. It was a plan for "copycat murders" that would make the police believe they had the wrong man in jail since similar "revolutionary" killings were still taking place while Bobby was behind bars. In our crazed condition, we convinced ourselves that the police would be forced to release our brother and we would all meet in the desert to begin new lives free from the world and its problems.

Vincent Bugliosi, the prosecutor, later totally rejected this theory and remained convinced that the Manson Family had had a wild and massive plot to bring about Armageddon and flee to the bottomless pit in the desert, from where Charles Manson—sometimes thought of as Jesus Christ—would one day be summoned to lead the world. It is entirely possible that some in our group—perhaps including Charlie himself—had in our satanic state slipped into such ideas. But to the best of my understanding, the copycat plan was the primary motive behind the most horrible rampage of killing and human destruction in California history—the Tate-LaBianca murders.

13

SLAUGHTER

Tex and I had been secretly snorting, or inhaling, Methedrine—crystal speed—for three or four days. In violation of the unspoken family code, we had kept our own private stash and were using it constantly.

I had become fond of Tex. He was a tall, string bean, bony Texan with beautiful blue eyes. Suave and at the same time very gentle, he was demonstrably grateful for favors and kindness, unlike many of the men at Spahn's.

He was important to life at the ranch because of his mechanical ability. He knew how to maintain machinery and had an uncanny ability to repair just about anything. To Charlie, he was valuable in maintaining our motor vehicles and especially in building and caring for dune buggies. This gave him an independence and high standing among the men at the ranch, especially Charlie. He was also popular with women, but seemed to prefer only one at a time.

It is unclear now, but this high standing probably was the reason we felt we could get away with keeping our stash. At any rate, Tex was as sold out to drugs as I was. He had an unusual way, for example, of maximizing the effect when he was tripping out. He would shake his head violently back and forth—his hair whirling and whipping. Then he would hold his head perfectly still while his eyes rolled and a strange, inhuman noise came from his mouth. He would become stoned beyond belief.

Tex and I, both stoned, were lounging around the boardwalk on the movie set with seven or eight others on the sweltering night of August 8, 1969. It was Friday night. Charlie walked up and called four of us aside—Tex, Pat, Linda, and myself. He spoke to each of us, together, yet separately: "Get a change of clothes and your knife and go with Tex. Do whatever he says to do."

I knew inside we were going out to kill someone. I hesitated. But Charlie looked at me. "I want you to go."

When I returned with my things, Charlie and Tex were talking. I was unable to hear what they were saying. Tex was apparently the only one who knew where we were going. I climbed into the front seat of the old Ford alongside Tex. Linda was the only one with a valid driver's license, but Tex did the driving. We were both stoned, but our senses were keen. We were alert. We knew what we were doing. We didn't know who lived there, but we were going to a house Tex had been in before—formerly the home of Terry Melcher, Doris Day's son. We were going to take all the money we could find and kill everybody there. We were racing out of control.

We looked at the fence at 10050 Cielo Drive. With a pair of wire cutters brought from the ranch, Tex had cut the telephone wires leading into the house before we parked the car at the bottom of the hill. Cielo Drive is a narrow street winding up sharply from Benedict Canyon Drive, a major thoroughfare running northwest off Sunset Boulevard in Beverly Hills out into Bel Air. It is a breathtakingly rugged and luxurious residential area, secluded and quiet. Suddenly that whole section, number 10050, was cut out of the world and lifted up into another existence. We were separated from the whole world. Perhaps for the first time in my life I was deeply aware of evil. *I* was evil.

But the four of us—darkly dressed, I in black jeans and a long-sleeve black shirt, and barefoot—didn't stop. Avoiding the high metal gate, we picked a spot in the fence and climbed over one at a time. As I reached the top, the hot air of the ninety-degree night smothered me. I looked around in a fraction of a second. It was crazy. Some multicolored outside Christmas lights were still up along a wall, and they were lighted.

I dropped down into a bed of ivy and fell to my hands and knees. Together we began moving up the hill toward the house, keeping low and quiet. The house was about one hundred feet away.

Suddenly headlights flashed across the yard. A car was coming down the driveway. "Get down!" Tex whispered sharply. "Stay here." I flattened myself on the grass and the sour taste of panic rose in my throat.

Tex disappeared into the darkness and in a moment I heard his voice. "Halt." Silence. Then a different voice sounded in the night. "Please don't hurt me! I won't say anything." Then came four gunshots in quick succession.

Tex returned immediately and motioned us forward. When we reached the car, a white Rambler, I saw a young man (Steve Parent, who had been visiting the caretaker, William Garretson, in the guest house at the rear of the property) slumped in the seat. Tex reached inside the car and turned off the lights. The four of us pushed it back up the driveway to the garage area to the right and rear of the main house.

We went to the house and three of us waited at a window next to the front door while Tex disappeared around back. In a few minutes he opened the window and Pat and I went inside. Linda remained outside to watch. Quiet in our barefeet, we went into the living room. At first it seemed unoccupied, but we saw a man asleep on a couch. Pat and I moved around behind the couch and Tex, a long .22-caliber revolver in one hand and a knife in the other, stood in front. A coil of rope was slung over his shoulder. Pointing the gun at the man's head, he said sharply, but not loudly, "Wake up."

The man, whom we determined later to be Wojiciech (Voytek) Frykowski, a playboy of Polish background, opened his eyes, understandably startled. "Who are you?" he blurted. "What do you want?"

Tex then, very matter of factly, uttered the words that still echo in my mind, "I'm the devil, and I'm here to do the devil's business."

Still holding the gun on the man, Tex told me to get something to tie his hands. He obviously had other uses for the rope still coiled over his shoulder. I looked all over the living room and went into several others. All I could find was a towel. I grabbed it and rushed back. Tex looked at me rather exasperatedly and told me to tie the man's hands. I did the best I could with the towel, but I knew it wasn't very secure.

Tex then told me to go check for other people in the house. I walked down a hall and passed a room where a woman wearing glasses was reading a book. I waved at her, smiled, and kept going. The woman, Abigail Folger, heiress to the Folger coffee fortune, smiled and waved back.

138

I continued on down the hall and came to another bedroom. A very pretty, pregnant woman was in bed, and a man was sitting on the bed. They were talking. They turned out to be Sharon Tate, the actress and wife of movie producer Roman Polanski, and Jay Sebring, an internationally known hair stylist. I was to learn later that this was the home of the beautiful Miss Tate and Polanski, who was out of the country at the time. A noted movie man, Polanski had produced the controversial *Rosemary's Baby*, a film about a woman who bore a child by Satan.

Miss Tate and her visitor continued to talk, apparently not seeing me. I found no one else in the house. Walking back toward the living room, I waved at the Folger woman again, and reported to Tex.

"All right," he said. "Take your knife and go bring them in here."

So once again, I walked back down the hall to the far bedroom where the man and woman were talking, only this time I burst into the room with my knife thrust out in front of me. I surprised them, and they seemed rattled. "Come with me," I said evenly. "Don't say a word or you're dead."

Walking behind, I herded them down the hall, and taking them into the Folger woman's bedroom, I ordered her to follow. And surprisingly, she came too, saying nothing. I held the knife menacingly in my right hand—although I write with my left—and my costume and bold manner obviously intimidated them.

In the living room, Tex told all of them to line up in front of the fireplace. At that, Sharon Tate started crying.

"Shut up," Tex shouted.

Sebring looked hard at Tex. "Can't you see she's pregnant?" She was very pregnant, and with the bikini panties and flimsy top she was wearing, it showed plainly.

Sebring stepped toward Tex and started to reach for him. Tex turned the gun and shot him twice. He fell over in front of the fireplace, apparently dead, or dying.

The Tate woman screamed, but then quieted into sobbing and weeping.

Tex told Pat to turn down the lights.

He continued talking, "Where's your money?"

The Folger woman spoke first. "I have some credit cards."

I moved swiftly and grabbed her, holding my knife to her abdomen. I walked her to her bedroom. "Please don't hurt me," she sobbed. "You can have everything."

"Shut up!" I spoke fiercely to her.

Tex took her wallet. It had seventy dollars in it.

"Is this all you have?" Tex demanded.

"Yes," she sobbed.

Tex's stony eyes passed from one to another. "Prepare to die."

Tex took the rope he had brought and tied it around the necks of all three. He threw the end over one of the living room beams and pulled it tight, forcing each of them to stand erect or choke.

Tex, looking vicious and cruel, yet blank and pale, turned to me. "Kill him." He motioned toward Frykowski.

I raised my knife to plunge it into his chest, but my hand would not come down. I tried to swing the knife down, but my hand wouldn't move.

The seconds flashed by. I yelled, "Tex, I can't do it!"

Suddenly Frykowski, still tied about the neck, but free of the towel around his hands, grabbed me and we began to struggle. Apparently the rope over the beam pulled loose and we fell to the floor, rolling and twisting.

I was fighting wildly but was aware that Pat and the Folger woman had begun to struggle also. There were

140

screams, yells, curses, wrestling, stabbing, and kicking as a desperate fight for life was waged in that luxurious house of horror in the hills of Bel Air. It was total chaos.

Frykowski grabbed me by the hair and pulled desperately, violently, literally tearing it out by the roots. He had me from behind and I flailed wildly with my knife, stabbing him over and over in the legs. Blood was everywhere.

Strangely, right in the middle of the battle for life, Linda came into the house, obviously terrified, horror-stricken. "Do something!" she screamed. "Sadie, can't you stop it?"

Still struggling, I somehow managed to converse with her. "No, I can't do anything!" I yelled.

And above everything, I could hear Sharon Tate crying, sobbing.

The fighting with Frykowski probably lasted only thirty seconds, but it seemed like an eternity, until Tex jumped in and began to battle Frykowski, too. He hit him over the head several times with the gun. I heard the crack of bone—Frykowski's skull. I thought he was surely dead. But he struggled on, and finally broke free, running out of the house and onto the lawn, screaming.

Just then, Linda came back in. "Give me your knife," I yelled. "I've lost mine." Apparently Linda did give me her knife, for I soon had another one. My own turned out to have fallen between cushions on the couch and was to be found by the police the next day.

Folger, Tex, and Pat all ran out onto the lawn after Frykowski, and it was there that the bodies of Miss Folger and her lover, Frykowski, ended up, unbelievably battered and punctured.

As they raced and clawed their way out of the living room, my burning mind recorded a scene I'd never forget. It was a picture of my good friend Tex—a gun in one hand and a knife in the other, both arms extended and a terrible mixture of scream and laughter coming out of his wide-stretched mouth. He was four feet off the floor, suspended in the air, a man possessed, driven. Even in that second I recalled the unusual words of Linda one night after she had made love to Tex: "I feel like I'm possessed." In that flash, I knew Tex was not a human being. He was another creature.

Suddenly, I was alone in the house with Miss Tate and Sebring's body. The bedlam had turned to silence. It was so quiet that I could hear the gurgle of Sebring's blood. Miss Tate had fallen on the couch and continued to weep.

I turned to her. "Shut up, you bitch. You're going to die."

Immediately Tex was back in the room. "Kill her," he said.

I grabbed her and held the knife to her. But that's as far as I could go. "I can't, Tex."

"Kill her!" he yelled.

"I can't."

He snarled, "Get out of the way, then." He plunged the knife into her.

Once again, it was very quiet. Everyone was dead. I could distinctly hear the sounds of death. In that quietness, I wondered why no one had heard the awful noises coming from the house—the gunshots, the screams. There was no explanation except one later given by the prosecuting attorney: The canyons play tricks with sounds, sometimes causing a soft sound to be heard distinctly a quarter mile away, while other loud sounds aren't heard a few yards away, even as close as the guest house where young Garretson was alone.

The three of us—Linda was gone again—looked quickly around the room. It was a shambles, and blood was spattered everywhere. Little was said, and we left through the front door. We were almost to the gate when Tex said, "Did anybody write anything on the door?"

"No, I forgot," I said. We had determined to leave a message that would hopefully establish a pattern that would recall the Hinman case and cause the police to suspect revolutionaries, probably black, and thus lead them to release Bobby.

I went back to the house alone. Inside, I saw Sharon Tate on the floor. Blood was all around her. I knew I shouldn't use my fingers because of the possibility of prints, so I settled on the towel we had used on Frykowski. I knelt beside Miss Tate and dipped the end of the towel into her blood. It was still warm. My mind began to race madly. I thought of her baby. I had a strong urge to remove the baby, to save it. But I knew that was impossible. Then I pictured myself tasting her blood. I nearly threw up at the thought and a wave of disgust swept over me for even having the idea. I found myself looking at the woman. She was very pretty.

I took the blood-dipped towel and went to the front door. On the bottom section, I wrote the word "Pig." Then I threw the towel back into the room and left. To get out of the door, I had to step in blood with one foot, so I hopped on the other foot down to the grass and wiped my bare foot back and forth several times.

I joined the others at the fence and we climbed over and walked quickly and silently down the hill to the car. Linda was sitting behind the steering wheel. Tex told her to get out of the way, and he got in behind the wheel. I climbed into the back seat.

All of us were angry at Linda for having left us. She remained silent as we changed our clothes and drove away. I had a lot of blood on my clothes.

My head was aching terribly, and I reached my hand up to

it. A large clutch of hair came away. Frykowski had battled with all his might.

There was little talking as we drove. We made several stops at embankments to throw away our soiled clothes and weapons. When I realized I didn't have my own knife, we talked it over and decided it was not worth the risk to go back and look for it.

Somewhere along the way we stopped at a house on a side street where we spotted a garden hose. We washed our hands with it until a man came out of the house and yelled at us, "What are you doing?" Tex told him we had just stopped for a drink of water. But the man persisted and reached into the car to try to grab the keys. Tex hit him and we sped away.

Back at Spahn's Ranch, we drove up to the boardwalk where we were met by Charlie and Clem. Tex told them we'd have to clean the blood off the car—around the door handles and the steering wheel primarily.

We went into the bunkhouse and Tex began to tell Charlie about the night. I couldn't hear everything they were saying, but I did hear Charlie ask, "Did you go to the next house?"

"No," Tex said.

Charlie became agitated. It was obvious he was angry. "Man," he said sharply, "I told you to go to every house on that street. Now we'll have to go back."

Tex was also angry, but I couldn't hear everything he said. I heard a phrase something like "it was crazy . . . everything went wild. . . ."

I couldn't believe my ears. "What does Charlie want?" Dragging myself into the next room, I fell on the bed exhausted. I felt as though I, too, were dead. I wasn't alive any more.

The next day I learned the identities of the people we had killed. Business was going along as usual at the ranch, but I decided to go into the house trailer parked alongside one of the buildings to watch the news on the television set there. The show contained little else but the account of "the Sharon Tate murders." I ran to get Pat and Linda.

As we watched, someone said—I believe I was the one—"The Soul really knew what he was doing this time." The Soul was one of Charlie's many nicknames.

I have no explanation for how hardened I had become in only a few hours. As I watched the TV reporters, I even laughed as they described the details of the horror.

That night, Charlie came up to me again. "Come on. We're going out again."

I knew he meant there would be more killing and I was immediately afraid. But I was obedient.

Charlie, Tex, Linda, Pat, Leslie, Clem and I drove off in the old Ford. Charlie was behind the wheel and he drove and drove, covering many miles, but I wasn't sure where we were most of the time. There was little conversation, at least about where we were going or what we were going to do. It was mostly light talk. I'm not sure about the others, but I was once again quite stoned on Methedrine and was pretty much preoccupied with my own thoughts.

At one point, Charlie stopped in front of a large church. "I'm going to kill a priest and hang him upside down on the cross," he said nonchalantly. No one said anything. In a few minutes, he was back. "Nobody was there."

We also stopped in a residental district, and Charlie got out and headed for a house. He returned soon, saying he had seen pictures of children on the walls through a window and didn't want to harm the little children by killing their parents.

Again, we drove away and continued for many miles, eventually coming to a stop in front of a house on Waverly Drive in Hollywood, not far from Griffith Park. I recognized the house. We had known a guy who lived there and some of us had been to one of his parties.

Charlie got out once more, but he didn't go to the house we knew. He went next door. He was gone for a considerable time, although none of us was keeping track of the time.

Charlie walked rather casually up to the car and motioned Tex outside. They talked for several moments and then Charlie told Pat and Leslie to go into the house with Tex.

I know nothing first-hand about what happened in the house, which was the residence of Leno and Rosemary LaBianca. I know that Charlie had somehow got control of the LaBiancas and tied them together in the living room. Apparently when the girls arrived, they took Mrs. LaBianca into the bedroom, where according to police reports, her body was found full of stab wounds, with a pillowcase around the head and a lamp cord wrapped around the neck. Mr. LaBianca's body was found in the living room with a pillowcase and a throw pillow over the head and a lamp cord wrapped tightly around the neck. The body contained multiple stab wounds, and a carving fork had been left protruding from the stomach. The word "war" had been carved into the abdomen.

Writing in blood had been left in three places. High on one living room wall were the words "death to pigs." On the opposite wall was the word "rise." And finally on the refrigerator door in the kitchen were the words "healter skelter," with the word "helter" misspelled.

In the car, meanwhile, Charlie, Clem, Linda, and I drove around some more. Charlie showed us the woman's wallet he had taken from the LaBianca house. He said he wanted to plant it somewhere in a black neighborhood to try to mislead the police. He finally drove into the parking area of a service station and told Linda to hide it in the ladies' room, which she did, putting it in the water tank, where it wasn't found for a long time. Charlie's efforts to arouse suspicions among the blacks failed, since the service station turned out to be white-operated and situated only on the fringe of a black neighborhood.

When Linda returned, Charlie asked her, "Do you know anyone we ought to kill?"

Linda, apparently trying to keep herself in Charlie's good graces, replied that there was someone in Venice she'd like to see dead. So Charlie drove to Venice.

Dawn was approaching when Linda, Clem, and I got out of the car and went into an apartment complex. Linda led us to a door and knocked. No one answered, so we left. I found out later that she had chickened out and purposely led us to the wrong apartment.

When we got back down the street, Charlie was gone. We soon realized that he had left us, so we decided to hitchhike back to the Spahn Ranch. First, we buried a gun Clem was carrying, and then with several rides arrived at the ranch in daylight. Meanwhile, Tex, Pat, and Leslie had also been left to hitchhike back from the LaBianca home. It was a weird thought: A gang of killers hitchhiking home from the scene of their crimes.

The killing did not end with the Tate-LaBianca murders. A ranch hand at Spahn's, Donald Shea, an aspiring actor whom we called Shorty, died shortly after the two nights of savagery.

Shorty apparently was thought to have known too much about the killings, having overheard a lot of our conversations. I have no direct information regarding his death, but it was believed and widely reported that he had been dismembered and buried near the ranch. His body was never found.

14
BUSTED

Something clicked. Metal on metal. I opened my eyes and looked into the barrel of a rifle aimed at my head. Holding it was a man in strange garb; he looked like a combination astronaut and frogman. It took five seconds for me to realize he was a policeman.

"It's all over," I said to myself, rising from the bed.

I wasn't alone in my fear. All twenty-five of our group at Spahn's ranch that August morning, one week after the Tate-LaBianca slayings, were experiencing the same treatment at that moment.

A two hundred-man tactical police force, including the famous S.W.A.T. group, swept down upon the ranch. They came in trucks, cars, helicopters, decked out in combat gear and camouflage, catching us completely by surprise. Our ragtag gang was no match for them, twenty-four-hour guard or not. Indeed, we were unable to offer any significant resistance. Charlie and Danny, a motorcycle gang member, were roughed up, so badly in fact that Charlie received two broken ribs.

They rounded us up into the street in front of the movie set and searched the ranch inch by inch. They tore up the place, breaking down doors, ripping up walls and floors, knocking furniture and belongings every which way. They later took pictures of the wreckage and told reporters we had been living there in that mess.

We learned that we were being arrested for auto theft—in connection with the vehicles we had been using to make dune buggies. But they were unable to find much evidence. Nevertheless, we were taken off to jail—the women to Sybil Brand in Los Angeles, and the men to the Los Angeles County Jail. Our children were taken into custody and prepared for placement in foster homes.

The Los Angeles police and sheriff's departments were beside themselves with bafflement over the Tate-LaBianca murders. Meanwhile, the killers were in custody right under their noses on charges that were quickly dropped. I was in Sybil Brand, a tomb of a prison, for only seventy-two hours. However, once released, I did not feel free. I continued to be more dead than alive. My feelings were vague, but I was afraid constantly. To my companions, however, I revealed only bravado. I was cocky and arrogant, openly defiant of the law and society.

From jail, most of us fled as quickly as possible to Death Valley. The desert was our only hope. But I had other things on my mind. As dead as I was inside, I still wanted my baby. From the last of August through October 9, I spent all my time working on ways to get him back. I finally found the name and address of the family he had been placed with, and I determined to kidnap him. First, I made several checks on the home, plotting thoroughly its layout and the surrounding neighborhood. My creepy-crawling experience paid dividends once again.

Early one morning, close to two o'clock, Tex drove Sandra

and me to the home. I left them in the car and went to the window of the baby's room, prepared to cut the screen and enter. But, oddly, the screen on the window was off, and the window open. I crawled into the room, and there was my baby. I have no explanation for it, but he was standing up in his crib, watching me enter. He merely stood, looking at me and smiling. I talked in whispers. "Hello, my sweetheart. How are you tonight? Are you glad to see your mommy? I've come to take you home."

He remained silent, but continued grinning widely.

I made my way in the dark, keeping low, to the kitchen and then to the refrigerator. I opened the door without a sound and took out the baby's bottle. It was full. I went back for my son, and then walked undetected out the front door. I had become a master in crime, a first-rate creepy-crawler.

We went from there out into the desert, to Barker's Ranch in the Panamint mountain range on the fringes of Death Valley. Barker's was a quarter to a half mile from Myers' Ranch, which was the one owned by Cathy's grandmother. We moved in and out of those small, rundown ranch houses and had begun, as well, to dig big holes in the ground and in the sides of the hills to live in and to store our goods in—food, weapons, gasoline, and vehicle parts. We had several stolen dune buggies and other vehicles to use for transportation as we waited expectantly for the police to link the Gary Hinman slaying with the Tate-LaBianca murders and thus release Bobby. But it didn't happen. Things just seemed to get tighter and tighter. We had been undergoing constant indoctrination from Charlie on survival—on how to hide from the police, who from time to time were nosing around trying to find out what we were up to, and on how to maim and even to kill. Quite a few of the kids with us had no knowledge of the murders already behind us. They still considered us a bunch of antiestablishment young people seeking a better world.

Immediately after my arrival at Barker's with my baby, two of the girls became frightened by all the talk about survival and killing. They ran away in the middle of the night, and several of us searched unsuccessfully until daylight for them. The girls, meanwhile, had stumbled upon Inyo County police and asked for protection. The next day came a full-scale raid on the Barker and Myers Ranches and our other hideaways out in the wilderness known as Golar Wash. The charges ranged from auto theft to arson. The raid was spread over three days, with the police apprehending more of us each day. My baby and I were among those seized the first day. A total of twenty-four people were arrested, including Charlie.

Since I saw those three days from my own perspective and was aware only of what was going on around me, I have pieced together many of the details of those hours and days from Prosecutor Bugliosi's account, which I have excerpted and paraphrased as follows:

On the night of October 9, officers from the California Highway Patrol, the Inyo County Sheriff's Office, and National Park Rangers assembled near Barker for a massive raid on the ranch, to commence the following morning.

At about four in the morning, as several of the officers were proceeding down one of the draws some distance from the ranch, they spotted two men asleep on the ground. Between them was a sawed-off shotgun. The two, Clem and Randy, were arrested. Though the officers were unaware of it, the pair had been stalking human game: Stephanie and Kitty, the two seventeen-year-olds who had fled the previous day.

Another man, Soupspoon, was apprehended on a hill overlooking the ranch. He had been acting as a lookout but had fallen asleep. There was still another lookout post, a well-disguised dugout, its tin roof hidden by brush and dirt, on a hill south of the ranch. The officers had almost passed it when they saw a girl emerge from the brush, squat, and urinate, then disappear back into the bushes. While two officers covered the entrance with their rifles, one climbed above the dugout and dropped a large rock on the tin roof. I was one of three women inside. We all rushed out to be met by pointed guns and handcuffs.

Those inside the ranch house—three other women—were caught unawares and offered no resistance.

Other members of the raiding party surrounded nearby Myers Ranch and arrested four women.

Two babies were also found (including mine).

A search of the area revealed a number of hidden vehicles, mostly dune buggies, mostly stolen; a mailbag with a .22 Ruger single-shot pistol inside, also stolen; a number of knives; and caches of food, gasoline, and other supplies. Also found were more sleeping bags than people, indicating there might be others.

The second phase of the raid occurred two days later. A California Highway Patrol officer and two Park Rangers arrived in the area before their support did and were hiding in the brush,waiting for the others, when they saw four males walk from one of the washes to the ranch house and enter. The patrolman spotted a sheriff's deputy from the backup unit approaching in the distance. It was already six o'clock, the dusk rapidly becoming dark. Not wanting to risk a gunfight at night, he decided to act. While one of the rangers covered the front of the building, the patrolman drew his gun and moved to the front door, flung it open and ordered all the occupants to remain still and place their hands on their heads. Arrested were three females and four men. There was no sign of the leader, Manson. The patrolman decided to recheck the house. Using a candle in the dark, he went into the bathroom. "I was forced to move the candle around quite a bit, as it made a very poor light," he said. "I lowered the candle toward the hand basin, and small cupboard below, and saw long hair hanging out of the top of the cupboard, which was partially open." It seemed impossible that a person could get into such a small space (it was later measured at three by one-and-a-half by one-and-a-half feet), but, without the officer's saying anything, a figure began to emerge. It was Manson, dressed entirely in buckskin.

Another man, an ex-convict, was found in still another part of the house.

On arriving in Independence, the county seat, everyone was charged with grand theft auto, arson, and various other offenses. Charlie was fingerprinted, photographed, and booked as "Manson, Charles M., aka (also known as) Jesus Christ, God."

There wasn't enough evidence to hold many of our group, so in a few days more than half were released. I was not one of them.

After two days, I was called out of my cell to talk with two detectives about the Gary Hinman murder. They said that Bobby had told them I had been at Gary's house and that they had found a fingerprint of mine. Actually one of the runaway girls had told them of my involvement. I then made up a story about having been there, but I said that Gary had been beaten up by some black men and that he had been alive when I'd last seen him.

"Stop kidding us, Sadie," one of the detectives said. "You killed him."

I was suddenly very afraid. I knew this was the end of the road.

I then said Bobby and I had been the ones at Gary's, but I insisted I didn't know who had killed him. They didn't believe me, and on October 13, 1969, I was booked on suspicion of murder and flown in a four-passenger plane to Oxnard and then taken by car to the Sybil Brand Institute, the women's house of detention in Los Angeles, which was to be my home for the next twenty-two months.

I wasn't going to have to run any more, dig holes in the sides of the hills, or watch for police airplanes. Deep inside, I was very afraid, and yet strangely, I was relieved.

This was our family, just a couple of months before my tenth birthday in 1958. That was in San Jose—mom would be dead in less than six years.

Here are my two brothers and I that same day. Mike was a budding teenager and Steve was about four.

This was taken on December 10, 1969, as I was being escorted from court back to the jail. It had been about a month since I had started telling Virginia and Ronnie about the murders.

UPI Photo

Here are Leslie and I with our X marks still showing.
This was taken on July 30th at the Hall of Justice
in Los Angeles.

Daye Shinn became my lawyer after I dismissed Richard Caballero. This picture was taken June 18, 1970, on our way to a hearing related to the Gary Hinman case.

In October, in the midst of the Tate-LaBianca trial, Charlie and I had to go to Santa Monica to enter pleas in the Hinman case. This picture was taken that day in the courtroom as Charlie walked silently past Daye Shinn and me.

Pat (*on the left*), Leslie (*center*), and I dressed up to come for the closing arguments in the Tate-LaBianca trial on December 29, 1970.

This is the new beatific me in my new cell just a few days before Christmas in 1975.

My smile is because of Jesus.

15

CONVICTION

I was booked into Sybil Brand, a genuine prison with no country-club trimmings, on October, 13, 1969. I knew I would never get out. I knew I'd never see the free world again, but that had little meaning to me then. There was very little meaning anywhere for my deranged mind and soul.

However, I was impressed, even if negatively, by Sybil Brand. It was a real jail—three stories of iron bars and cellblocks. The doors to our cells were opened at 4:30 in the morning, and we had breakfast at five. Unless appointed trusties with jobs, we had nothing to do until the lights were put out at nine o'clock at night. It was one of the toughest places I had seen, and I had seen plenty of toughness and meanness. I saw several women die there from disease and other causes. Burned into my twisted mind was the sight of one woman undergoing a seizure and falling from her top bunk, cracking her skull on the floor.

I was close to screaming myself into insanity, but somehow I knew I had to be tough. I had a compulsion to prove I was as tough as anyone there. Even in my totally defeated and broken self burned the need to impress people. I was beset by twin drives—the need to be tough to survive in the midst of harshness, and the need to feel accepted. Behind both of those drives lay fear that was nearly paralyzing, the same fear I had felt when I was first arrested with Al up in Oregon. Could that have been only three years earlier?

When it became obvious that I was going to be there a while, I was checked into Dormitory 8000 on November 1. This was a large room, a dormitory, with four rows of bunks running the length of the room. It contained forty-eight to fifty-five women, charged with every kind of crime imaginable, some gravely serious, like mine, some far lighter.

My pals from the desert were in other dormitories. We rarely saw one another.

I was assigned a bunk opposite a tall, buxom woman named Ronnie, a pretty, but hardened former call girl in her thirties, who was charged with forging a prescription. Coming into 8000 with me that day was another call girl who had known Ronnie quite well. Her name was Virginia—a woman about my size and build, with short, reddish, curly hair. She had been picked up for parole violation. These two women, whom I seemed to get along with better than any of the others, were to affect my life profoundly.

Virginia and I were thrust even closer together when we were assigned to the same work duty. We became trusties and were assigned as runners, carrying messages between prison authorities. When activity was slow, we sat in the message center and talked.

It had been nearly three weeks since I was arrested and something welled up within me, actually tightening and pushing outward against my chest. It grew and grew until it burst. I *had* to talk to someone about those nights of horror in the hills of Hollywood and Bel Air.

All the women knew I was in jail on a murder charge, but I didn't look like much of a murderer to them. They thought I was a little kid. So they tested me, trying to get something out of me, trying to see how tough I was. They often called me "Crazy Sadie," and with good reason, I guess. My memory is extremely fuzzy on many of those days, but I believe I often walked around in something of a fog, and then would break out laughing and singing, for no apparent reason and sometimes would jump into one of my go-go dance routines. I was "crazy" all right but lucid often enough to want to project an image, to grab the spotlight. The craving again became my downfall.

The great pressure within my chest finally gave way fully near the end of my first week in Dormitory 8000. It began when Virginia and I were waiting in the message center.

"What are you in for?" she asked.

"First-degree murder," I replied.

She looked skeptical.

"Yeah," I continued, "a man snitched on me. He was picked up and thrown in the L.A. jail." I was referring to the Hinman murder and Bobby, not knowing the runaway girls had provided the information on me.

Unable to shut up then, I told Virginia more about the murder in the next couple of days. Finally, she asked me point-blank, "Did you do it?"

I can remember looking her right in the face and smiling until the corners of my mouth stretched tight. "Sure," I said.

I then babbled on with a fraudulent account of what had happened, saying I had actually stabbed Gary over and over, which was a lie. Why did I lie? Why this need to put the spotlight on myself? I was wallowing in my filth and everybody else's, too.

And then came the point, two days later, when I erupted fully. It was late afternoon, and the work day was finished. I walked over to Ronnie, who was lying on her bed, and sat down beside her. She had done a lot of time and was knowledgeable; she had her head together about prison life. I wanted her to like me. I began rambling and went on for forty-five minutes, covering almost everything I had ever done, and ended up knocking the police for stupidity.

"You know," I said, "there's a case right now that they're so far off on that they don't know what's happening."

There was a long pause. "What are you talking about?" Ronnie asked. Her dark brown hair was very long and was pulled back along the sides of her head and was hanging loose in back. She watched me closely.

"That one on Benedict Canyon," I said.

Again, a long pause. "You don't mean Sharon Tate?" Ronnie's mouth actually fell open and stayed that way.

The dam within me burst wide open. "Yeah," I said slowly. And the torrent came, full of lies and innuendoes, full of glory-seeking. I was to be a big shot at last, taking credit for the killing of the pregnant Sharon Tate and all sorts of atrocities.

But it didn't end there.

One night I went over and sat down on Virginia's bed and poured out the same garbage. The clincher came when I said, "I bet I could tell you something that would really blow your mind."

"I don't think so," she said. I didn't know it then, but Ronnie had already told Virginia some of my story and urged her to pump me to see if I told the same story. They perceived they might be able to negotiate their way out of jail.

But I didn't need any pumping. I was determined to establish myself as something special. "You remember the Tate deal?" I asked.

She nodded.

"I was there. We did it."

"Really?" She revealed only moderate interest. "Anyone can say that, you know."

Then I laid out everything in happy hysteria. Virginia understandably got a lot of it mixed up, confusing Charlie and Tex, for example. And because of my lies, she thought I had stabbed Sharon Tate several times in the chest. She quoted me as saying, "It felt so good the first time I stabbed her. . . ."

Within a week of my playing the blabbermouth, the Tate-LaBianca cases blew wide open. I was folding clothes in a big room at Sybil Brand just before supper when a woman burst in and said the official word was that I had killed Sharon Tate and was going to be so charged. In hours, I was moved into isolation, where I remained for three months.

Alone, in cellblock 4000—the mental observation tank, steel and concrete—I began to feel the seriousness of my situation sinking into my sick brain. I lay in my hard, single bed at night, listening to the guards slowly making their rounds of the catwalk—tap . . . tap . . . tap . . . slowly . . . slowly. The lights were never put out, only dimmed. "I've failed again. I've given up sacred information to outsiders and betrayed my own people. I'm going to be fingered from both sides. The world will never understand me. They will hate me. Charlie, Pat, Leslie, Tex, Mary—they will all hate me. They will never trust me again.

What am I going to do?"

A yawning, pulsating sickness filled my stomach. I knew I had dug a deep hole, so big and so deep, that I'd never be able to crawl out. My mind turned to blackness.

In a proceeding that I am unable to recall at all, Richard Caballero was assigned as my attorney of record in the Hinman case. As we spent more time together in the lengthening days that followed, I realized I had never met, or even heard of, a lawyer like him. Richard, a former deputy district attorney, was the most serious-minded and dedicated man I knew. He eventually came to the conclusion, which he shared with me one afternoon, that I was not in my right mind.

"There is a force working in your life that is stronger than you are," he said. "And I want to get you away from it."

I didn't know precisely what he was talking about, but I believed he was right. I presumed he was referring to Charlie's power.

As for my case, which soon included the Tate-LaBianca murders, Richard wanted to try to save my life, hoping to work out a deal with the district attorney's office that would allow me to plead guilty to a lesser crime and get off with a life sentence. Much of the time during those days was taken up in meetings with lawyers and with Prosecutor Bugliosi, who was handling the Tate-LaBianca case but not the Hinman. I was even taken out of jail on more than one occasion, to make a tape of my "confession" and to visit by car the areas of the crimes.

Finally, Caballero struck a deal with the district attorney. He felt it was a good bargain for me. If I testified before the grand jury, the prosecution would not seek the death penalty for me, and my testimony would not be used against me or the codefendants when we went to trial. I was wobbling all over the place in my attitudes toward testifying, toward my codefendants, and toward myself. I just didn't know what I would do from hour to hour. But I agreed to the deal. At least I wouldn't die.

Meanwhile, I began to receive messages from Charlie through my visitors, the members of our group who were not in jail. He was working on me subtly, trying to bring me back under his domination, trying to get me to deny everything I had said. I eventually refused to testify at the trial, although I did go before the grand jury and tell everything as accurately as I could remember it at that time.

Finally, I was so strung out that I asked to see Charlie. Caballero did everything he could to talk me out of it, but failed. And on March 5, nearly five months after entering Sybil Brand, I was taken to the Los Angeles County Jail to see him.

Sitting opposite me at a table in the big visiting room, with a large divider between us, Charlie looked pretty much as he had. He had a beard and shoulder-length hair and was dressed in jailhouse blues. He was friendly but hard as steel just beneath the surface. I was frightened.

With Caballero sitting to my right and a deputy sheriff with him, Charlie looked at me with his piercing eyes early in the conversation and spoke to my insides. "Sadie, are you afraid of the gas chamber?"

I knew he was pressing me as to why I had talked. "No, I'm not afraid of it now," I said, smiling. In that instant I was back under his control. I knew it, and he knew it. But I was still afraid.

He then launched into a sort of doubletalk, with real words dropped in every now and then. The others had practically no idea what he was talking about, but I grasped most of his meaning, I believe. The essence of his remarks, which were tantamount to directives, was that I should fire Caballero, drop any moves toward an insanity plea, and refuse further discussion with Bugliosi.

As his eyes burned into my face, I was overwhelmed with yearning for his acceptance, his forgiveness. At the end of our fifteen-minute meeting, I was not fully certain that I had received either.

But the next day I sent word to the judge that I wanted a new lawyer. I was firing Richard Caballero and hiring a Korean-born lawyer, Daye Shinn. Then I proceeded to deny everything that I had told the grand jury. My deal with the D.A. was blown sky high.

I might be executed ultimately, but I had taken a step or two toward getting myself back into the family's good graces—maybe.

Finally, on June 15, 1970, the trial of Charlie, Pat, Leslie, and me began, with jury selection, in a court presided over by Judge Charles Older. Tex had fled to Texas during all the confusion over the Barker arrests, the lack of evidence, the release of many of our group, and my talking. From there he fought extradition successfully for some time, but eventually was returned to be tried himself. Linda, who testified for the prosecution, was not on trial.

From the outset the trial received full coverage of all its weird details. Little new can be added even with the advantage of hindsight. However, I was left with several strong memories.

First, I was ashamed of that nine-month trial. The crimes we were accused of were horrible, brutal, the worst imaginable. But what took place in the halls of justice was also horrible and brutal. It seems so obvious, with the benefit of hindsight, that on display were three young women clearly not in their right minds who were in slavish obedience to a madman. Every defendant in the case was mentally and spiritually sick, deeply ill. We were not to be excused; we were guilty. But we were desperately sick, legally so, and all the authorities refused to acknowledge this. We were treated as though we were intelligent, criminal masterminds.

For our part, throughout the trial, we did everything possible to disrupt the legal process. We shaved our heads to protest. We fired our lawyers. We loudly ridiculed and vilified the judge, the prosecutors, society, everyone. Charlie shot paper clips at the judge, who kept a bodyguard nearby. I even managed to knock prosecutor Bugliosi's stack of papers and briefs onto the floor one day. He momentarily lost control of himself, took a swing at me (fully reported in the papers the next day) and snapped through clinched teeth for all to hear: "You bitch!" I walked arrogantly across the room, hips swinging vulgarly, relishing a small victory.

One of our most sensational acts—for which I still bear the scar—came near the end of the courtroom proceedings. Charlie arrived one morning and brought gasps from many spectators. He had carved a bloody X in his forehead. Outside, our colleagues distributed a typewritten statement from Charlie.

"I have X'd myself from your world," it declared. Other bits and pieces said:

"I am not of you, from you. . . . I stand opposed to what you do and have done in the past. . . . You make fun of God and have murdered the world in the name of Jesus Christ. . . . My faith in me is stronger than all of your armies, governments, gas chambers, or anything you may want to do to me. I know what I have done. Your courtroom is man's game. Love is my judge."

The following weekend, Leslie, Pat, and I used matches, red-hot bobby pins and needles to burn X's into our foreheads. If it was good enough for Charlie, it was good enough for us. What an ugly mess we were!

One very serious thing that was blamed on us and our colleagues—but which I am convinced to this day was not done by us—was the death of Ronald Hughes, one of our lawyers. Hughes was a big, bearded, long-haired, good-natured man with a reputation as a "hippy lawyer," although he had never tried a case when he was taken on by Leslie as a replacement for a dismissed lawyer.

On Monday, November 30, Hughes was absent when court convened. Much investigation revealed that the burly lawyer had gone to an area called Sespe Hot Springs some distance northwest of Los Angeles where he had often spent weekends camping. Flash floods had occurred that weekend. It was assumed by everyone, especially Bugliosi, that the Manson Family had done Hughes in. Actually, I believe the lawyer died an accidental death. His body was found by fishermen after the completion of the trial wedged between two big rocks in the Sespe Creek.

It was midday on Monday, January 25, 1971, when we received word that the jury had reached a verdict, having deliberated for ten days. Pat, Leslie, and I were taken to the courtroom. Soon Charlie was brought in. He was smiling, and winked at us. We all returned the wink and giggled loudly.

Soon the jurors filed in, and I found my hands and lower arms growing tense, heavy. My breathing slowed to almost nothing as the foreman handed a sheaf of forms to the bailiff, who then handed them to the judge. "The clerk will read the verdicts," he said.

Time stopped in the courtroom. The court reporter, who hadn't smiled in nine months, looked straight ahead—unsmiling. Judge Charles H. Older, graying, hefty, his double chin hanging over his collar, slouched ever so slightly against one side of his chair. Bugliosi sat erect, expectant, in his vested suit. Flourescent lights struggled valiantly against the natural darkness of the room's brown wood paneling, and the air conditioner maintained its incessant nine-month hum. I looked momentarily at the red carpet, vaguely aware of the two female guards standing only a few feet behind me, with Pat and Leslie to my right. One male guard stood behind Charlie three people to my left. Were they ready to clutch us?

Time resumed as I heard the clerk read a long, one-sentence passage that my mind struggled unsuccessfully to pull together. Then he said loudly and clearly:

"We, the jury in the above-entitled action, find the defendant, Charles Manson, guilty of the crime of murder of Abigail Folger in the violation of section 187, Penal Code of California, a felony, as charged in Count I of the indictment, and we further find it to be murder of the first degree."

He continued on for more than half an hour, reading the verdicts of guilty of all charges for Charlie, Pat, Leslie, and me. Three of us—Charlie, Pat, and I—were guilty of one count of conspiracy to commit murder and seven counts of murder in the first degree. Leslie was guilty of one count of conspiracy to commit murder and two counts of murder in the first degree.

Next, under California law, came a so-called penalty trial in which it was determined whether we would be sentenced to death or to life imprisonment. It was a chaotic, dragged-out affair in which we did all we could to throw everything into confusion by changing our stories all around and trying to prove Charlie innocent.

On March 29, with shaved heads and bloody crosses on our foreheads, the four of us were escorted into the courtroom for the verdicts. In each case, the penalty was death.

I was immediately filled with fury. Several things were spoken loudly by the four of us. I can only remember that I shouted out: "Better lock your doors and watch your own kids!" I was overcome with hate in that very instant for those who had judged us. I thought they had no right to judge me or anyone else. They had done too many wrong things in their own lives. They were my enemies. I hated them. And I was certain that the world would fall apart just as we had proclaimed and that each of my enemies would receive his just reward.

I had no realization of what had just happened to me—no deep-down realization that I was to be executed for my crimes. Acceptance of that fact would take several weeks.

Charlie, Clem, and Old Bruce were subsequently convicted for the murder of the actor-ranchhand, Shorty Shea.

16

DEATH ROW

The second huge steel door swung open. There was death row.

It was a narrow corridor, thirty-three feet long. Everything was the same color—cream. My mind quickly counted the tiny cells. It seemed there were five on each side, but closer inspection showed one to be a shower room and the opposite one a bare cubicle with a little table in the middle of it—a visiting room obviously. One cell was for the guards, known as "staff"—one man and one woman. They looked at me quizzically as my escort, big, old, bushy Mr. Morrell, led me in.

"This is Susan Atkins," he said, his jolly, watery eyes twinkling as he gave me a big smile. It seemed genuine.

Suddenly two other faces were watching me. Pat was standing looking out of the first cell on the right. There was Leslie in the second one on the same side. "They're right together," I thought, dreading the hostility I was certain would arise from their opinion of me as a "snitch."

I mustered as much courage as I could. "Hi!" I said, probably too loudly, and grinned broadly.

They spoke almost simultaneously, "Hello." It was very cool. Each stepped back from the doorway of her cell. The woman staff led me down the corridor, past the two girls, who were sitting on their beds, to the fourth and last cell on the right. An empty cell separated me from Leslie and Pat.

"Is this it?" I said aloud.

"This is it," Pat answered. "The last stop."

I turned into the cell, nine feet by eleven, and stared at the interior—a metal-framed single bed bolted and cemented to the floor at the far end, an open toilet with no seat, and a small sink in the near corner. I couldn't restrain a chuckle. "It looks as bad as I do," I thought to myself. I was a sorry sight, I was sure, standing there in a gray, ankle-length strong-dress, so named because of its strong resistance to tearing, with a bald head and a still-bloody X on my forehead.

The woman slammed a door behind me. I turned around. It was made of bars and a grill, with an opening for passing things through. An awesome steel door, with an eight-inch-square window at head height, was ajar. "What about that one?" I asked the woman. "Aren't you going to close that one, too?"

"That one stays open all the time except for emergencies—except when you want it shut to use the toilet."

Ugh. I looked at the open john. Not even a cover. The woman went back to the head of the corridor.

And that was death row at CIW—the California Institution for Women. It was a low, sprawling, military-like institution near the city of Ontario, forty miles east of Los Angeles. I had been impressed by the setting on the way in—a plateau of farmlands with mountains almost everywhere you looked. It was really the boondocks, dominated by "Old Baldy," a massive, ten-thousand-foot mountain only a few miles in the distance.

"Hey, Pat," I said loudly. "What do you do all day?"

The answer was even and emotionless. "Nothing." I noticed the strange echo of our voices along the hall of our cold, stark home, the Special Security Unit—SSU.

"Where did you get your scarves?" I asked. Each was wearing a brightly colored scarf that hid her baldness and X.

"Our parents brought them."

I was surprised. "I thought the past was supposed to be severed, forgotten." I didn't say my thoughts aloud, asking instead, "You're allowed visitors?"

"Only parents and lawyers. No friends. And your mail is censored." Pat was the only one answering my questions. My nervousness intensified and began to show in my voice.

"When do you eat?" I asked.

Suddenly Leslie's voice rang sharply along the corridor, "Why don't you just stop asking so many questions? Just shut up and watch."

My stomach sank. The hostility had been laid bare. I sat on the bare mattress and did my best to put away Leslie's remark. "There aren't any sheets or blankets," I said mildly.

"They'll bring them to you." It was Pat's voice again.

Before long, the woman guard appeared with two blankets, two sheets, a pillowcase, two towels, and a washcloth.

"Hey, can I have a cigarette?" I asked her.

She went to the staff room and returned with a cigarette, handing it to me through the door opening.

"Can I have a match?"

The watchwoman lit the cigarette through the door. "You can't have the matches," she said, and then stood at the door as I smoked. "When you're finished," she went on slowly, "don't put it out. Give it to me." She stood at the door until I had finished.

The old fury rose in my throat, and I immediately hated all the staff and all authority. I cursed the watchwoman without speaking. My anger, which was all over my face, didn't seem to faze her, however.

A few minutes passed and the male and female staff brought lunch to us, sliding it through the slot in each door. I stared at the plastic tray. There was one frankfurter, hash-brown potatoes, green beans, ice cream, milk, coffee, placed in plastic dishes and accompanied by plastic knives, forks, and spoons.

"Not bad," I mumbled softly. The food at Sybil Brand had been terrible. I ate quickly, pushing aside the hot dog. Like most of my colleagues, I had stopped eating meat a year and a half or so earlier.

Finishing the meal, I yelled for another cigarette.

"Just a minute," came an answer. I waited twenty minutes, my rage rising higher and higher until I was ready to blow it at the woman. But Morrell brought the cigarette. As I smoked, I asked him, "When am I going to be let outside?"

I expected a short retort, but instead, the aging correctional officer, who stood six-foot-two or three and must have weighed two hundred and twenty pounds, answered warmly, "Right now, my friend."

I looked up into his face. He had a big wad of chewing tobacco in one jaw. His eyes still twinkled.

He opened the door for me and I looked out into an enclosed yard, about fifty feet wide and twenty deep. Stepping through the doorway, I took a deep breath of fresh air. I hadn't seen the outdoors up close in nearly two years. I walked into the afternoon sunshine and held my face up to it;

I had grown very pale and thin during my early imprisonment. Spotting a patchy piece of dirt near the right corner of the barbed-wire fence, I walked slowly to it and sat down. I picked up a small handful of the thin dirt and let it run through my fingers over and over. After a few seconds I scooped some into my hand and lifted it to my nose. I had forgotten what dirt smelled like.

Completely lost in my moment of return to nature, I sat and played in that little patch of dirt like a child. I don't know how many minutes passed—probably only a few—but I became aware that I was crying. I looked up into the pale-blue, Southern California sky, and I saw out of the corner of my eye that Morrell was watching me tenderly.

In a few moments, I noticed other things in the yard. Right behind Morrell was a tree, beautiful and green, and there was a second one, too. And there, straight ahead from the door, was a concrete bench. My eyes swept over all the other low, brick buildings, the strong, high fences, the lawns, the sidewalks, that made up CIW. "It's like a campus," I thought. But it was far away despite its nearness.

I got to my feet and walked to one of the trees. I touched it gingerly and then put my arm around it. "Nice tree," I said, and hugged it.

I turned to the correctional officer. "How long can I stay out?"

"An hour for now. You can come out one at a time for an hour. But always with a guard."

At the end of the hour, as I was being escorted back into my cell, I asked if I could stop and talk with Pat and Leslie for a minute.

"Not right now," Morrell answered. His eyes were tender, but his expression was serious. I could tell he was concerned about my relationship with my two co-defendants. I had picked up some whispers along that line as I was being skin-searched and showered that morning at the Receiving Guidance Center.

"Let's see what'll happen now," I had heard one woman say.

"She's in for it now," I thought another said.

Pat and Leslie had been at CIW about a month when I arrived after being sentenced for the Hinman murder, and they had had plenty of time to plan a strategy for dealing with me, whom they considered to be their "personal snitch." Our togetherness front had collapsed after our trial. There had even been talk of their planning to kill me.

Back in my cell, I slept until supper, which consisted of beef stew on noodles, creamed corn, two slices of bread, coffee, sugar, milk, and chocolate cake. Again, I skipped the meat.

By nightfall, we had a new, lone watchwoman for the night. She was kind enough, but distant, keeping a close eye on all of us and making notations in a logbook. She seemed to be interested in anything we said or did that would cast light on our attitudes. It was a strange sensation, to know that all your words and actions were being monitored.

On death row in California, residents were allowed the luxury of television sets, although in that first stage the three of us shared one, placed on the wall opposite our cells. I could see most of the screen by sitting to the far right of my door and peering left. It was uncomfortable but provided one way of passing time in those early days. Later, we would really move into luxury when each of us was provided a set.

That night, in late spring of 1971, we watched the news, but I have no recollection of what the world was concerned with at that time. I know the Manson Family was no longer

174

big news.

I interrupted my TV watching long enough to take a shower at the far end of our unit, near the staff office. I stood under the hot water and let it roll off my pale, skinny body. Prison pallor had definitely taken it over.

"So this is it until I die." By then, I had pretty well settled the matter in my head. I was ready to pay for the crimes I had committed. I was ready to die in the gas chamber as prescribed, and I didn't care when they took me. My only thoughts about it were whether my knees would buckle at the last minute and I'd have to be carried in. I also wondered what I'd say at the end. I had no expectation of survival. I was scared and confused, but not about the gas chamber. It centered on my aloneness. I had betrayed humanity, I had betrayed my colleagues, and I had betrayed myself. There was no one left. My alienation was complete.

The water beat down on my back. "How long will this take?" I thought. "Will they continue to freeze me out for the rest of the time? Will I be able to keep from going crazy?" That was a strange thought. "Am I already crazy?"

We watched television until eleven-thirty when the lights were put out, except for the bare light bulb in each of our cells. Occasionally in the night, my nervous sleep was broken by the soft, rubber-soled tread of the watchwoman's shoes pacing up and down the concrete-floored corridor. Step, squeak. Step, squeak. Step, squeak.

Work on the Special Security Unit of the CIW began during the penalty phase of the Tate-LaBianca trial. The workers weren't sure they were preparing a death row or a maximum security suit, although the strongest hunches were that it was the former. At any rate, a lawn was provided and a gigantic fence erected. It made a good yard for us, twenty-four times around equaling one mile. I walked it regularly. There was also ample space for us to plant our own flower gardens. Our capabilities in making things pretty, as well as our embroidery talents—which were revealed by Pat and Leslie before I arrived—gave us rather an ambiguous reputation. How could those "Manson women" who had done such foul things on the one hand produce such beauty on the other? Our embroidery became so good that national publications wrote about it.

And we became very meticulous about our own appearances and the cleanliness of the entire unit. Pat's dad brought a cut rug for our visiting room, and we added decorations we made ourselves. We eventually got bedspreads for our very unattractive beds, and even were allowed to make and have our own clothes, where once again we were ingenious in drawing color and beauty out of very little.

We were really the beastly beauties. Pat, at five-foot-four and a year older than I, was not a classic beauty, but comely and attractive nonetheless, except for the slumping, round-shouldered manner in which she walked. Her long auburn hair was very thick and provided a good framework for her blue eyes. She was educated, well-read, and articulate, although her speech had a cold, reserved quality to it, especially with those she knew very little.

Leslie, on the other hand, had the effervescence, the big, broad smile, the excitability of a collegiate queen. She was tall—five-six-and-a-half—and very thin, and carried herself with exceptional elegance. Her smiling, beaming face and brown eyes were framed by dark brown hair, worn shoulder length with bangs.

We soon were allowed to keep one package of cigarettes and a book of matches in our cells, which was quite a breakthrough. The potential for destruction with the matches was rather great. And at the end of our first six months there, we were allowed to keep small cans of foodstuffs and snacks in our cells, but all cans and pulltops had to be returned to the staff.

Inside our cells we were permitted to have cardboard boxes for tables to set things on. It took about three-and-a-half years for us to get additional furniture—a desk, closet, and wooden box to cover the toilet.

Despite our refinements indoors and out, SSU was still very much a prison. We were under constant surveillance, and security was tight. There was a hotline telephone, for example, placed between the two heavy doors leading into our wing from the other part of the building. I understood that if the receiver were merely lifted, alarms would be set off in the San Bernardino, Chino, and Ontario police departments, bringing armed policemen in helicopters and cars. In minutes, they could have the unit sealed off.

A few months after my arrival, the population on death row was increased again, first by the arrival of Claire, who had been convicted of killing an elderly woman during a burglary, and a short time later Jennifer, sentenced for killing the wife of her lover.

Claire, who had spent three-and-a-half years on a hospital death row, brought a lot of prison savvy with her. In short order, she opened our eyes to additional privileges we were entitled to. She was a short woman, with short blond hair and piercing blue eyes. Agitation gripped her as she paced the floor of her cell telling us to stand up for our rights. And, of course, as she fought for things for herself, the prison authorities had to include us, too.

And even more privileges came with beautiful Jennifer, a

tall, very proper and sophisticated woman in her early twenties. Time out of our cells, for example, increased gradually from one hour to five hours at certain periods.

One of the most significant events in my entire life at CIW came immediately after my arrival. A Roman Catholic chaplain came to see me, bearing a brown leather Bible. "Susan," he said, handing it to me, "this was sent to you by a woman named Horvath. She sent one to each of you girls."

I looked at it. "Susan Atkins" was inscribed on the front.

"Hah!" I said sharply. "A lot of good that'll do me now."

I tossed it onto one of the boxes in the corner, and gave the chaplain a big smile. "Thanks anyhow."

After he had left, I went to the box and picked up the Bible, opening to the front flyleaf. Sure enough, something was written there. "Jesus, my prayer is that you reveal yourself to Susan Atkins."

"Who in hell is Shirley Horvath?" I muttered angrily, flipping the book back to the box.

I threw myself onto the bed, and grabbed my embroidery. I jumped back up and threw down the embroidery. "I'm going crazy!" I yelled inside myself. "These games we're playing are driving me out of my mind!"

Here I was, waiting to die, and we were playing all kinds of games about *our privileges*, and about embroidery and sewing, and about gardens and flowers—and now, a Bible from some weird little old lady! These people can all go to hell!

My mind was still a mess, but over the weeks and months, I was coming to see that I was being eaten up by my guilt and my loneliness. Even my body was deteriorating badly. I had had gonorrhea so many times that the prison medical authorities wanted me to have a hysterectomy. But I refused. And my teeth were getting uglier and uglier, and painful, too. I had taken so many drugs that my entire mouth was rotting away. I had to have tons of dental work.

But my guilt. What was that about? Was I sorry for what I had done to innocent people? No. I was sorry mainly for the betrayal of the people I thought I had loved. And I was being forced to live with two of them in a space the size of someone's living room. My twisted dreams at night never ended. I was alone. I was hated. And I hated in return.

My letters to my remaining family were full of that hate—full of attempts to inflict pain. I was determined, in my pain and madness, to infect everything and everyone with pain and madness.

Had that Los Angeles reporter been right? Someone had told me what he wrote, probably Leslie or Pat. Was he right? "Watching her behavior—bold and actressy in court, cute and mincing when making eyeplay with someone—I get the feeling that one day she might start screaming, and simply never stop."

17

LIGHT IN
THE TUNNEL

The radio played softly, tuned to a local music station. I looked at the embroidery in my hands and was amazed at the progress I had made on the bedspread. The purple was good with the yellow and white.

The news announcer's voice penetrated my consciousness. "From the state capital, this story: The California Supreme Court has voted six to one to abolish the death penalty in the state. Citing cruel and unusual punishment. . . ." That's as much as I heard before the words repeated in my mind—"voted to abolish the death penalty in the state. . . ."

"That's us!" A loud voice came from Leslie's direction. "That's us! No gas chamber. . . ." Her voice choked. Pat was talking loudly. I couldn't piece together what she was saying.

Almost unconsciously, I felt myself slipping off my bed toward the floor. I was on my knees. And the tears came. In seconds, sobs were rising from deep in my chest, and I was weeping audibly, not loudly, but openly. And for the first time since my mother's death, I spoke to God. I remember distinctly; I called him "God," not "Father" or "Lord." It was only two short sentences: "Thanks, God. I want to thank you for letting me live—and all the others, too."

I stayed on my knees for several minutes. There were no interruptions. I'm certain that all across California at that moment, similar scenes were taking place. I merely stared at the blanket on my bed, and then at the embroidery.

"They can't kill me," I said to myself. "They can't kill me! I've got a whole life ahead of me. What will happen now?"

Death row sprang to life. All five of us talked at once. Even the staff joined in. For the first time in two years, I heard real joy and happiness in the voices of Pat and Leslie. All the cynicism and bitterness seemed gone. Their laughter had a tinkle to it.

"I told you they weren't going to kill you." It was Claire talking from across the corridor. "I told you it would eventually be abolished."

She was right. She had spoken often as our jailhouse lawyer, but I had never paid any attention to her. I had fully expected to die. And I was surprised at the impact the news had on me.

The relief was almost palpable in SSU. All of us babbled and laughed. "Now they'll have to put us on mainline," Claire said. That was an unexpected thought.

"Hey, yeah," said Leslie. "They can't keep us in here now. We'll get out with the others."

"I wonder what kind of jobs we'll get," said Jennifer. And that was something else to think about. New vistas were opening in rapid succession. We'd be able to hold jobs and not just sit in our cells all day and night.

Late that afternoon, I lay in my bed, staring at the cream-colored ceiling, and once again my thoughts began at the center of my life—me—but then moved in circles, around and around, before drifting out toward someone, something, else. Yes, it was God. What about God? Why had this happened to me today? It was just like other times in the past, when I probably should have died. Why didn't I die? When I was just a baby, I became very sick—the diagnosis was scarlet fever—and the doctor told my parents I might die. But it turned out to be measles, and I recovered. When I was four years old, I was riding in the back seat of a car between my father and my aunt. We were crossing the Golden Gate Bridge when we were struck head on by a truck. I was the only one to escape without a bruise. There were the times when I was stoned out of my mind on grass or acid, driving up and down the California freeways at ninety and a hundred miles an hour. I should have been killed, but I wasn't. There was the crazy time of delivery of my baby, and I survived. And now this. Nine people in their graves for whom I was partly responsible. My life was spared again.

The swirling increased in my mind and I was unable to concentrate. Everything was mixed up. I was full of hate and bitterness; yet I was alive. I blinked my eyes and the ceiling came into focus again. "What day is it?" I thought. "February 18, 1972."

Within three weeks, Claire and Jennifer were moved out of SSU in their first step toward life on the mainline campus.

"What about us?" Pat, Leslie, and I said, almost in chorus to the staff that day.

"We're told you will not be moved," the watchwoman said evenly despite her obvious discomfort. "You're too great an escape risk. You're too famous."

Boom! The curses and epithets thundered around the entire unit. I'm sure the staff had never heard worse talk from any convict.

The next morning Pat shaved her head in protest. She said she had heard from Charlie during the night. "Charlie told me to," she said simply. Leslie and I followed her action immediately.

Reaction came quickly. The superintendent of the prison, Mrs. Carlson, arrived and stood in the corridor, facing us. "Your little act of rebellion will not get you moved," she said. "You seem to think your 'rights' are being violated. Well, let's have an understanding on this. You have a 'right' to two meals a day and a shower, and you are to be let out once a day. Anything else is a privilege."

Hatred seethed along the thirty-three-foot corridor.

Attitudes in SSU deteriorated badly over the next several months as we watched things pass us by. The United States Supreme Court ruled in June similarly to the state court that the death penalty violated the Constitution in that the way it was administered was cruel and unusual punishment. But nothing seemed to affect us. We were becoming vegetables, and we knew it.

This condition was apparent to all watching us, and one day a light in our tunnel of darkness became visible in the person of a happy, smiling woman named Karlene Faith. She arrived at SSU and met with the three of us.

"I'm from the University of Santa Cruz," she said, "and we are offering college courses to residents at CIW, including you. They will be offered with credit toward a degree."

She looked at the three of us, who were still showing the effects of vegetating. "Do you think you would be interested?"

"Why not?" Leslie said. "Give us some more information."

Karlene, small and frail, smiled her very happy smile—she was in her early thirties—and told us she would be able to bring in other instructors over the months ahead, and we'd be free to study just about anything we wanted—literature, philosophy, journalism.

The cloud of hatred seemed to dissipate a bit, and we agreed we'd like to sign up. As Karlene talked to each of us about our desires and needs, she and I were left alone for several minutes.

"Karlene," I said softly, "my mind is empty—sometimes confused and messed up—but really empty. And you have an opportunity to teach me anything. I'm like an open vessel."

Her smiling face became very serious. "I will do my utmost not to abuse your emptiness. I will try not to infringe on your rights to learn and grow."

One of the most important courses for me in those early days was one on women's studies. I suddenly found myself free from the male oppression I had so willingly walked into in my middle teen years and had violently sealed in my relationships with Charlie and others in the family. For the first time, I got a view of my sexual degradation, for example. I began to glimpse how I had allowed myself to be domineered in the most primitive fashion by other people. In my drive for freedom, I had entered into the worst bondage possible.

I unexpectedly found that I enjoyed reading and writing. My mind began to open up. Philosophy was fascinating and I read deeply, although my understanding often faltered. Unhappily, I knew deep inside that I was still too dependent on other people, only this time they were people like Karlene and another instructor, Jean Gallick. And I was touched by the love and affection of Mrs. Smith, an occupational therapist from the Psychiatric Treatment Unit at the prison, who came twice a week to work with the three of us on handcrafts and sewing.

Friendship began to take root in these relationships, too, especially with Jackie Christine, a counselor and psychological therapist who came with Karlene. Occasionally the dirt within my existence was scraped away enough for thoughts of goodness and human worth to be considered. These thoughts were nurtured by certain watchwomen and correctional officers who were regular parts of SSU life.

Although the freeze from Pat and Leslie toward me showed no signs of thawing, the two of them were revealing signs of easing into thought patterns and mannerisms of individuals, not cultish, family drones. Change was coming in them, ever so slowly, although they refused to let me participate in it. One night I even heard them discussing the possibility that "helter skelter is not coming down after all."

18

ESCAPE

The early morning fog was beginning to lift, and patches of blue were spreading across the sky. Dew was still on the grass—mostly crabgrass, actually—but Catherine and I didn't mind. It was going to be a beautiful spring morning and our anticipation overcame any discomfort from the hard ground or the dampness. I plucked at the crabgrass between my knees and occasionally glanced into Catherine's brown eyes. She didn't look thirty. The loss of nearly forty pounds had left her at the well-proportioned, size-nine figure she had displayed during our days at Spahn's Ranch.

She was talking about her new man. "Spider is such a beautiful man, Sadie, so much more together than Charlie ever was."

"Susan," I interrupted. "Please call me Susan, not Sadie."

"I'm sorry," she said, smiling, "but don't be so touchy, woman. We don't have time to be hassling over names right now. There are more important things to be discussed."

Catherine had always been intense, but she was more so then—in 1973. She and Mary, both central figures from the Manson days, had arrived at SSU just a few weeks earlier, sentenced for an armed robbery conducted right after our conviction in the main trial. They had staged the robbery to get guns to try to break Charlie out of jail. Their charges didn't seem to merit SSU treatment, but they, like Pat, Leslie, and me, were considered high security risks.

Catherine, who had also been known as Gypsy, and Mary had been welcome additions to SSU for me. The cool treatment from my two codefendants had never abated, and the newcomers provided me with someone to talk to at last. While we were all civil and formally polite to one another, there had been a definite three-way division of the five of us—Pat and Leslie, Catherine and Mary, and me, pretty much alone. I had begun to drift toward the latter two, just for the sake of companionship.

Catherine was still talking. "I want to know if I can trust you or not to help me and my partner."

It was strange that she should be asking if she could trust me. I hadn't completely made up my mind to trust her and Mary.

Catherine spoke with a warmth that occasionally reached ferocity about "freedom." She in fact intimidated me. "We've got to fight our way into freedom," she was saying again. "It can't be found in prison."

That was obvious, I thought, but her intensity gave it deeper meaning. I was beginning to understand that she was not merely an outlaw. She was a revolutionary.

"It's funny that you should ask me if you can trust me," I said, as she paused. "My name is not the most trustworthy one in this prison, you know." I smiled wryly. "Can you trust me, you say. Hey, I'm not sure I trust myself, or even that I trust you."

I'd never seen a harder look on a woman than the one that covered her face in that instant. It caused me to shudder.

"If you blow my scene, I'll kill you. So don't play any games with me. Either you're with me, or you're against me. Which is it, Susan?"

I tried not to look frightened. I had more than held my own with the old Gypsy. But this was a different woman.

"I'm with myself, Catherine," I said softly but firmly. "But I'll do what I can to help you get out of here, if that's what you want. I may even decide to go with you, but I'm not committing myself that far at this time. If you trust me and I blow it, I know where I stand. Right?" I paused, and added, "Right!"

There was a long silence. I looked up. The sky was practically all clear, and the slight spring breeze was warming. I pulled on the crabgrass in front of me.

"Okay, girl," Catherine said without looking at me, "this is what I want you to do. I want you to sit up tonight and watch the perimeter man and clock him. I want you to tell me tomorrow morning how many times he drives around the perimeter and how long between the times he passes SSU. All right?"

I was still equivocating. "What on earth for, Catherine?" It sounded dumb, but I was sincere.

The hardness returned to her face. "Look, do you want to ask questions and play games, or do you want out of this hellhole? You just do what I tell you and as you prove yourself to me, I'll tell you more. A good con doesn't ask too many questions, Susan."

She paused, and her face softened slightly. "If you remember nothing else about what I'm into and who I'm with, girl, you remember not to ask questions. Just do what you're told, and you'll be taken care of."

Deep in my stomach was the feeling that comes after you've had the wind knocked out of you. It was that old, old

189

feeling of mine—fear and the beginnings of loneliness. I was cold again. But I refused to show my feelings. I had to stay tough. Catherine had learned things I wanted to know. Besides, she was company, for good or for worse, and if I was going to keep my mind from slipping into the pit that so often beckoned to it, I needed someone to talk to. She claimed she was "a pretty together white witch," with real powers—and maybe she was.

"Say, Cathy," I drawled after nearly a minute of silence, "tell me more about Spider."

I had pushed the right button. We alternately sat and reclined on our little lawn for an hour as she spun out a fantastic tale of her "new warrior . . . Prince Charming . . . everything a man ought to be. . . ."

He was in one of the major prisons . . . "the best, the most popular man in the joints . . . the most respected among the together revolutionists . . . the general of a new army."

"He actually kidnapped me one day while I was sitting on the corner waiting for Charlie to get out of jail," she said, "and I've never been the same since."

I couldn't believe what I was hearing. Was this Charlie all over again? She let me read one of his letters, and to my surprise he named me as one who should join them. I perceived he was far ahead of Charlie in his cunning. He was more serious about revolution, about violence, then any of us had ever been. Yet much of his rap had the ring of Charlie to it.

"Let's walk," Cathy said suddenly. "I don't like sitting around where the cops can listen in. Besides, Spider says we've got to stay together physically; it's our best weapon against these pigs."

So up we got from the sun-warmed grass and began to walk the L-shaped yard. I felt lazy, but Catherine took off like a runner, her hair flying behind. She was walking, but at a tremendous clip, her arms pumping like an old-fashioned steam locomotive.

"Hey, Cathy, I thought you said walk! You're nearly running. Wait up!"

"Either catch up or be left behind, Susan," she said sharply.

I jogged enough to catch up. I knew she wasn't talking only about her walk. And the thought of being left behind scared me.

We walked for forty-five minutes, and it wasn't long before the staff was watching every step. Our sergeant had a hound dog's nose for trouble, and he knew something was up. He had worked too many years with men in prison to relax his never-turn-your-back-on-a-con attitude. My legs were feeling like lead so I welcomed his call for us to come in, but I wasn't going to let him know it.

"All right, ladies, inside. It's lunch time." He stood at the door like a sentry as we filed past.

"Baker, when are you going to give up?" I asked, my nastiness flaring fully.

"When all the cons are buried six feet under and never see daylight, woman, so what do you think of that?"

"Nothing, you - - - - male chauvinist, nothing!"

As I stepped inside the door, Catherine spoke quickly to me, "Cool it, Susan, the man is only doing his job."

I expected, and received as soon as we were back in our cells that afternoon, a lecture on how to con the guards and keep them off our backs. Despite my experience, I still was too messed-up to be very prison-wise.

That night, after the final count had been taken and all the good-nights spoken, I sat up in my bed and stared out the window into the night. Four rows of vertical steel bars and four of horizontal covered the window. A screen covered them from the inside. The outside was well-lighted. I could see the perimeter road, beyond the large field area outside our own small yard. First there was our barbed-wire fence and then the high barb-topped fence twenty-five or thirty yards beyond. And then . . . freedom.

I shook my head. "No way," I thought. There was no way, it seemed to me, that Cathy and Mary could get through those bars on our windows, over the SSU fence, across that large open space with no trees or bushes, and over that outside fence with its rolls of barbed wire on top, placed there just for us after we had arrived. And besides that, there was the electronic beam along the fence and the spot man in his little tower a quarter-mile away.

There were the headlights. That was the perimeter man, making his first round in the car—10:10. We had gone back to wearing watches since the Manson days. How were they going to cut the bars? And what about the fence? "What if I go with them, and we're busted?" I asked myself. "They'll never let me see daylight again!" I shuddered inside.

How long does it take that creep to go around? "There they are" . . . the headlights—10:17.

"I wonder if Pat and Leslie will try to go with them?" I shook my head negatively.

So Spider thought I was worth trying to help, huh? I began to fantasize. "Snap out of it, Susan." The thought broke through to my consciousness. "This is no game. This is for real. These people aren't playing. What are you going to do? If you're busted, or get them busted—if you blow it one more time, girl—you can start counting the daisies and prepare to make fertilizer for some oak tree."

There were the headlights again—10:45. "He's sure not consistent," I said into the darkness. Suddenly I heard noises. "Oh oh, bed check." I pulled the covers over my shoulders and closed my eyes. The watchwoman passed by and returned to her office.

"This is just like old times," I thought, noticing the feeling of fear in my stomach and my rapid breathing. Flashes of creepy-crawling burst into my brain, then dissipated. I wasn't sure if the feeling was good or bad.

There were the headlights again—11:03. "Man, I'm not used to this. I'm sleepy." Headlights—11:15. . . . Headlights—11:20. . . . And on into the night.

"To heck with this. I'm going to sleep."

"Well, give me the rundown, woman." Catherine was eager as I stood outside her window. It was my turn to be outside with Mary that morning. "Is he consistent in his trips around the joint?"

"Nope. It's anywhere from three and a half minutes at the fastest to twenty minutes between trips. I think the guy on the perimeter must stop and talk with the guy on the spot. You'll have to ask Pat about that. Her room overlooks that scene. I can only see the roads and haystacks."

Catherine pursed her lips. "Okay. That's good enough. Now I want you to draw out a map of SSU for me. I need to send it to Spider so he can tell me which is the best route to take. I want every phone in the place marked, where the staff's office is and a timetable of when they make their security calls. Here is how I want you to write it."

She held up a plastic glass half full of a pale liquid. "You'll draw it with this. It won't show on the paper till it's heated. Then he'll make it out. We'll just send an innocent little letter."

I didn't do anything for two or three days after that. I was still wrestling with whether I could trust Catherine, although I felt myself drawing closer to her and Mary all the time. Pat and Leslie were still maintaining their Susan freeze, and I needed someone to trust in. Not to trust is not to live, I thought. Crazy idea. I'd misjudged people so many times, but I figured, "One more time." Maybe I'd win the prize this time—a real friend. Sometime later, walking with Mary the endless circle we made in our yard—this time at a far more reasonable pace than Catherine's gallop, although Mary's long, slim legs still kept me moving—I inquired about Gypsy's man. "Mary, do you love Spider, too?"

Her cool, blue eyes peered out of their narrow slits in the morning's bright sun, and her customary frown turned into a look that said, "Don't come too close, Susan!"

But she said, "Why do you ask?"

"I asked my question first, Mary."

"It's none of your business, Susan," she said evenly, "but yeah, I love him."

"What about Charlie, Mary?" I asked rather innocently. "Did you get tired of his trip?"

Her fierce look blistered me as she stopped and turned on me. "If you never mention him again to me it will be too soon. I can't stand him and I don't want to talk about the - - - - creep; you understand?"

Her fuse was short. "Yeah, all right, Mary, I hear where you're coming from. So how is Pooh-Bear?"

"His name is Michael, and he's fine. I don't call him Pooh-Bear anymore."

"Hey, Mary, there's no need to be defensive with me, I'm not out to hurt you."

She put her hands on her hips, and stared hard into my face again. "Oh yeah? Is that why you went to the grand

194

jury? Don't talk your trash to me. You're going to have to prove to me you ain't going to hurt me any more."

I started to walk away. I was quivering like jello inside, but I still had the capacity for a tough exterior. "I'll see you later, Mary. I don't want to be your whipping boy today, all right?"

Mary and Catherine may have been closer to me than Pat and Leslie during those mid-SSU days, but things obviously weren't going to be lovey-dovey.

Summer came and went in 1973, leaving me with a bit more confidence—although it was shaky—a nice tan, and the feeling that I could really regain a good reputation as a together woman in this world. I'd made maps, written out procedures, obtained information no one else in the unit had the guts to seek. Getting into a procedure log when the staff wasn't around, for example, wasn't easy, and more times than not I'd thought I'd surely get busted.

The fog season—one of California's blessings or curses, depending on your point of view—was rolling in, and it was time to make the big move. The needed hacksaw blades and other equipment had arrived, something I discovered while walking in the yard late on a windy afternoon. The wind was unusually cold.

"You'll never believe me when I tell you we won't even need to go over the fence," Cathy told me through chattering teeth.

I looked at her calmly and said, with more confidence in my voice than I'd felt in years, "Try me, Cathy."

She grinned with delight and whispered into my ear, "We have a brand-new set of wire cutters."

"Oh yeah? Should I even ask?"

"Sure you can ask but I'm not going to tell you." Her grin widened. "Use your imagination, Susan. Spider has taught you that, hasn't he?" She was referring to my inclusion in a lot of his communications in recent weeks.

I pulled my ski hat down over my shoulder-length hair, envying Cathy's long full hair, which she continually flaunted. "I'm starting to compete with her!" The realization hit me unexpectedly. "I can't get back into that! Stop it!"

I thought about how Mary had got the blades in when she returned from making a court appearance in someone else's case—in her rectum. But not wire cutters, surely! Cathy's only visitor had been Jeanie. I looked at Cathy, and she was laughing. She was dying to tell me as soon as I'd admit I didn't know.

"All right, I give up. I thought I knew. But not wire cutters. That's impossible."

"That's not the only place, you know," she said, giggling. "Will it help you if I explain that the handles unscrew from the cutters and that it's only about five inches long and two inches wide when apart?"

"You mean to tell me, Cathy, that Jeanie carried those things inside her vagina, and old Baker didn't pick it up on the metal detector."

"That's what I mean to tell you, Susan. Baker is so busy looking for things that he misses everything. That's why I talk nice to him and don't want you yelling and swearing at him. It makes him mad, and we want him to like us and trust us. You get him all riled up and he wants to bust you."

She paused a moment, then looked at me knowingly. "And furthermore, if it ever comes down to it, don't be afraid to give a little bit more. What's more important—your chastity or your freedom?"

That set Catherine off on another of her lectures. I just

wasn't up to it and said so, edging away toward the door. She continued on walking in the cold wind, and talking. The last words I heard before she turned the corner were "It gets cold outside late at night." Everything she did was calculated, and everything seemed to work. But still, I wondered, how had they passed those hidden wire cutters while sitting in the visiting room in front of a staff?

I was curled up on my bed and had the blanket pulled up to my neck, reading one of Karlene's philosophy books. Capitalizing on our ever-increasing freedom to move about SSU during certain hours, Cathy walked into my room quietly. The look on her face startled me. I thought I'd done something wrong. Paranoia still prevailed. But, lightheartedly, I said, "Hi. What's the serious face for?"

Without blinking, she said, "It's decision time, Susan. Are you, or are you not, coming with us?"

Silence.

"If you decide to go, you know that because of your name, if they see you, they'll shoot to kill. And once you're on the other side of the fence, you're either with us, or you're on your own. You know everything I know about how to get out. You've proven yourself to be valuable. Spider's told you that. So if you decide not to come with us, you can come later, on your own. But you must understand that, once I'm out there, there's not going to be a whole lot of time. I'm going to be busy. I'm going to bring it down fast. I was born a revolutionist. I lived through the underground scene in France during World War II. My parents died in the underground, and I'm not about to stop now. I believe in what I'm fighting for. If you don't, then tell me now, sister, because I'm ready to make my move."

I knew something about Catherine's childhood. It had been full of pain. She was the daughter of a Hungarian musician and a woman of German-Jewish background. They had fled from the Nazis to France, and there had fought in the underground after the fall of that nation. They ultimately committed suicide during the war. Catherine was adopted by an American family when she was eight, only to have her adoptive mother commit suicide after being stricken with cancer. Catherine cared for her blind father, a psychologist, until he remarried, and then she went off on her own, marrying, divorcing, playing in small movie parts until she met Bobby and, through him, Charlie. She was one of the most talented members of the Manson group—an outstanding violinist and a magnificent singer. She was experienced, and she was tough.

"I don't need any albatrosses around my neck, Susan, and I can't carry your load for you. There are people out there who will hide you if you make it. If you don't make it, well, you'll have gone down fighting instead of lying here dead in your head."

I still didn't answer, so she rambled on. "I want you to know that all you have done for us so far has been appreciated. I've taught you as best I can. I thank you for staying up and typing those nights while I was working on getting my bar out. If I'm busted before I make it and you choose not to go, they can't implicate you one bit. You can merely say you didn't know what was going on. But, if you try now, and get busted with me and Mary, you'll never be given another chance by them."

I sat on the bed, and picked at the bedspread. "In all honesty, Cathy, I've really weighed it all. I've considered the chances. I know I can't stay here with them, Pat and Les. They drive me crazy. You know I can't handle their games

198

any more, and the thought of staying in SSU the rest of my life blows my mind."

I stopped. I *had* to go on. Could I? "But I'm not ready to go with you yet. *If* I do go, and *when* I do go, I'm going to have to do it on my own. I can't join you and Mary and Spider. That is too much like the past. I don't want to be on your trip. I want my own trip. Can you dig it? I'm together enough now, I think, to know I've got to stand alone and make my own decisions. This is my first decision—I'm going to stay behind."

I was exhausted with my spiel..Exhausted and afraid. Was I right?

Catherine spoke. "I hear you, sister. You've come a long way. But, seriously, Spider will be proud of you. He'll be disappointed that you aren't coming out with us, but he'll understand. And your stand, when you make your move, will make a lot of dudes inside want to have a woman like you on their team. Don't worry about finding a man. He'll find you, Susan."

She was very close to being as tender as we once had been toward one another. But she pressed on, "I'll write you through your attorney if I need to contact you for anything. All right?"

I nodded.

"Tonight," she said softly, "I need you to type real loud one more time. Pat is going to turn up her stereo loud for us and we should be all the way through the bar tonight. Mrs. Barnhouse will be on, and she ain't too smart, you know, so I'll tap on the wall when I need for you to stop typing. Mary will be in my room around midnight. Her lock is all ready."

She hesitated. "This is it, sister, time to get it on. Check you later."

With that last word, the together witch left. She knew her

business, and I respected her. But the old affection was gone. The only thing I was really attracted to by then was her power to make things happen. She was just like Charlie—and apparently Spider. If she pictured things in her mind, they seemed to happen.

I hammered on the keys till my fingers were sore. I'd been at it for nearly two hours. Suddenly, I felt something in the air. Something was wrong. I stopped typing, and Pat's stereo was suddenly turned way down. Leslie was saying something to Pat as I got up and went to my grill door.

Mrs. Barnhouse was standing in front of Cathy's cell. "Don't move, you! It's all over! You've had it!"

Confusion rolled in like a whirlwind. All the lights went on, and staff people filled the corridor. For four hours, a storm raged such as CIW had never seen. Two women had come within a fraction of escaping from the highest security this medium-to-minimum-security prison had to offer. The screen was off its brackets. The last bar needed to clear the window was all but an eighth of an inch through. And in one cell were the two women, a pair of wire cutters, two backpacks with makeshift camping gear. All unheard of.

I sat quietly on my bed. I wondered about all the privileges we were going to lose—the ones we had worked for for two years. We'd just have to start over.

But what about Catherine and Mary? They, too, would just have to start over. I shook my head as I thought about the second plan they had already laid out should the first go awry. Nothing was outside their calculation.

19

THE BRINK
OF INSANITY

It was winter. And, despite Southern California's reputation, it was cold and windy. But in my cell, my coldness was not entirely from the weather. I had even felt it in the hot grip of summer.

I had the covers over my head, refusing to face the early morning light. An image of a pair of pliers flickered in my mind. They were clamped tight against a rod or bar or something. It looked like metal at first, but it was softer. It was like dirt or clay. It was cracking and crumbling under the pressure of the tightening pliers.

That was me . . . caught in the middle. The squeeze was on. But who was squeezing the pliers?

The attempted escape and failure had polarized things more clearly in SSU. Pat and Leslie were just about finished with Mary and Cathy. "They didn't give a damn about us, and what it would cost us, when they tried to go out of here and blew it," Leslie had complained bitterly during one of those rare moments when she would talk to me. "We're all lumped in with them in everyone's eyes, and we'll suffer for their screw-ups."

Meanwhile, Mary and Cathy saw the other two as "dead skunks in the middle of the road," a line borrowed from a song playing on the radio a lot in those days. It was funny at first, until the deadly seriousness sank in. We still hadn't escaped from our habit of deriving reality from the unrealities of recorded music.

"I'm stuck in between," I thought. "This is crazy. Is this just going to be one endless road of attempts and failures at breaking out of here, with Pat and Leslie yipping and yapping from the other side? What if they do break out? Can I take this endless monotony of Pat and Leslie's ignoring-Susan game? How long can I stand up to all this crap anyway?"

I rolled over, but kept the covers over my head. "Why don't I just blow it? Nobody gives a damn anyway . . . None of these crazy women care . . . And the staff . . . They're just - - - - pigs paid to watch me and make sure I don't go anywhere . . . I'm losing my mind!"

A hurricane raged in me. "What if I go crazy? Who'll clean up my room?" That was uppermost in my mind, and there was nothing funny about it. "What about my embroidery?" I thought. That wasn't funny either. "I've got to be able to function, at least. No one can know I'm going - - - - crazy. If I just nod my head and act like I understand and am right there with them, they'll never know the difference . . . 'cause they really don't care. Not even Cathy and all her fine talk. She's just using me anyway, and I'm the duck that's going for it."

I flung the covers back and quickly stood up, my heavy nightgown falling to my ankles. I looked out into the corridor. "Why don't they open my door? I've got to get outside."

I yelled into the corridor. "Mr. Henry! Please open the

door! I've got to get outside!"

Our middle-aged guard, Mr. Henry, came quickly down the hall. He looked into my room. "Susan, are you all right?"

"No, damn it, I'm not! Will you please let me outside? I've got to get some fresh air."

I didn't realize it until I started to move, but my face was wet with tears. My nose was running. I could hardly see.

"Okay," the kindly guard said, "come on."

The tears were hot, like lava, on my face. I felt like someone deep in the throes of the flu. He opened my door and then the door to the yard. I plunged out, barefooted and without a coat. The cold air hit my burning face with a whoosh. It stung. My hot face and breath formed a mist all about my head. It was like fog on the moors.

I stepped across the ice-cold pavement onto the yellowed grass. It was freezing. I hugged my sides with my arms and burst across the yard. "I've got to maintain!" I yelled inside myself. "I've got to maintain!"

I spoke sharply to the guard. "I'm going crazy, Mr. Henry!" It wasn't a scream; it was merely a statement. "I'm going crazy."

The waves broke over me and I sobbed uncontrollably. It seemed that the sobs were outside me at first, but then I knew they were from down inside my bowels. My cries mingled with the twittering of the morning birds— damnation and beauty running together in the wintry morning.

"I've got to stop," I said to myself. "No one must see me cry. They mustn't see me blow it. Who's going to get me dressed? Who's going to take care of my room? Oh, my God, I'm losing my mind!"

Suddenly, I stopped. "Mr. Henry, what day is it? Please tell me what day it is."

He stood close to me, a fatherly man, deeply anxious. "It's going to be all right, Susan. It's going to be all right."

I pushed him away. "No! No! It's not all right. I'm blowing it and I don't know why. No one can help me. I'm losing my mind."

I was caught completely off guard by a soothing voice, beautifully low pitched—a woman's voice. "Susan. Susan. Listen to me." The words were like a soft violin. And I felt the reassuring touch of Cathy's hand on my arm. I turned and through blurred, burning eyes met Cathy's firm, steady gaze. My head felt swollen from the explosions within it as I wrestled with the words coming from her full, pretty lips. "Susan, listen to me."

I could tell she feared I was gone, so I struggled for control, to give her a sign of recognition. "I'm blowing it, Cathy. I'm blowing it." I spoke as softly and clearly as I could manage.

Her face held even. "Okay, so you're blowing it. Come on inside where it's warm. You can blow it in there just as well."

She led me back into the unit, like a mother leading a child who had gone astray, past doors that seemed to be full of peering eyes and quizzical, although slightly frightened, looks. Mutterings and mumblings rolled into my flooded mind. "She's gone crazy. At last. So what else is new?"

Cathy led me into the visiting room. But where was Mr. Henry? Oh, he was probably making some coffee. That was all we ever did anymore—make coffee, eat, sleep, make coffee. This was crazy. Why hadn't they just killed me and gotten it over with?

"Cathy." The words spewed out. "I'm not able to maintain any more. It's like one long acid trip, and it's a bummer, man, a real bummer."

Cathy said nothing for several seconds. We both sat at the

small table in the visiting room.

"Susan, if you decide to go crazy, *know* that you are deciding to go crazy. It is *your* decision."

She paused, and her tempo increased slightly. "These people here will take care of you. You don't have to worry about what you will wear, or when to take a bath, or what to eat, or anything. They'll take care of you. So if you're worried about not being able to function, don't worry about it. Just let go of the branch and fall, baby, fall. Or else, pull yourself up and get back to the edge and hold on."

She seemed so confident. That was the most impressive thing about the moment; yet her words made sense in my drowning mind. "If you let go, you'll only have to land once. If you get back up on the ledge, you may have to jump to get over this gaping hole in your life. But one thing is for sure—you can't hold onto a branch forever, Susan."

Cathy got up from the table and walked around the little room. Her steps were soundless on the carpeted floor. She was still in her nightgown.

"I've told you before, woman, you have four ways to go. Do you remember that time out in the yard a few weeks ago? And you were wondering what you should do because of my first bust. I told you I'd try again, remember? And I invited you to go with me—the way was still open. That was one way. Or, I said, you can sit here in prison and rot or die, because you're not a good convict. Your reputation out there on mainline ain't exactly Susie Cream Cheese, you know. Or, I said, you could become a Jesus freak and preach your way out of prison. Lots of people are going that route. You see them all the time on TV and they're always writing to you to try to save your soul."

She laughed. But I didn't. I wondered inside, "And what's so bad about someone wanting to save my soul?" I didn't dare say it out loud because I was no match for her philosophy. She believed all souls were saved already, or something like that.

"Or," she continued as she paced, "you can go crazy and flip out into never-never land. The chance you take there is this: There's no guarantee that you'll ever return to reality."

She stopped speaking and walking, staring down at me in the chair. "It looks to me, Susan, like you've begun to make your choice. Is this what you want? If so, then let go of the branch and fall, baby."

She turned abruptly and walked out of the room, passing Mr. Henry, who was bringing a cup of coffee to me.

Like a zombie, coffee cup in hand, I walked back outside into the cold air. There were no leaves on the trees. They were like gray skeletons. The grass was like dirty straw stubble. Standing transfixed, looking out across the distant cow pastures and then on to the blue-gray mountains, I spotted a spider's web. It was woven between two of the steel strands in the fence around the SSU yard. As I watched, the web seemed to take the shape of a whirlpool, swirling down and away into grayness.

"I'll be damned if I'll go crazy," I said half-aloud. "I'm not going to let go."

I'm not sure if I continued speaking aloud or not. I know Mr. Henry was watching from a distance, but no one else was near.

"I'll die if I escape. They'll no doubt shoot me. I'm not clever or tough enough to make it on the run for long. And I can't stand rotting in prison forever. What does that leave me? Become a Jesus freak and preach my way out?"

Even in my twisted condition, I laughed. "Who would believe me if I turned to God? The foulest mouth in the prison . . . the one with the deepest hate for everyone and everything here . . . the one with the temper tantrums and gross attitudes toward anything good . . . the one with so much guilt and self-condemnation buried under an attitude of I-don't-give-a-damn . . . the one who feels guilty just for feeling guilty . . . Who would believe somebody like that?"

There had to be another way.

I could feel the stains on my face. It was stiff and scratchy. The coffee mug was cold in my hands, but I could feel the sun starting to warm my back.

"I'll just have to take it a step at a time," I said, turning to look at the grim SSU building. "If I don't turn loose of the branch, then I've got to find reality. I've got to find the truth. Does anyone know the truth? What is that, anyway? It's a dumb word."

My eyes landed on Mr. Henry. "I've got to stop thinking," I said to myself, "or I *will* go crazy. I'll start thinking tomorrow. Yes . . . tomorrow."

I went back to my bed.

Mary and Cathy made one more effort to escape. Again, they were unsuccessful. They got their bars sawed through, but they never got outside their rooms. They had managed to hide their hacksaw blades in some book bindings after the first debacle, and no amount of searching by the staff—even in our flower gardens out in the yard—with metal detectors and all other modern devices and techniques turned up anything.

Much of the relaxed attitude that had developed among the staff and us over the previous two years vanished—at least for a while—both Mary and Cathy received bad reports, called CDC 115's, for their files.

But eventually, the storm passed and Catherine was

ultimately released from the prison. I had no explanation for her early departure beyond her own claims that she was a "white witch" who could postulate anything and see it come to pass, whether with prison authorities or anyone else. She also was a master con artist.

As for Mary, she was not released from the prison, but she was eventually removed from SSU and placed in the mainline population at CIW.

The three of us who had declined to join in the escape attempts remained in the Special Security Unit. Such are the vagaries of prison life.

20

THE
BLOWING WIND

It was early in January, 1974, and a number of currents within my life were moving at the same time—all related perhaps, but not always obviously so. I had made an all-out commitment to find the "truth" and to being honest in that search. Cathy and Mary's second escape attempt was still in the planning stage, and I was equivocating on what I might do regarding them, although I felt pretty much as I had before—this was not my time.

In addition to my embroilment with "truth," I was caught up in one of those crazy affairs that happened so often in prisons. I had decided that I wanted to be "real" as well as truthful and honest, and reality in my jangled mind meant possibly settling down with one man, with whom I might one day live out the remainder of my life, no matter how many years it took. I fell overboard with a man who had begun to write to me from another California prison. I believe I genuinely fell in love with him—to the extent that that's possible from afar—even though I sensed somehow that he might be playing me for a fool. I was so blinded that I figured the reality of my love would convert any frivolity on his part. I felt that genuine love was stronger than any game that could be played on me.

I wrote over and over to this man, Johnny, about our love and, among other things, the need to develop "Christ consciousness" as the center of our relationship if we wanted it to work. Johnny wrote back, "That is where I'm coming from, too, Susan," and I believed it. As it turned out, neither of us had the slightest idea of what we were talking about. I had come across the term "Christ consciousness" in my philosophy readings in connection with the University of Santa Cruz workshops. It sounded so good that I adopted it. Johnny also latched onto it.

One day I received a letter from Johnny, nearly a year after we had begun writing. I opened the envelope and read hungrily. It was a typical letter, but strangely the name "Susan" didn't appear anywhere in it. It was full of the name "Carol." It dawned on me. I had received someone else's letter. It was from Johnny all right, but it was not for Susan. Johnny had mixed up the letters.

It turned out that he was quite a man. He had been carrying on romances with women all over the state. I, in my first attempt at total honesty, had walked right into dishonesty.

I crumbled. My little dream world of a white cottage and pretty flowers and a normal life with a true husband collapsed. I took several giant steps backward emotionally. I thought I had reached the point where I could make decisions for myself, trust my own feelings and judgment, and move into reality and truth, but that confidence blew up in my face. Wrong again. Forever wrong. I would never trust anyone again. Never.

And then, along in here, overlapping with the numerous forces working at that time, came Old Bruce from the family days.

I had first met Bruce, who was four or five years older than I, when we were moving around Topanga Canyon. Shortly after our meeting, we became lovers and shared our lives quite intimately until we went to Spahn's Ranch. Then Old Bruce—to be distinguished from New Bruce, the father of my son—disappeared for about a year. Having traveled around the world, he ended up at Spahn's for lack of anywhere else to go.

Many of the girls at Spahn's thought Old Bruce was conceited and arrogant, which was probably true, although he was always kind and gentle to me. Many put him down because he looked quite a bit like Charlie—although Bruce was far more rugged and stocky—and no guy was permitted to stack up well against Charlie. Bruce was only about five-foot six and a half inches tall, which strengthened the resemblance, and he always looked as though he were on the verge of growing a beard—pretty raggedy.

He was valuable to Charlie in the dune buggy days because of his welding skills and his overall competence in getting things done.

Bruce, sentenced to life in the Hinman-Shea cases, was in Folsom prison. Since we were codefendants in the Hinman matter, we were allowed to write to each other as long as we dealt with the case. I received a message in February, 1974, that he wanted to write to me, and I arranged for permission for us to exchange letters.

It wasn't long before we were writing on a regular basis, first two or three times a week, and then practically daily. I told him about my commitment to truth and honesty, and he constantly held me to it, snapping me back on track after my escapade with Johnny. "I reckoned you'd snap sooner or later," he said in his first letter after my blow-up, and urged me to get on with my quest for truth. Probably the most important thing about that letter for me at that moment was the way he ended it: "Peace and be cool. I love you."

He seemed so calm and very cool himself, unlike the man I had first encountered six years earlier. From then on, he asked questions that reached down inside me, questions that challenged my pledge to seek truth above all things. He had an incredible way of saying something that he believed to be truth, which would infuriate me and my warped sense of reality, and then hanging on until I argued myself back and forth and around to his original statement.

He kept me constantly puzzled, refusing to lay anything on me as "the only truth," but telling me just enough about what he thought to spur me on to think through the truth myself.

It didn't take long for me to see that Bruce had an unusual consistency about him. His attitudes toward life—the horrible past, the difficult present, and the uncertain future—seemed to hold firm and not wobble the way mine did. In short, he seemed much more together than I was, and I determined to keep writing and nagging at him until I had what he had.

Because of the necessity to maintain at least a facade of communication about our legal situations, our letters contained a lot of references about other cases and were rather restricted and cautious, especially at first. But this was gradually eased, although we continually included legal references.

A significant breakthrough in our discussions, for me, came in a letter from him dated May 6, 1974. It gave me a rare insight, although still not as plainly spoken as I'd like, into love and how Bruce felt about me, the result, by the way, of my hounding him on the subject. I had really badgered him on whether he loved me or not. It's embarrassing to look back upon it, but my insecurity was so monumental that I wanted his love and affection spelled out in black and white. And his style wasn't black and white.

But he gave me a sweet taste of his love for me and I felt warm all over as I sat on my bed reading his efforts to reassure me. He said he had always felt I was "a special person" and his deepest desire was for me to realize it. And he brought it all the way down to the personal level. I had felt in previous letters that he might have been speaking of a platonic love, but the cloud lifted from me as he said he meant it "personally" when he said he loved me—he loved me for myself. I smiled as he attributed a lot of this love to the fact that I was like him, on the down-to-earth side. How could he think of someone like me, who had spun off in a dozen different directions all at once, as being on the down-to-earth side? But he was seeing that, inside, that was the way I wanted it.

But he didn't stop there. He turned mysterious on me and started additional questions flowing. First I was excited and then doubtful about his feeling that he would see me sometime. He carefully said that only time would tell whether we'd be free together, but he raised all kinds of strange feelings within me as he wrote of such things as the world as we knew it coming to an end and of his refusal to look at the world and the future in terms of himself and his own desires. He seemed to be looking himself right in the eye but still not taking himself too seriously. He was smiling at himself for a change.

He ended that letter with "peace and blessings to you," his first use of the word "blessings." I was immediately aware of it, and very curious. He had a way of dropping in little things like that with no further discussion, and it would take several days for my letter to raise a question and several days more for him to respond. Meanwhile, he was moving on to fresh things.

It was two days after Mother's Day that year that he drove hard against my relativistic way of seeing things. Actually the letter had been written on Mother's Day itself, and he had raised many varieties of emotion within me with his best wishes. My son was living with foster parents somewhere in the United States, but I had no idea where and no expectation that I would ever see him again. But, still, I was his mother, and I loved him longingly.

Bruce spoke of his belief that there was an absolute best way to live, an absolute best way to go, and that his problem was to find out what that way was or, better still, just to come into a realization of the way. But then he went on to say that a man alone could not figure out that best way, any more than clay could figure out how to become a pot. He said most men, in seeking solutions, had left out a necessary part of the equation. Did he mean God? It appeared so. For he went on to say that he prayed for the strength to do what was right, adding that he believed he was being made strong enough to do right.

That was troubling for someone who had been the centerpiece of her own life for as long as she could remember. Bruce was too full of "absolutes" for me. Yet he wasn't harsh, as most people were who spoke of such things; he was very gentle. And he spoke of *praying* for the strength to do what was right. Could that be rugged, self-sufficient Old Bruce?

Two days later, without flattery, came more tenderness and hope. He seemed to be constantly seeing possibilities for good in me. I had raised the issue of innocence and simplemindedness, two characteristics I believed had left

214

me. But Bruce felt they had only retreated and held out hope for "innocence reborn"—born not out of blindness or ignorance but out of love and grace. Wow! How good that sounded! Was it possible?

He continued with enigmatic language that told me he not only *saw* good in me, but also *expected* it to come forth. He seemed to have some insight into my future. It was spooky.

For example, he hooked me with his own story, how he had tried so hard for years to put his own head together, getting nowhere, except to Folsom. And then "someone" he couldn't yet see had readjusted his head. Was he talking about God again? I lay back on the firm mattress and read more. He shifted gears to point right at me, declaring that he *knew* I soon was going to "super-relax" in my head long enough to look at myself squarely and laugh and cry at everything. And then, he said, I would see the way I was going. He urged me to check it out very carefully.

Strangely, he closed the letter with "Take care, beloved sister." *Beloved sister*? I thought I was more like his lover!

He startled me a little more within a few days when he began to write about change coming in the world—the end of the age and things like that. We had both been through a lot of talk of that sort, and I wasn't sure I wanted to get into it anymore. But Bruce had an interesting point in one letter. He spoke of civilization getting ready to become something new. He said the source of his information was something that had been written by "some agency" that had never been wrong. I eventually figured out he was referring to the Book of Revelation in the Bible. But hadn't Charlie got a lot of his wild talk out of Revelation?

However, Bruce peristed in his monologue about the deterioration of the world—the corruption, the failure of governments, the rise of despots. He said one of the things he wanted most for me was to understand that we were approaching the end of the age, that drastic changes were coming. He spoke at length about the Four Horsemen in Revelation and then concluded that so-called religious leaders had rarely told the people the truth about God or Christ or what the Bible said—about what was going to happen. He came down hard on those he said were telling things designed to suit their own ends, those who caused pain in the name of Christianity, those who ultimately produced hostility to the whole truth of Christ with slick and tricky misconceptions.

He concluded that letter tenderly—and I found tears flooding my eyes as I sat alone in my cell—by saying simply that he believed he was one day going to break through into understanding about life and that he wanted those he loved with him in that breakthrough. But, he said simply, it would have to be my choice that led to my breakthrough. He couldn't force it on me.

It was only two days later, June 12, that he gave me a clue as to why he was thinking so much about the future of the world. He recommended a book called *The Late Great Planet Earth*, by Hal Lindsey, a best-selling volume about Bible prophecy. It was to be instrumental in drawing me more and more into what the Bible had to say about our time.

But then, after getting me all turned on about the future of the world, Bruce seemed to do a quick shuffle and left me hanging. In a nutshell, he said he didn't know what the particulars of the future would be, but since God made the future possible, all he really had to do was trust God.

That was the way with him. From mysteriously complex to the utterly simplistic. I reflected on this as I sat on my bed one day, keeping absolutely quiet about my letters from Bruce. I still wasn't independent enough to want my fellow

216

SSU residents to know what I was up to. Furthermore, I wasn't even sure myself what I was up to.

"Bruce seems to start to say something definite and then he backs off," I thought. "What is he trying to do? Maybe he doesn't really know what he means, and yet . . . he seems so calm and assured. What is he trying to tell me?"

It was late afternoon. I curled into the corner of my bed and re-read a section of his letter dated June 10. He jabbed at my impatience. I chuckled and winced. He wished it were as simple as a snap of the fingers for me to find fulfillment and satisfaction. But, he said, the best thing for me to do was to dig into the Bible, especially the New Testament, disregarding what I had been led to think about it, and find some answers for myself. He hammered hard at the earlier theme that we had been given concepts that were not true, that in fact we had been tricked and were carrying hostility toward Christianity as a result.

I tossed the letter on the bed and stared at the ceiling. Then, reaching to the box near the head of my bed, I pulled down another of many letters I was receiving from some woman named Elizabeth Burson. Like all the others, it contained a tract, but for some reason I had not thrown this one away. "This woman never gives up," I thought.

I had taken a lot of razzing from my codefendants because of the letters from the Burson woman and others, including Shirley Hoffman, for whom I'd babysat in San Jose years ago. The old joke continued about "everyone wanting to save Susan's soul."

"Why don't they leave her alone?" Cathy had said rather loudly recently. "They don't seem to realize her soul has been spoken for—she's already been saved." I could sense rather than see the strange smile on her face, and I wasn't really sure what she meant. I knew I wasn't "saved" in the sense that all those ladies were talking about in their letters. I was lost, even though I couldn't admit it to anyone else—not even myself.

At that very moment, sitting alone in the late afternoon light, I knew momentarily that I *was* lost. "I'm lost. I'm going to hell," I said. But the thought quickly evaporated.

I took out the tract from the Burson woman's letter. It was entitled "What Is Life All About?" That was some question! I began to read. It made one quick point: Every person was meant to know God, to love Him, to serve Him. Life was to be lived with God through the death and resurrection of Jesus Christ.

I threw the letter back on the box and slept fitfully until suppertime.

Bud Mardock looked much as he had in my junior high school years in San Jose. Casual and conservative, still young looking, he seemed even more open than he had been as my school counselor. He sat opposite me at the visiting room table, leaning back in his straight chair and surveying me.

"It's been a long time, Susan."

"Yes." I wasn't sure what to say, but I didn't want him feeling sorry for me. I had to keep up the facade.

"Things are pretty much the same in San Jose," he continued after a moment. If he felt awkward, he didn't show it. I was amazed at how relaxed he seemed. "It's bigger and busier, but all in all a lot the same. You'd feel right at home."

"Not me." I smiled and spoke a bit too sharply. "School and I didn't really get along."

"I know," he said, smiling broadly. "But it wasn't all that

bad in junior high."

"You're right," I conceded. "It wasn't all that bad at that point, but it was headed that way."

He told me a lot about the kids I had grown up with—who was married to whom, who had gone where. He told me about his family, about his teaching career. And after half an hour, he said, "Susan, I felt I had to come down here to tell you something I should have spoken about before." He still seemed very relaxed, but just a trifle shy at the moment. "I want to tell you about Jesus Christ."

Zonk! Not him, too! Everybody had flipped out.

"I know about Jesus Christ," I said, trying to remain cool. I looked him in the eyes, but they held level.

"I'm glad," he said softly. He continued to look into my face. "I'd like for you to know him real well."

I noticed he hadn't said "know *about* him real well."

"I'd like for you to know that he loves you and can put your life back together for you. He did it for me."

This was crazy. Cathy was right. Everyone was trying to save my soul. And I got on a high horse about it. Who did they think they were?

"I hear you, Mr. Mardock. That's where I'm coming from. I'm with God. I believe in him. I'm on your side, but I'm doing it my way."

He remained so very casual, almost loafish. There wasn't a trace of harshness or criticism on his face. This unsettled me and caused me to ramble on. "Jesus was all right—I really agree. He was a good man, a good teacher. He had a lot to teach mankind."

Mardock waited patiently as I charged on, trying with all my might to hold up that facade. I suddenly realized he wasn't saying anything; he wasn't arguing back. I thought of Bruce. He didn't argue back either; he just laid things out calmly.

A bit flustered, I pulled my elbows back off the table and placed my hands in my lap.

"That's all true, Susan," he said at last, evenly, gently. "But he was a whole lot more than that."

He stopped, apparently expecting me to charge in again. I remained silent.

"He was the savior," he said. "He died for us. He took away our sins. He set us free. He wants us for himself, for his Father. He wants us to live the way we were meant to live and he's made it all possible. All we have to do is accept it."

There was a long silence. I could hear Pat and Leslie talking down the corridor. Outside, I could hear the birds and had a flashing vision of the Saturday morning brightness outside the SSU walls.

"I'm really into that kind of positive thinking, Mr. Mardock," I said as brightly as I could manage. "I hear your philosophy. It's all right. I've been doing a lot of thinking about God, and this Christ-consciousness thing is really right on."

I knew I had to get this guy off my back. He was a good man, and I didn't want to hurt him. The best thing to do was to agree with him, and let the whole thing go.

Mardock listened to me for several minutes, and then we talked about the weather, the musical scene, the movies, and several small things. Finally, he got up from his chair, and the visit was over. He was ready to walk out through the big steel doors. But he reached across the small table and grasped my hand. "I love you, Susan," he said softly, a smile flooding his face. "And Jesus loves you very, very much."

I battled with all my strength to hold back tears. "Why don't you get the hell out of here?" I screamed within myself. But I said nothing. I think my face was blank.

Summer was in full swing when Bruce became more pointed in his letters. We were writing almost every day. I was hitting him hard on what I detected as male chauvinism. I was even a little bit aware at the time that I was setting up a straw man, based partly on other people's opinions of Bruce five and six years earlier. Actually I was trying to find a way to needle him and deflate his rather strong Christian posture. He didn't rattle easily.

I was falling more and more in love with him—my old and predictable condition. He seemed to be so stable, and as always I desperately wanted something to grab hold of. But I still kicked up my heels to try to establish a facade of independence, still wanting him to be more overt in his expressions of love to me. Bruce told me he loved me, but his expressions had a quality to them that I had not experienced.

I sat on my bed on the last day of June and read page three of his most recent letter over and over. I didn't know if I liked it or not. He repeated his contention that he loved me, but then, it seemed to me, he muddied the waters. If he had to choose between my personally loving him and my experiencing the love and grace of God in Jesus, he said, he'd choose the latter and let his own desires go down the drain. His greatest purpose, he said, was to tell everybody he knew about his experiences "in the love that Jesus gives."

It was odd. That was as close as he ever came to telling me about his "experiences." It sure sounded weird—"the love that Jesus gives." What did that mean? Did Bruce love me or not? Never mind about the love that Jesus gives. No matter how much I pushed him, he wouldn't get explicit about what had happened to him. But something certainly had happened. This was definitely not the "Old Bruce" from

221

Spahn's Ranch. He was a new man.

In August, as the country convulsed over the crazy and confusing Watergate affair, with President Richard Nixon finally resigning on the ninth of the month, Bruce's challenge of my thought processes and my trite and cliche-ridden philosophies intensified. He refused to "tell" me things, but he pricked and probed at my understanding and forced me to think for myself. Day after day, he laid before me good, reasonable thoughts about women's rights, children, grace, trust, nature, beauty, divine guidance, morality, marriage, gluttony, the Bible, love.

But his most telling arguments centered on the subject of Jesus. I'm not sure if it was the force of his arguments, or my receptivity to the subject matter itself, but something brought a new tenderness and a new understanding into my rattled brain when he spoke about Jesus. And he almost always used the name "Jesus," not "Christ." Even on paper this seemed to make a difference.

I felt the back of my neck tingling as Bruce told me that even he himself was not trustworthy—he couldn't even trust himself. But, he said very simply, he did trust the love that Jesus had for him and the love Jesus showed through him. And, furthermore, it was that Jesus, he wrote, who provided the way for a personal relationship between an individual and God. I remember that these words stung my eyes: "He is a personal Master, or Lord, or whatever we may call him." How could that be? He had to be crazy! But then he showed how Jesus had made the truth known to him in the Bible, how he had made it possible for him to end speculation and to grasp reality. And he then challenged me on the point with a suggestion that the next time I read the Bible, I should pray a short prayer asking that I find what I was looking for. "Jesus will help you," he declared flatly.

And then the clincher. Jesus—I could almost hear Bruce saying it flatly and evenly in that soft drawl of his—Jesus is not a concept, or a philosophy, or a religion. Jesus IS. I stopped when I read that. Jesus is. JESUS is. Jesus IS. It sounded okay any way you said it. But I wasn't sure I knew what it meant. And the tenderness only lasted a few moments.

With hindsight, I see I was so nervous and jittery as Bruce hit closer and closer to my conscience that I flared back with everything possible to divert him. At one point, I even went into a lengthy and crude speculation on "the love life of Jesus." It made no sense and contained no truth.

It was past midnight when I dropped off to sleep one hot, muggy night late in August. My brain was sore from its gymnastics with Bruce, Hal Lindsey, and God. I plunged into a deep sleep right away, and I began to dream.

I was in a playground. In the middle of the scene of swings, slides and seesaws lay a dead person. I strained to see who it was. It was Bobby. Why was he there . . . and dead? What had happened to him?

Suddenly the scene changed. The playground was gone, and I was in a huge room, bigger than any I'd ever seen. Masses of people filled the room. It was a sea of people. They picked me up over their heads and started walking with me, carrying me somehow out of the big room, out into the open.

There in the open space—wide and colorful, clean and pure—was something, a being. It wasn't a human, and it wasn't an animal. It was a being, and all the people began falling down and bowing down before it. What were they doing? I soon realized they were worshiping the being. "That must be God," I heard myself saying.

Beautiful plants were growing out of the ground. They were everywhere. Everything was beautiful. And the being walked around stepping on the beautiful plants. But he didn't hurt them. They came right back up into their beautiful shape. Everything was beautiful.

The being was talking, but I couldn't understand it. "What am I doing here?" I heard myself saying. "This guy is really on a trip." My voice dripped with arrogance.

The being then walked over and tapped me on the head—right on top of my head. He was larger than I had realized. He looked into my face and said: "The trouble with you is your indifference to me. I want you to think about your indifference."

I was instantly awake. My heart was in my throat, and I felt I might choke. Perspiration covered my body, but nonetheless I felt chilly. I was afraid and cold.

21

BORN AGAIN

I turned the brown, leather Bible over in my hands. It was still soft and lovely after three and a half years lying unused in my cell. I opened to the flyleaf. "Who is Shirley Horvath?" I thought. "Why did she send this to me?"

"Please read Isaiah 43:25," the words said. I thumbed through the pages until I found Isaiah and then chapter 43 and verse 25. The language of the King James Version was hard for me. "I, even I, am he that blotteth out thy transgressions for mine own sake and will not remember thy sin." I read it twice.

I looked back at the flyleaf. "Jesus, my prayer is that you reveal yourself to Susan Atkins." At the very bottom of the page were these words: "Believe on the Lord Jesus Christ, and thou shalt be saved . . . Acts 16:31." I had paid very little attention, if any, to that in 1971.

Following Bruce's suggestion, I had sent away for a correspondence course from the Berean School of the Bible. And, ignoring another suggestion from him—that I concentrate on the New Testament—I decided to begin my reading at the beginning of the Bible. But the course

225

material hadn't arrived, so I plunged ahead without it—right at the beginning of "the first book of Moses, called Genesis."

Recalling Bruce's instruction, I bowed my head and tried to pray, "God, help me to understand the Bible. If you're there, show me what to believe."

It was hard going at first, but interesting. And I plowed on—Adam, Noah, Abraham, Moses.

I put the Bible down. The unit was unusually quiet for an afternoon. I was still taking precautions against anyone discovering what I was up to, but there were no voices, no steps. All was quiet. My mind tried to fathom what I had been reading. Imagine Noah—making an ark out in the desert. The people must have thought he was crazy, but he was just obeying God. What they must have thought when it started to rain! Only eight people out of the whole population of the earth were saved. All the rest were corrupt and violent. They had turned their backs on God.

For reasons that were completely unknown to me I began to feel pain there in my cell that afternoon. I was feeling sorry for God. "That's crazy!" I thought.

And old Abraham. He fascinated me. Pack up everything and go, God said, and he did just that. He finally got a son, and then God told him to sacrifice him. And he prepared to do so. "I wouldn't be able to do that!" I thought. "What did Abraham have anyway? Faith, they say. I don't see how he could do that."

And when God used Moses to deliver the children of Israel from Egypt—that was too much. I was afraid I might shout out loud, and my colleagues would discover what I was up to. I felt like breaking into an old high school victory cheer as he led them safely out. And then—the parting of the Red Sea was the coup de grace. "How did he do that?" I wondered.

I was stunned as I reflected on those people whom God loved so much turning on him and his servant, Moses, with their complaints that they didn't know where they were going. They complained about food, and he gave them food. They complained about water, and he gave them water. Before long, I was feeling very sorry for God.

And then . . . the golden calf. Moses was receiving the Ten Commandments at Mount Sinai, and the children of Israel built an idol and worshiped right in the presence of God, who had loved them and saved them. How could they do that? As I sat staring at the wall, I could feel the tears on my face. I was weeping . . . weeping for God. "Who am I, to cry for God?" I thought. "How presumptious can you get?" I was suddenly confused. I was too small and inadequate for such emotions. I was furious at those people for turning their backs on this wonderful God and sinning right there in his presence.

Suddenly the bomb fell. I saw something clearly for the first time. I was just like those children of Israel!

How many times had I cursed God? How many times had I worshiped an idol? How many times had I sinned at the foot of Mount Sinai?

I grabbed the brown, leather Bible and turned quickly to the Ten Commandments. Exodus, chapter 20—I had it marked. There was not one I had not broken. I had broken them all . . . willingly. "*I* broke them all," I said half-aloud. "No one broke them for me."

I closed my eyes, and my mind was clogged with a huge mound, right in front of me. It was massive pile of dirt, and garbage, and filth. There in front of me I saw twenty-six years of sins.

"This is crazy," I said, and got up from the bed, putting the Bible up under my pillow. "I can't think like that. I'll go crazy again."

I picked up the latest of the Burson woman's tracts. It was one sheet folded to make four small pages. I opened to the centerfold, and my eye landed on a block of boldface type. It looked familiar, but I didn't know what it was.

Behold, I stand at the door, and knock: if any man hear my voice, and open the door, I will come in to him, and will sup with him, and he with me.

I read on for one more sentence. "Those are the words of the Lord found in Revelation, chapter 3, verse 20," it said. "They are for you today."

That Burson woman never stopped. She had only recently told me she had been praying for me for three and half years, she and the Bible study group at her church in Sierra Madre, California. Why should an elderly woman, a grandmother living alone, do that for someone she didn't know, someone convicted of murder?

It was September 27, 1974. I was in my cell, locked in for the night. Everything was quiet. The thoughts tumbled over and over in my mind—about Bruce and the changes in his life, about the huge mound of sins I continued to see in front of me when I closed my eyes, about my ghastly crimes against humanity. I even thought of that little green room, the gas chamber, where I had expected to end my life. "I deserved to die there," I whispered.

After several minutes of silence in the dark, a new sentence formed on my lips—an entirely new spoken idea for me. "I want to be forgiven," I said, barely audibly. The thought burned into me, refusing to leave.

Can society forgive me for such acts against humanity? Can it take this guilt off my shoulders? Can serving the rest of my life in prison undo what's been done? Can anything be done?

I don't think I asked any of those questions aloud. I believe they were all in my mind. But they were plainly articulated. And the answer to each was plain: "No."

I looked once again at my future, my alternatives: Stay in prison. Escape. Commit suicide. As I looked, the wall in my mind was blank. But somehow I knew there was another alternative. I could consciously choose the road as many people, especially Bruce, had been pressing upon me. I could decide to follow Jesus.

As plainly as the daylight came the words, *"You* have to decide."

I turned onto my side and tried to think. Very quietly, I slipped into the most solemn moment of my life. Everything was absolutely quiet and unrushed. It seemed that time stopped, and I knew one fact beyond all others: This was my last chance. I don't pretend to understand the theology of it, but I knew for a certainty that, at that moment, I had the opportunity to give my life to Jesus Christ and I would never have another opportunity.

The moment held still. "Am I asleep?" I thought. No. I was fully awake. I turned again onto my back.

"Behold, I stand at the door, and knock. . . ." Did I hear someone say that? I don't know. But the statement was there. All else stood still.

"Okay. If you're there, come on in."

Total stillness . . . and then: "All right. I'll come in, but you must open the door."

This was incredible! I talked back to the voice. I assume I spoke in my thoughts, but I'm not certain. "What door?"

Child of Satan–Child of God

"You know what door and where it is, Susan. Just turn around and open it, and I will come in."

Suddenly, as though on a movie screen, there in my thoughts was a door. It had a handle. I took hold of it, and pulled. It opened.

The whitest, most brilliant light I had ever seen poured over me. I was standing in darkness, but the light pushed the darkness completely out of sight. It vanished behind me. There was only light. And in the center of the flood of brightness was an even brighter light. Vaguely, there was the form of a man. I knew it was Jesus.

He spoke to me—literally, plainly, matter-of-factly spoke to me in my nine-by-eleven prison cell: "Susan, I am really here. I'm really coming into your heart to stay. Right now you are being born again and you will live with me in heaven through all eternity, forever and ever. This is really happening. It is not a dream. You are now a child of God. You are washed clean and your sins have all been forgiven."

I was distinctly aware that I inhaled deeply and then, just as fully, exhaled. There was no more guilt! It was gone. Completely gone! The bitterness, too. Instantly gone! How could this be?

For the first time in my memory I felt clean, fully clean, inside and out. In twenty-six years I had never been so happy.

I have no idea how long I lay awake in the night. When I did slip off into unconsciousness, I slept soundly for the first time in many years, free of nightmares—unafraid and warm.

22

BEGINNING OVER

I stared into the mirror. I looked pretty much the same in the bright morning sunlight as I had when I brushed my teeth the night before. But there was a difference. It was in the eyes. I looked intently into the reflection in the mirror. There was a light in my eyes. They weren't hard and flat as I remembered them from recent days. There definitely was a light in them.

Suddenly, I smiled. And that was new. Indeed, it was so new that I laughed out loud. I could look at myself in the mirror and smile!

As I dressed, I wondered what would happen next. What would Pat and Leslie say? Ugh! They'd laugh if they knew. "I can't tell them," I said to myself. "What if they think I'm a Jesus freak?" What about my image? "I'll be embarrassed," I thought.

The ideas vanished as quickly as they had come. "Who cares?" I said, smiling at the face in the mirror. "I've been saved!" What strange talk! Saved? I looked back into the mirror. "But you had been lost, and you know it. Now you're saved." I smiled back into the mirror. There definitely was a light in my eyes.

For better or for worse, I *didn't* talk to anyone about my experience with Jesus for a couple of weeks. I couldn't even bring myself to say outright to Bruce that I had accepted Jesus Christ as my Lord and Savior. But it only took a few days for him to detect that something had happened. For one thing, I wasn't arguing with him any more. I sounded more and more like him. For another, I was falling even more deeply in love with him—and not only as a Christian brother—and it apparently was showing.

Two weeks after my conversion, I received a letter from Bruce with several direct questions: Did I believe Jesus was the Son of God? Did he die to save me from my sins? Was he raised from the dead in order that I might have new life in him? Was this Jesus my Lord and Savior?

With that, I made my first open expression of commitment to Jesus Christ—my first "confession," as the Bible called it. To all of Bruce's questions, I answered yes, and inexplicably my relationship with Jesus took on an even deeper reality. It seemed nailed down somehow—just as the Bible said.

Once again, Bruce had sparked me into new freedom. Fears of others somehow learning that I had been "born again" began to diminish. I was ready to tell.

And the opportunity rushed in when the other SSU residents and especially the staff noticed that foul-mouthed, vilifying, hateful old Susan Atkins had stopped swearing. I hadn't even been aware of it myself. I hadn't uttered a clean, wholesome sentence in years, but unexpectedly, without my trying, my filthy ways were changing.

One day the sergeant in charge of our unit made a

determined effort to rile me and bring back the old Susan. We had argued on a daily basis for years, but for some time now I had seemed to be playing some new jailhouse game. He wanted to crack it.

That afternoon he laid into me heavy with one vulgarism and cuss word after another. I squared around in front of him and a trace of a smile played on his lips expectantly. "Here it comes," he seemed to think.

"Sarge, I don't have time to argue with you any more," I said softly and evenly. "I don't want to fight any more. You have a job to do, and I respect you for it. I won't give you any more hassles. That's all over. And I ask you to let me alone and respect me in the same way. I only want to love people and live for Jesus."

Blop! There it was. Out in front.

Sarge's expression didn't change. But he said nothing as I walked away. I didn't look directly, but Pat and Leslie's eyes were wide as I went to my cell. There would be jokes and needles later—from them as well as from Sarge—but for that moment, all was quiet.

I sat in my room, holding my Bible. Now that everything was out in the open, what was I to do regarding the people around me? "I can't force this on anyone," I thought. "What would I have done if Bruce had tried to force this down my throat?"

I sat for a moment. "All you can do is pray." The message was as clear as spring water.

And that became my routine. I spent hour upon hour in my cell, reading the Bible, Hal Lindsey books and others that I discovered, and the tracts that continued to pour in. And I prayed many times each day. I prayed for Pat and Leslie, for all my former colleagues, even for Charlie. And I prayed especially fervently for the members of my natural family. I cried over and over to the Lord for reconciliation with my father, my brothers, and my aunts and uncles. The prayer that was most often on my lips was for my baby. "Keep him safe, Lord. I don't know where he is, but you do. Please bring him to yourself."

Occasionally I would lead a conversation with Pat or Leslie around to Jesus, but inevitably came the stone wall. So it was back to prayer.

Meanwhile, inside me came confidence. It grew and strengthened, aided by Bruce's new thrust with his letters. The hints and intrigue were gone. He talked plainly and simply about the Father, the Lord Jesus, and the Holy Spirit, about the world, and about us. What a relief it was for me to understand him at last. When he said that, even in prison, he was freer than he had ever been before, I understood him fully. Real freedom comes from God. When he spoke about letting your life, not just your mouth, be the main instrument for spreading the word of Christ's power and love, I could see his point. I agreed with him that the Lord didn't need us, but that he could do wonders through us.

Soon I began to long for someone to talk to face to face about what had happened to me. The chaplain visited me, and that was good, although I was a little disappointed to find he wasn't walking on cloud nine with me all the time. He had many other people and things besides me to worry about, so our time together was rather short. But he opened up his library to me—his Bible dictionaries, commentaries, histories, anything I wanted—and this was invaluable. I soaked in everything my new young mind would take.

But I yearned for someone like myself, just an ordinary human being who had found new life in Christ. I needed to talk, to ask questions, to laugh, to cry.

I knew about a program for prisons in the state that sounded as though it might offer some hope for my longings. It was called the M-2 Sponsor program, set up to provide prison residents with visitors from the communities. The idea was to find a person who would visit regularly with a prisoner, taking the time and the responsibility for caring about someone who had no one else to visit them. My visitors were very infrequent, almost nonexistent, so it seemed I fully qualified.

I asked for a questionnaire and filled it out. When I got to to the space where it asked what type of person I would like to have visit me, I wrote in large capital letters, "A CHRISTIAN."

As I folded the paper, I closed my eyes. "Dear Jesus, please send me just the right person—a friend."

One month passed. Then came the word that I was going to have an M-2 visitor. I got so excited I couldn't stand in my room. Then I got so nervous I couldn't sit down. I was both happy and afraid. I hadn't talked to a full-blown "Christian" since my conversion, except for the chaplain. What if she didn't like me? What if she thought I was crazy. Maybe I was all wrong—a phony.

My heart was pounding when I walked into our little visiting room and waited for my visitor. Suddenly, there she was, walking in the door. She was smiling. And her eyes had that light! It was just as I had seen in the mirror.

We shook hands, and I guess I was smiling all over my face. It had been so long since I had smiled like that; I was afraid my face would break.

We sat facing one another. "A real, live Christian!" I thought. "I wonder what I look like to her."

Those thoughts banished immediately.

"I'm Stephanie Schramm." The voice was light and well

modulated. The smile persisted. "The M-2 people have gone over your situation carefully—and they've screened me from top to bottom. And they've asked me to come to see you."

I didn't say anything. I just wanted to hear her talk.

"I'm a housewife, and a mother of three, and I guess I'm about your age, maybe a few months older. I found the Lord two years ago myself. Isn't it exciting?" Her smile was so alive I could hardly stand it. She was naturally pretty, but her real beauty exceeded the mere facts of light brown hair, pretty white complexion, strong full mouth, and tall, womanly figure. When she said, "Isn't it exciting?" I jumped inside. It was more exciting right at that moment than anything I'd ever known.

"You know, when they talked to me about you, I naturally had heard of you, and I was a little skittish at first." Not a trace of judgment or hostility showed on her face. She merely smiled openly and looked me right in the eyes. "But I finally said, 'Lord, if you're her Savior, you're mine, too, so I'd better go see her.' I knew that if you had really met the Lord, you were a new creature, just like me, and I wasn't going to worry about the past. I was just going to rejoice with you about your new life."

I was so dumb, and so excited, that I still didn't say anything. I just looked at her. And I believe my mouth was hanging open. All I could think was, "I'm just like her. I'm a Christian. I'm born again. This is for real!"

If Stephanie was troubled by my silence and awkwardness, she didn't show it. She kept on talking. "Susan, I'd like to say this to you, and I hope you'll understand me: The love of Jesus shows all over you. It's in your face, in your eyes, and I heard it in your voice when I walked in. You are full of the Lord at this moment, and don't you forget it. I naturally had some reservations, some questions, but they're gone. I love you as a sister in the Lord."

That did it. The dam burst. My eyes filled with tears, but I didn't break out crying. I was too happy. I giggled, I'm sure, and I began to talk. It was a torrent. I told everything that had happened to me—all about Bruce, the tracts, the Bible, the encounter with Jesus in my cell. On and on, it spilled out. I was completely unconcerned about the staff woman sitting with us monitoring the visit. Nothing was going to stop that first time of sharing my experiences with Jesus.

There were to be regular visits with Stephanie from then on, the first and third Wednesdays of each month—hours of talking and listening, learning and growing. But there was nothing quite like that first face-to-face encounter with a sister in the Lord.

My first step toward the mainline prison population came in an answer to prayer. I was to be allowed to attend the prison church services. I had been meeting with my *one* Christian friend for a month. Now, I was to be with others, if I had the nerve.

It was November, 1974, a brilliant fall day with the temperature reaching into the seventies. I had worked my courage to its peak. My staff escort carried on small talk as we left the unit and headed across the yard to the low, very ordinary building where the church services were held. What would happen when one of "the Manson women" walked in? What would I do?

The escort opened the door. The room was full and the service was in progress. Looking straight ahead, trying desperately to appear relaxed, I walked in. I felt stiff, straight as a board. My knees didn't want to bend.

Chaplain Waltcott was making announcements as I sat in one of the folding chairs about midway into the room. When he had concluded, he continued talking in a quiet, normal voice: "We have someone with us today who has not been with us before. Would you all please welcome Susan Atkins."

The women looked at him. He smiled rather shyly. And then all eyes turned to me. I didn't know what to expect, but in an instant they all began to applaud. It continued on for several seconds. Somehow, I knew I should stand, and I did, but I wasn't sure my legs would hold me. I had not been in such a large company in nearly four years, and I hadn't been in church in nearly eleven.

As I stood, the applause died down. I was crying and was very quickly becoming an unattractive sight, I was sure. But I took a deep breath and blurted out, "I thank Jesus that I'm here with you all. Without him, it wouldn't have been possible." What an understatement! How dumb could you get!

For the first time in my life, I heard a chorus of "amens" and several exclamations of "praise the Lord" and "thank you, Jesus." It was delightful, but I continued to cry.

I remember very little of the service and nothing of what the preacher said. But I know I was very happy. And that happiness heightened at the end of the service as dozens of women came up to me and hugged me. Almost without exception, they said the same thing, "It's so good to see you out of SSU." What a difference from what I had expected. I had become convinced that the entire prison population was hostile to me. None of that showed.

My joy was rampant through those days. My relationships with Pat and Leslie were still far from satisfactory, but I was in peace most of the time. There were many moments of faltering and a good deal of uncertainty about the future, but I lived in optimism most hours of the day and night.

It was December 3 when I eagerly opened Bruce's letter. My first Christmas as a Christian was approaching, and we had been wallowing in excitement and expectation. Each day's dialogue added to the holiday spirit.

I read quickly, my eyes flashing back and forth across the page. It took me nearly five seconds to realize something was wrong. The letter was different. It seemed to be about his mother.

I stood up and continued to read. He was quoting extensively from a letter from someone . . . his aunt. What was this all about? His mother had been concerned as to whether she should write to me, as Bruce had suggested. She had prayed about it . . . with the aunt. God spoke to them . . . through unknown tongues . . . or prophecy . . . or something. My eyes refused to move past the next sentence. They were stuck.

"On the authority of Jesus Christ the Son of God, Bruce is not to write to this woman."

That was me! They were talking about me! Bruce was not to write to me! My eyes burned. Fireworks exploded behind them.

I fell onto my bed and finally managed to read on. Bruce said he had come to accept the words as being from God. He had accepted and had found peace. Curses flashed across my mind. How could he do that? I thought he loved me! How could he do that? We just have to trust in God's love, he said. I exploded inside. He doesn't care! What does he mean, he'll just have to leave me in God's hands?

Child of Satan–Child of God

Bruce went on to talk about Abraham and his obedience. And Job and his suffering. And Jacob, who waited fourteen years for his wife. And living by faith, not by sight. I couldn't handle it.

He became very tender, but for that moment I was aware only of sharp, jagged rocks, and glistening shark's teeth, and rusty, broken knife blades, slashing and tearing at me as I twisted and turned. His words of continuing love and concern, his compassion for my condition failed to penetrate my exploding universe.

23

POWER TO LIVE

I stood on a tightrope in the middle of my tiny cell, ready to fall to either side. I was dizzy. A plunge was certain.

I saw myself plainly. The possibility existed, and was very evident, that I would fall into the dark chaos that had so long surrounded me. I grabbed the pillow from my bed and squeezed it with both arms. Pressure pounded outward against my eardrums. My head was full and churning, tightening second by second as scraping and screeching sounds began to rise. I knew I might scream, but I am quite certain I remained outwardly silent.

"Again!" That was the only word I said for several seconds and it didn't escape my body. "Again! Again! Again! Again!" Once again, I had grabbed hold of someone, and once again, he had failed me. "Nothing is real." I said aloud, almost in a hiss, as my jaw muscles began to tighten.

"That is not true." That was aloud, too, but I'm sure I didn't say it. But I heard it, and I stopped moving, talking, and thinking.

"I have said I would not forsake you. And I have kept my word."

Contrary to my historic pattern, I purposefully stepped down off the imaginary tightrope and slipped on down to my knees. Everything seemed cracked inside me, but I closed my eyes—I squeezed them.

"Oh my God, my Father, Lord Jesus—don't let me forsake you again." I spoke in a whisper. I'm sure it was audible for some distance around me, but I didn't care. SSU was absolutely silent. I had to hang on. "I don't want to forsake you again. I've done that so many times. Don't let it happen again! I don't want to go back there!"

I felt a terrible pain in my chest, right in the middle. It was heavy. But I held still. I fought the panic.

"I will never leave you, Susan"—there it was again—"as long as you do not run away from me."

I stood still. I would not run.

I have no idea how many minutes I stayed that way and fought against death. It may have been only two or three minutes—it may have been twenty or thirty—but soon I was completely covered with the feeling that everything was going to be all right. There was a loss—a suffering—but not *all* was lost. No. All was gained—I knew that, but I did not understand it.

I eventually got off my knees and sat on the edge of my bed. I looked at Bruce's letter on the pillow, where I had dropped it, and picked it up. It was a very tender letter. I could see Bruce in my imagination—tender, kind, yet strong and obedient to what he believed Jesus was saying to him. He had written as gently as he knew how, but he had been decisive. That was the way. I realized I didn't even know how long he had been following the Lord—how long it had taken him to achieve that obedience. He refused to disclose, then and to later inquiries from others, the circumstances surrounding his acceptance of Christ. But he had learned well.

Once again I spoke to the Lord. "Jesus, help me to understand this. Help me to be as strong as Bruce is. I don't know why you've done this to us, but I accept it as best I can. Give me the strength to accept it all the way."

My mind became clear again, and the thoughts raced. I even smiled, and shrugged my shoulders. "Well, here you are. Still in prison. And things look as bad or worse than they did three months ago. You're still in isolation, and you may be here the rest of your life."

I shrugged again. Things really *weren't* the same.

It took several weeks, but I eventually understood why Bruce had been led to stop writing to me—at least I understood it from my standpoint. I had become very dependent on him, and on Stephanie, too. I was in danger of becoming less and less dependent on the Lord Jesus. I was in danger of liking to talk about the Lord and to be with his people more than talking with him and being with him. In my childish ways, I was putting people and things between him and me. The Lord did not want that.

Before arriving at this understanding, of course, I passed through several stages of self-condemnation. What had I done wrong? What sin had I committed that the Lord was punishing me for? Why didn't Bruce like me? Why didn't God like me? But I finally discovered, and hung onto, a scripture that solved this for me. It was in Romans, chapter eight, verse one: "There is therefore now no condemnation to them which are in Christ Jesus, who walk not after the flesh, but after the Spirit."

If God wasn't condemning me, why should I condemn myself?

The situation seemed obvious. For a time at least, Jesus wanted me to see things all the way through with him. He wanted me to walk alone with him for a while, and I was going to—with his help.

Christmas had come and gone, and I was finding great enjoyment being alone in my room, talking to the Lord almost constantly, and then, unexpectedly, singing to him. I found myself making up songs to the Lord. I was quite adept on the autoharp, and spent many hours playing and singing the songs that seemed to come to me from out of nowhere.

And I read and re-read the Bible, amazed at the Christian life that was presented there. I had been elated that salvation existed. But there was so much more. The writers spoke so confidently about knowing and understanding the Lord better, about living a life pleasing to him, worthy of him, about serving him, about ministering to others.

Further thoughts on ministry came to me at night as I lay in bed, as was so often the case, somewhere between full consciousness and sleep. Two thoughts ran closely together, one right on top of the other, and caught me by surprise. "Jesus is coming back soon to claim his own" and "you are going to have a ministry."

I fully believed Jesus was coming, and soon. But a ministry for me? That seemed far-fetched as I looked at the bars on my window. The thought persisted, even in the days ahead, but I saw little that I could do with it except file it away.

In my reading during that time, I began to come across references to "speaking in tongues" and "the Pentecostal experience." I didn't know what to make of them. I had just barely noticed a couple of references in the Bible to "tongues," but they had had no meaning to me. Bruce's last letter had contained a similar reference. As a child, I'd heard about "holy rollers" and people who shouted and groaned in church. But I knew nothing first hand. In the book I was reading, the author seemed to speak favorably about speaking in "unknown" tongues and about "gifts of the Holy Spirit."

On her next visit, I asked Stephanie about it. "Have you ever heard anybody talk in tongues?" I asked out of the blue.

She looked surprised. Her face beamed for a moment and a new twinkle came into her eyes. "Why do you ask?"

"Well, I've come across the expression several times, and I don't know what it means. Do you?"

Again, the twinkle. "Yes."

"You mean, you've heard somebody speak in tongues? Who?" I thought it was funny.

"Me," she said, smiling.

"You? You're kidding!"

"No, I'm not kidding. I've spoken in tongues. In fact, I speak in tongues all the time."

Wow! This calm, young woman, this very normal, Christian lady, this mother of three young children, this leader in the PTA—she spoke in tongues! I was shocked. "Tell me about it," I said.

"Well," she said, "it's really not a matter of speaking in tongues so much as it is the baptism in the Holy Spirit."

Something else new. But I didn't interrupt.

"The Bible teaches us that Jesus baptized the early disciples in the Holy Spirit," she continued, "and he's still doing it today. We're having a whole resurgence in the body of Christ of people being baptized in the Spirit, filled with the Spirit, filled with power, just the way they were in the early church. Speaking in tongues, or praying in tongues, is just *one* of the manifestations of this baptism. There's prophecy, healing, miracles, interpretation of tongues—all those things. It's just like Paul's teaching in First Corinthians."

"You mean this is going on today?" I was astounded—and excited.

She nodded her head.

"That's great. Tell me some more—tell me about yourself."

She then told me about her own baptism in the Holy Spirit shortly after conversion, about the church she was involved in, about the "charismatic renewal" occurring across the country. I took it all in, but I didn't know what to make of it. I was still a trifle put off.

Stephanie agreed to bring me some books on the subject on her next visit. We would talk further.

One of three books she brought was *Two Sides of the Coin* by Charles and Frances Hunter. One was *Beyond Ourselves* by Catherine Marshall. I don't remember the name of the other. I put the Hunters' book on the shelf and dipped into *Beyond Ourselves*. It wasn't specifically about the baptism in the Holy Spirit but was very powerful on complete surrender to God.

I hadn't proceeded far when, again at night, I was overcome with the desire to be closer to God, to know him better. I was convinced I wanted to be fully, totally God's own. I had made up my mind, and I didn't want to turn back. Nonetheless, I had serious reservations about the experience called the baptism in the Spirit. "You dummy," I thought. "You haven't even been baptized in water, and now you're talking about this."

But my longing wouldn't go away, doubts or no doubts. I knelt down beside my bed and took out my list of people I was praying for. I prayed through the list and then began to talk to the Lord about my own condition. I stopped abruptly and said aloud, "You have not because you ask not."

Bowing my head right down to the bed itself, I prayed, "Dear Jesus, if you want to baptize me in the Holy Spirit, here I am. Have your way. Make me willing to take what you want to give me. Amen."

I went to bed.

It was early in February. I was just on the edge of dropping off to sleep, thinking about the Lord and the scriptures I had just been reading—"Let not your heart be troubled: ye believe in God, believe also in me" (John 14:1). I was very sleepy. But something was happening. Something was washing over me. I could feel it, and I opened my eyes to look. I could see nothing in the dark. But I tingled all over, and I knew what it was. It was the love and the peace of Jesus. It was washing over me, more intensely than on the night of my conversion. I was floating, but when I opened my eyes I was still in bed. But I knew I was floating. I began to feel a rising sensation, as though I were rising in an elevator.

I immediately thought of another scripture I had read in the last few days—something about testing the spirits to see if they were from God. So there came another first for me. I thought a second and spoke into the darkness: "If this isn't from God, and Jesus, then I want no part of it and I demand that it stop in the name of Jesus."

I held my breath for a moment. The wonderful rising sensation continued. I was being lifted up in huge, soft hands, higher, higher, and higher. I was like a little baby in its father's hands. This time, I kept my eyes closed—tight. I

247

was rising. "There was never a trip like this," I thought.

Once again, I heard the voice of Jesus. It was unmistakable. But he wasn't talking to me this time. I knew he was talking to the Father. I couldn't understand the words, but I didn't care. I heard other voices—high, tinkling, sparkling voices; low, mellow, rich voices. They were angels, I knew. And they were singing.

I was immersed in love. I knew I was truly loved, and I knew I truly loved. For the first time, I understood love. There was nothing outside it. All that came into it became it.

I remembered nothing else until morning. When I opened my eyes, I saw sunlight, slanting into my room across my face from the window. And I heard myself saying, "Praise you." The love was still there. I loved Pat and Leslie. I loved the staff. For the first time, I was willing to stay in prison as long as God saw fit for me to stay. "I will never worry again about anything concerning my life," I said in my mind.

It was ten days later, and I had finished the Catherine Marshall book. I had never experienced such peace and security as in those ten days. Each day seemed to bring something new—a new understanding, a fresh wave of love for the Lord. I wasn't sure exactly what had happened to me the night I felt I had been lifted up by Jesus into the presence of the Father. But it was good, and I was eager for more. I was still seeking to know more about the baptism in the Holy Spirit.

And that led me into the Hunters' book, *Two Sides of the Coin*. I read carefully of their experiences and was fascinated by the chapter teaching the reader how to receive the baptism in the Holy Spirit and the gift of tongues, which they described as a heavenly prayer language. That sounded good. They even had a prayer asking for the baptism on one page. I prayed it, and waited. Nothing happened. I closed my eyes and waited some more. Nothing. I got uptight then and started to read on, but the next chapter was on "what happens after you receive." I wasn't going on to that until I had been baptized in the Spirit. So I put the book back on the shelf and spoke aloud: "Lord, I'm not reading any further until you answer my prayer."

With that I picked up a book by Andrew Murray on obedience. I read all the next day, sitting in my room, then walking out in the yard, reading as I circled. I had walked a lot of circles in four years and didn't need to watch where I was going. Throughout the reading, I knew obedience was the key to my walk with the Lord. Since infancy, I had been short on obedience. I had rebelled, gone my own way, spat at authority. That had to end.

I finished the book that night, determined to do everything within my power to surrender my entire being—body, mind, and spirit—to the Lord. I immediately remembered a line from some of my recent readings, perhaps the Hunters, about surrendering even the tongue, which the Bible describes as our most unruly organ—a fire, full of deadly poison. That made sense. And that led to thoughts of speaking in tongues and, ultimately, of the baptism in the Spirit.

I began to talk to the Lord. "I'm not going to give up until I have what the Bible—your word—promised me. I'm surrendering everything to you, my tongue included. You can have my voice, my mouth, every single part of me."

Then an idea occurred to me. "Jesus, I'm going to step out on faith. I'm opening my mouth and you'll have to do the work."

In the darkness, I opened my mouth and stuck out my tongue. I wiggled it, and began to make funny noises like a little kid. But the funny noises didn't continue. They shifted, almost like shifting into another gear, and became wordlike sounds. They sounded good, just like words, but I didn't know what they were. They were pretty—fairly low and quite mellow. The gibberish seemed definitely to have turned into a language.

It continued for several minutes and then thoughts came roaring into my mind. "You are playing games, Susan. Stop it. That's just you doing that. What makes you think that's God?" I was knowledgeable enough to recognize Satan. He was shooting lies at me. But, still, I wanted to be sure. So, just as I had ten nights earlier, I spoke a simple prayer, "Jesus, if this isn't you, then I don't want any part of it. Take it away if it's not you."

I waited. And then I began again. It was just as beautiful as before. And then good thoughts began coming into my mind. I began to understand what had been happening to me. It was very clear and positive. Ten nights ago I had received the baptism in the Holy Spirit and hadn't known it. I had truly been lifted up in the hands of Jesus like a baby and immersed in the Holy Spirit. And right before the Father. That's why I had been so swept over with love. I had been swept over with the Holy Spirit, who is God, and God is love, the Bible says. I began to chuckle even as I continued speaking in unknown tongues. "You dummy! You've been seeking and seeking the baptism in the Holy Spirit and you already had it. But now you've got the evidence." I could see it all.

I rolled over onto my back and my hands almost automatically reached toward heaven. I reached right out to God and my new language poured from my mouth, making one more shift after a few minutes. The talking turned to singing. I was singing in that language and it was beautiful. My faith was deep down inside me and it was pouring out.

24

GOING PUBLIC

Several Bible verses had been rattling around in my head since I discovered them three months earlier. One was from Mark 16:16: "He that believeth and is *baptized* shall be saved. . . ." Another came from Peter as recorded in Acts 2:38: "Repent, and be *baptized* every one of you in the name of Jesus Christ for the remission of sins. . . ." And there were others, all adding to my conviction that I wanted to be baptized. And I wanted it the way I believed Jesus had been baptized—by immersion. I couldn't go to the River Jordan, but I wanted it as much like the early church experiences as possible.

I had been baptized as a child, but I was disturbed by the fact that I hadn't known what it meant at that time. Now that I knew more about it, I wanted a believer's baptism by immersion. And *that* would take some doing in the Special Security Unit of a prison.

I talked to Chaplain Waltcott about it, and he said he would be happy to baptize me by sprinkling with water at one of the regular church services. However, when I insisted on immersion, he said he'd help in any way he could, but he wasn't sure how it could be done.

I talked to Stephanie about it, and we agreed to pray. I also mentioned it to the people in SSU and triggered a lot of kidding and joking. A typical remark among residents and staff was, "They ought to dunk her three times and pull her up only twice." I knew a public baptism in that place would take courage that I might not possess. I knew the ridicule would be heavy.

Occurring nearly simultaneously with my yearning for baptism were thoughts about an old friend I hadn't seen in eight years or more—Sargent Wright, the man who had visited and prayed with my mother just before her death. I wanted very much to talk with him. I vaguely thought he might be related to my hopes for baptism. But he had left my hometown and I didn't know where he was. Once again, the chaplain came to my aid and located Sarge for me at a church in Pasadena, not too far from the CIW. I wrote a brief letter to him, explaining that I had come to know Jesus Christ as my Lord and Savior and wanted very much to talk with him.

Sarge's response was immediate and warm. "I'd been thinking about you even before your letter came," he said. "I wasn't all that surprised, therefore, when it came. I want very much to come to visit you."

With the paper work and screening out of the way, the Reverend Sargent Wright was given permission to visit a former member of his church family who had gone so far astray as to land in prison for murder. It's hard to imagine the thoughts that went through his mind as he entered the two massive doors at the entrance to SSU and was escorted into the tiny visiting room.

I had put on my best dress and was nervous and eager. In he came and the sight of him surprised me. He looked less like a minister than anyone I'd seen. He had on blue Levi pants and a Levi jacket, the very picture of informality and the total opposite of the man I had become accustomed to seeing in a long, black robe.

"Hello, Susan." His face was warmer and kindlier than I'd ever seen it. He took my hand, bending forward to kiss me on the cheek.

"Hi, Mr. Wright."

"I'm Sarge," he said. "You remember that, don't you?"

"Yes, but it's been a while."

Sarge, as before, was a warm, gentle man whose strength as a minister was in simply loving people and meeting them where they were, without placing demands upon them. It was extraordinarily easy for me to tell him what had happened to me, even the bad parts. He smiled widely as I told him about accepting Christ and growing closer to him every day. But his happiness was not like mine. It didn't gush all over for everyone to see. He was more like the chaplain. He merely listened, and watched me closely, and let a twinkle play around his eyes. I had expected him to jump up and down with me. But Sarge was even cooler than he had been before. I was beginning to understand something of his maturity and confidence in the Lord, but I still had a tiny speck of trouble with people who could remain so calm while such explosive things were happening before their eyes. I had to settle for knowing that Sarge was rejoicing with me inside.

"Sarge," I said during a pause. "I've wanted to talk to you for sometime now about my mother."

His expression didn't change.

"It's been more and more on my mind, of course, in the last four months, but I have always been curious about it."

"What do you mean, Susan?"

"I mean, about my mother's death—just before she died.

253

It always seemed to me that something happened to her just before she died—about two or three weeks before she died. I came in one afternoon and you were praying with her, and she seemed different after that. Did she accept Christ at that time?"

Sarge put his elbows on the arm of the chair and propped his thumb under his chin. "Yes, Susan, I believe your mother accepted Christ, and I believe she was sincere."

His eyes were very clear, but very tender. "I believe in my heart that she's with Jesus right now."

My eyes didn't remain clear as his had. They filled with tears and I'm sure became red-rimmed. But I smiled. "Praise God," I said softly. "That's the best news I've ever had. I had thought it was so, but I wasn't sure."

I was at mid-sentence when I knew Sarge was the one who should baptize me. I placed both my hands on the table, palms up. "Sarge, I want to be baptized—immersed—and I'd like to have you do it for me. Will you?"

Again, the broad smile. "Will they let you do it?"

"I think so. The chaplain is agreeable. But we'll need a tank or something."

"That's great, Susan. Sure, I'd like more than anything to do it if you can get it approved. You'll have to do some real searching to find a portable tank, but they can be found."

We set a tentative date—February 23—only three weeks away. "I'll keep you posted on the tank," I said.

The date was just four days away when the chaplain called. "We've got a tank," he said. He sounded as excited as I was. "It's being provided by a couple of people involved in the M-2 Program—a Mr. and Mrs. Beckendam—Pete and Carol Beckendam, I think it is."

"Praise the Lord!" I shouted into the phone. "Then we can go ahead on the twenty-third."

"Yes, Susan," he said happily. "We can go ahead."

Sunday morning, February 23, started off just as the previous three days had ended—rainy and foggy. But by 10:30 the fog had burned off, and the day turned bright and sunny. The sky was a sparkling pale blue and every cloud had vanished. By noon, the temperature had reached into the low seventies. What more could I ask? There was an answer to that question—courage. For the first time in four months, I was doubtful and insecure, even after the assurance the Lord had given me so forcefully. I was once again afraid, and at the center of the fear was my old enemy, my image.

In just an hour or two I was going to make a public spectable of myself. I was going to let it be known far and wide that Susan Atkins was one of the Jesus people. A Jesus freak! A sap who couldn't make it on her own. I could hear it. Very few outside SSU knew anything about my conversion, and those who did had not thought much about it either way. But now I was getting ready to let everything show. I was getting ready to say out loud in front, "Jesus Christ is my Lord." Even as I said it that very moment, it was like a blast. That was serious stuff—"Jesus is Lord."

There could be no turning back then.

I knelt beside my bed once again, as I had so many times in those last few weeks. I needed courage to take my stand publicly. "Lord Jesus, I am fully committed to you. You know that. But I'm afraid right now, Lord, about telling the whole world. The whole campus will know in a few hours. Then it will leak outside to the streets, and there will be all kinds of wild stories. Please help me, Jesus."

The struggle was won. Once again, I knew I belonged to Christ. I'd been forgiven and I'd been granted the ability to forgive myself. I had to go with Jesus.

When I arrived at the religious center—the Corral—I discovered that the baptism was to be outdoors and that the tank had been filled with cold water. I shrugged. The Lord had been good in bringing a springlike day in the middle of the winter. He had also been good in performing the impossible feat of opening the prison doors to allow ten people to be present as witnesses. I couldn't believe it, but all of them were there.

The sight of Sarge's wife, Lucille, brought tears to my eyes. She had known me as a child, and I'm sure she had been stunned by my crimes. But her embrace at that moment was strong and genuine.

I was introduced to Mr. and Mrs. Beckendam, who had provided the tank. Their eyes sparkled and danced as they greeted me. There was Stephanie and her mother and Tory, a tennis professional I'd met through the prison program, with her friend, Jan. There was the chaplain, and there was a special older woman named Lois, with whom I'd grown close since my first attendance at the Sunday church services.

"Okay, Susan," Sarge said, "all you have to do is get into this choir robe, and away we'll go."

Then Sarge, the chaplain, and I went into a little room, and they talked to me about water baptism. I heard everything they said, but I had gone over all of it so many times in the last month that I'm afraid very little sank in. Instead, my mind played over and over the notion that I was getting married. "I'm getting ready to say, 'I do' to an eternal life commitment. But I'm saying 'I do' to God. That's something else."

We walked outside. The long white robe flopped around my bare legs. I carefully stepped into the tank, about six feet by three by three, and gasped, but only for an instant. The water was very cold, but in a twinkling it became warm, at least to me. Sarge said it was cold.

"Susan," Sarge's voice was strong in the open air, "have you accepted Jesus Christ as your Lord and Savior?"

"Yes, I have." I kept my voice as firm as I could. "Jesus Christ is my Lord and Savior. I commit myself to following him forever."

Sarge took my left hand in his and I knelt because of the shallowness of the tank. He then placed his right arm across the back of my shoulders and gripped my right upper arm tightly. "I baptize you in the name of the Father, the Son, and the Holy Spirit."

He leaned me forward, and I went under the surface. The water streamed off my face and body as I came up, laughing and crying at the same time. I threw my arms around Sarge, and he joyfully hugged me back.

Being welcomed into the family of God was the neatest experience!

25

TEMPTATION

My escort opened the door to SSU and I walked back into my home, but I don't believe my feet were touching the ground. After my baptism, I was in the clouds even in my dark hole. I was freer than I had been an hour earlier, soaring like an eagle. I understood an often-quoted portion of scripture even better: "Then said Jesus to those Jews which believed on him, If ye continue in my word, then are ye my disciples indeed; and ye shall know the truth, and *the truth shall make you free*" (John 8:31-32).

But the contrast between my own condition and that of the others in the unit, including the staff, was immediately overpowering. As I passed down the corridor, again before ever-watching but silent faces, I felt the cold, hard wall of bitterness. How could I be so free at last in the midst of such unhappiness? I knew why: "Our soul is escaped as a bird out of the snare of the fowlers: the snare is broken, and we are escaped" (Ps. 124:7). I had put my experience out for all to see, and my prison walls had been smashed. I had taken my first step toward becoming a transparent individual.

My conversion, my baptism in the Holy Spirit, and my

water baptism had worked together to prove a very important point about the Christian life to me: The Holy Spirit—the Spirit of Christ—is a missionary spirit. He is concerned about others. That was why I was feeling that wall of bitterness so keenly. That was why I found myself praying day in and day out, with tears flowing constantly, for the salvation of all those around me—Pat, Leslie, the staff, all others whom I encountered irregularly. I often felt an ache in the pit of my stomach for those in my life who did not know the Lord Jesus.

In most cases, all I could do with any consistency was pray, but I had found a new, easy boldness in my steps of obedience to the Lord. I had a willingness to speak the name of Jesus in front of everyone, and I did so whenever I felt the slightest direction from the Holy Spirit.

My words were not always well received. They frequently were thrown right back into my face, now and then with curses and growls. But criticism and condemnation rolled off before any penetration would occur. Again the scripture was supporting my experience and day by day adding to my conviction about the total reality of the Christian life. St. Luke had written so accurately in the first chapter, eighth verse of the Book of Acts: ". . . ye shall receive power after that the Holy Ghost is come upon you: and you shall be my witnesses unto me . . . unto the uttermost part of the earth."

But the total reality of the Christian life—being in the world yet not part of it—had some aspects that I wasn't ready for, despite the biblical warnings about their existence. And I was to learn very quickly two distinct truths: We Christians in ourselves are very frail even when

260

born again and baptized in the Spirit, and the devil, Satan, is a roaring lion, constantly slashing at God's people. I had to learn that temptation and failure do not just automatically vanish.

It was summertime, and I was waiting impatiently at the front-door window of the unit for a staff escort to my daily arts and crafts class, a delightful time of entrance onto the mainline campus for me. He was late.

Ah, there he was! But my heart sank. It was Mr. Adams, the temporary who had made me so uneasy the day before. He had rather rudely said he wanted a cup of coffee and when I'd taken it to him had complained that it was bitter. The old Susan had started to rise in my throat and I could hear the words coming, "If you don't like it, go - - - - yourself." But I had swallowed them quickly and told him I was sorry. Another staff, Mr. Estrat, was walking up the pathway with him.

"Come on, beautiful." It was a sexy voice—a deep baritone. Unfortunately—or fortunately maybe—Adams' overall looks were not quite as stimulating as his voice, which was as seductive as any I'd heard. But he *was* good looking, and his baby-blue eyes were very appealing.

The three of us climbed into the little golf cart that was used to transport residents to distant buildings at CIW. I was sharply aware of the two of them as I squeezed between them, but I quickly turned my mind to what I would be working on at the pottery wheel that day. However, they had other thoughts.

"You'd better be good or we'll take you out in the back of one of these buildings, beautiful, and thump on you." It was Adams. I looked straight ahead.

"I'm always good, and I'm not really in the mood for being thumped on today, thank you very much. Besides, I don't fool around like that—any more."

"What do you mean, 'fool around,' Susan?" Adams pressed on sarcastically. "I'm not talking about fooling around, are you, Mr. Estrat?"

The other guard replied, "No, Jack, when we do something it is serious. Right?"

"Right."

I looked first at Adams, who had spoken last, and then at Estrat. "All right, you two, I know when you're jiving and when you're not. And you may be jiving, but I'm not. I honestly don't fool around anymore. I used to when I was out in the free world but since I've been in prison, I haven't fooled around with anybody."

It sounded a bit silly, and they laughed but said nothing. I charged ahead to keep them from mocking me further. "There hasn't been anyone to fool around with really, of course, but since I've found Jesus and he saved my soul, I couldn't think of fooling around with anyone, let alone a married man. The Bible says that is adultery for that man, and I sure don't want to be the cause for any man to go and sin against God—let alone sin against God myself. So please cool the conversation. Okay, Mr. Adams?" I looked at him and then straight ahead again. "I don't play games any more."

Adams said rather softly, and with that seductive tone of his, "So who's playing games?"

I kept quiet and went into the building to work on the ceramic wheel.

The clay lump was being slowly transformed into something resembling a pot, and I watched it intently. Without planning, my eye caught a glimpse of Adams seated on a high stool over near the window. He was silhouetted, and I couldn't see the features of his face. But I sensed I was being closely, curiously watched. It seemed that I could feel his eyes going over my body. I suddenly wished I hadn't worn my cut-off jeans so tight. I hadn't felt that stare in years and I was afraid I might blush, something I hadn't done under the greedy eyes of men since high school days.

To my dismay, I felt something out of the past rising up inside me, wanting to flirt with Adams. "This can't be," I thought. "I'm a new creature in Christ." But it kept rising. It would be so easy to lead him on. "Resist the devil and he will flee from you" (James 4:7). I said the words forcefully within myself. And I quickly turned to a fellow ceramic worker and began to talk to her about the Lord. I'm not sure what I said. I merely talked rapidly, on and on for nearly an hour, until my work on the wheel was finished. As long as I talked about Jesus, the temptation to flirt seemed under control. I mumbled to myself, "Thank you, Lord, for protecting me," as I picked up my sweater and headed back out the door with Adams, who continued to watch me with those hooded, baby-blue eyes all the way back to SSU.

Back in my room, with my door closed, I dropped to my knees by my bed and prayed, "Lord Jesus, please forgive me for even giving a thought to flirting. I put off the old woman and put on the new. It is not I who live but you who live in me." The words, the Bible verses, the sobs poured out of me for several minutes. I stayed in my room the rest of the afternoon and night, turning gratefully to a Christian television station that had become increasingly important to my growth in recent weeks. I had become so addicted to it, in fact, that it had begun to affect my speech patterns when praying or speaking about the Lord. Several of my Christian friends had asked me why I seemed to slip into a Southern accent when praying or praising the Lord. I had never been to the South. It dawned on me one night that I had been learning about prayer and ministry from several television ministers—Pat Robertson, Jim Bakker, Paul Crouch, for example—and they were all from the South. In normal conversation, I sounded like a standard-brand Californian. In prayer, I became a Southerner.

My door lock snapped, and I opened my eyes. Daylight. I looked at my clock. "That's funny. They've unlocked the doors a half-hour early. Praise the Lord! I'll get out and get a cup of coffee and have an extra half-hour for reading. The quiet, early mornings had become especially important to me in my study of the scripture and praying. I usually accomplished a lot before the day's activities began.

I leapt out of bed and was immediately talking to the Lord, bounding out of my room and into the corridor. Violating my custom, I didn't put on my bathrobe but strode out into the hall dressed only in a thin, summer nightie. I flew into the room with a hotplate and found coffee already brewing. That was unusual. It sure smelled good.

Without another thought, I rushed back to my room, grabbed my cup and headed back for the coffee. Then came that low, sexy voice from yesterday. "Bring me a cup, too, Susan."

I wheeled around and there were those baby-blue eyes. I was stunned, and my mouth dropped open. Three seconds passed, and I realized I was standing in front of a clear window. The sunlight behind me provided a detailed silhouette for Adams. He looked unabashedly from my breasts down to my thighs. I felt my face flush, and the blood in my feet seemed to turn to ice water. I felt naked, and embarrassed. I didn't know what to do. Finally, I forced my cold feet to move, and I made it back to my room, grabbing my robe and flinging it around me. My pulse pounded. I had the feeling that I had just made love, and I abhorred it. My

2

1

3

4

5

6

7

8

9

10

11

12

13

14

15

16

17

18

19

20

mind blackened for an instant. I forced the words out: "Jesus, please help me."

From behind me came the voice again. "You look terrible in the morning, Susan." He was blocking the door, and I forced myself to look into his eyes. It was obvious he didn't mean what he had just said. His eyes were all over me until I finally got the robe tied. I tried to force out the words, "Please move out of the way," but nothing came out. Then came the terrible realization, the horrible truth: I was strongly attracted to him. That flash must have reached into my eyes because I knew instantly that Adams recognized it. He moved to the advantage. "So why are you blushing? It's only natural, Susan. You're attracted to me and I am to you." He paused, and smiled. He was attractive. "So now, what do we do?" He put the question bluntly.

I ignored it, and with panic in my voice and eyes, I said, "Ah, Mr. Adams, if you'll excuse me, I'd like to get some coffee please. I don't know what you're talking about."

My lie was obvious, but at least he moved and I went to the coffee. "Jesus, help me," I said to myself again. "I have lust in my heart for a married man. Show me the way out, please, Jesus."

The coffee was warm and good—a bit of reality in a very unreal situation—and I returned to my room, placing the coffee on the desk and crawling back into bed. I picked up my Bible and opened to John's Gospel, staring at the pages without comprehension. My mind was scrambled and I was unable to concentrate. And I needed God's Word more that morning than any other.

"I really should stay in my room," I thought, "but I want to talk to him. Maybe the Lord brought him here for me to witness to. That's it. I'll tell him about Jesus this morning and, 'Lord, please, help him to accept you and to get his eyes off me.' "

It all sounded fine as I rehearsed the thoughts in my mind while getting dressed. The other staff would arrive in a few minutes, and then maybe I could take Adams out into the yard for a talk. "I'll share my story with him."

Something wasn't ringing true, and I knew I should stay in my room that day, reading the Bible and watching TV, but I ignored the warning. After all, wasn't witnessing more important than anything?

"Mr. Adams, would you please open the back door? I'd like to go out this morning please."

Pat and Leslie were stirring as he answered from the end of the corridor. "Just a minute. Let me get my coat." He acted very official, logging my exit in the record book and walking briskly to the back door.

I couldn't look him in the eye. But I had to clear something up. So as we stepped out into the morning air, I talked while looking off at the mountains in the distance. "Mr. Adams, why did you unlock my door so early this morning?"

"My name is Jack, Susan. Please call me Jack, not Mr. Adams. I unlocked your door this morning because I wanted to, and you have no idea how hard it was for me not to go into your room and wake you up myself."

He looked at me. "Do you know you're blushing, woman?"

"Yes, I'm quite aware I'm blushing, and would you please stop talking like that. It isn't right. You're a married man, and on top of that, I don't even know you." How dumb that sounded! Married or single, what did it matter? "Besides, I feel guilty just being out here talking to you."

I sat down at the outdoor table, facing the unit. He sat opposite me. "You don't have to feel guilty," he said softly. "You haven't done anything wrong except to want me, and I want you. There is nothing wrong with that."

He paused. "Susan, believe me, I may be married, but as far as I'm concerned, I'm not sure that piece of paper called a marriage license has any meaning. I don't think I love my wife. And I sure don't want her the way I want you."

"Mr. Adams—Jack, what you're talking about is adultery and lust, and I don't want to be a part of that regardless of whether I want you or not. It isn't right. The Bible calls it sin. God says it's sin. And I'm feeling guilty for even what has happened. I can't help it."

Suddenly, he looked like a little boy. "Susan, guilt is relative. You haven't done anything wrong. Honest, I wouldn't steer you wrong."

There it was again. That old monster—relativism. Hadn't I been down that road enough? No guilt. Everything was relative. Nothing was wrong. That was crazy! God said it was wrong; Adams was trying to say it was not. "But I'm not buying it this time," I thought. "God is right. Adams is wrong."

But then came the old witnessing thought. "I've got to help him see he's wrong. I've got to convince him. Lord, please help me to help him."

I tried to talk, but he wouldn't let me. He turned to flattery, then logic, then innuendo. Where was my witness?

"Excuse me, Jack, I need another cup of coffee. Would you like some more?"

I knew I had to stay out of the mind trap he was laying for me. As I pushed the door open with my foot, returning with a steaming cup of coffee in each hand, I was face to face with him on the doorstep. His grin was the epitome of confidence as I practically fell into his arms. "This is absurd," I thought, "just like one of my old movie scenes from the past. But this man's attractiveness is overpowering me." I was waffling back and forth with the regularity of a pendulum.

I handed him his cup and we returned to the picnic table, still seated opposite one another. He was suddenly very quiet and thoughtful. I stared over the rim of my cup and finally could stand it no longer. "What are you thinking?"

"I'm thinking about how much I could really dig knowing you better, and wishing you were on the streets and not in here."

I let the remark pass and sat silently for several seconds. "Jack, how long are you going to work back here in SSU?"

"Just for today as far as I know. They have me on a relief schedule. Why do you ask?"

"Just curious, that's all." I knew immediately I had given him the idea I wanted him back here. In fact, my emotions were mixed. I was thankful I wouldn't have to endure this temptation for long, but at the same time I was definitely attracted to him.

Pat and Leslie soon came out for their morning walk, laughing and talking. They took one look at us and obviously sized up the situation, walking on by without a word. Right behind them came Mr. Henry to join Adams and me at the table. That gave me an excuse to go back inside. I needed to be alone for a couple of minutes to get my thoughts sorted out, but in my mind was the slightest tinge of hope that Adams would follow me. I was near to slipping out of control. I had read about backsliding, but I had never believed it could happen to me.

In three minutes, he was beside me again in the room where we kept the coffee, asking for a fresh cup. The visiting room was just across the corridor, and SSU was empty. We were alone together. Simultaneously we moved to the visiting room, cups in hand, but instead of sitting at the table, I went to the overstuffed chair near the bookshelf we had been allowed to bring in as the unit rules were eased. I reached for a book of poetry—feminist and counter-culture poetry, entitled *Monster*—and turned to one that looked good at the beginning, trying to ward off what I knew was coming. Before he could say anything, I began to read.

Gulp! I hadn't expected the poem to be so seductive, vulgarly and basely so, in fact. It seemed to invite him to come ahead. And that's what he did, stepping toward me and holding out his left hand, which I—virtually out of control—took with my right hand. He pulled me up to him and kissed me.

A war raged within me, but I wanted to be kissed, even though I knew it was wrong. I had not been held and kissed with such passion in five and a half years. And I returned the kiss with equal passion, frightened that such emotions still churned within me. Suddenly I pulled away, ashamed and conscience-stricken. I grabbed each side of my head and thought I would collapse.

"Susan," Adams said in that soft, low baritone, "this is bigger than either of us, and you know it." There was another class B movie scene! What corn, but there was truth in it.

"Excuse me." I turned and walked quickly out of the room, knowing he would follow me, but by then genuinely hoping he wouldn't. As he stood by my cell door, Pat and Leslie walked into the unit from outdoors and I silently thanked the Lord for the interruption. Capitalizing on the break, I said, "Mr. Adams, would you please excuse me. I would like some privacy."

I shut the door, as though to use the toilet, and collapsed on my bed in sorrow. I just sat, stunned and ashamed, very far from Jesus, I thought. I felt that one kiss—but more than that: lust in my heart for another woman's husband—had separated me from my Savior. And, tragically, the lust was still there. I felt something toward him, something dark that I didn't want to see in the light. "Oh Father, I feel so dirty again," I sobbed. The cell was quiet. I felt desperately alone, and my insides were full of tightness and pain.

It was after lunch when I asked to be let outdoors again, this time to turn on the sprinklers that watered our lawn and gardens. And, of course, it was Adams, not Henry, who hurried to let me out. I went silently from sprinkler to sprinkler, turning them on, certain that his eyes were watching my every stretching and bending move. The cool water sprayed over the parched grass.

When he opened the door and I brushed past him, fixing momentarily on his blue eyes, I realized my passion for him was not over. The old Susan was gaining the upper hand. I wanted him.

Once again, the unit was empty. Henry had accompanied Pat and Leslie into the backyard, so I led the way once more into the visiting room. I turned to Adams.

"Jack, please sit down. I *must* talk with you."

He sat at the table. I continued standing for several minutes before sitting in the easy chair. "Please listen to me. You've got to understand. I think I could love you, but it wouldn't be a godly love and that isn't good enough. This whole thing is harming your wife, and me—and you, too. So please understand, I can't let this go any farther than it already has, which is too far."

I fixed my eyes upon his. "Do you understand where I'm coming from, Jack?"

He had good timing, keeping me waiting just long enough. "I hear you, Susan, but that doesn't change and can't change what I feel for you. I feel like I'm taking advantage of you, Susan, and I don't want to do that. But what we feel for each other is not wrong and you have not sinned."

270

I interrupted him. "You may think not, but I know better inside my heart."

He started to get up. I shoved out at him with my right hand. "Please. Sit back down. I don't want you to come near me."

"If you don't come to me, then I'm coming to you. Which way is it going to be?"

"You just stay put, Jack. Please."

He crossed the room in one step, placed a hand on each arm of the chair and leaned down to kiss me. Again, I let him, but I fought with all my mental strength to resist. I put my hands on his broad shoulders and shoved. He was much stronger than I, but allowed himself to be pushed away. I looked up at him.

"I don't know if it's you or the fact that I'm just starved for affection. I'm not in any condition to make that determination, Jack. But I do beg you: Please don't do that again. I can't handle the changes. Please respect that."

He hesitated, looking into my face, and then backed away to the chair behind him. "Susan, I'll be leaving here in about ten minutes, and I don't know when I'll see you again, or when I'll be back on the unit for any reason. But please don't forget me. I feel very deeply for you, and I'm sorry that I'm not able to control it. I won't forget you."

There was not a sound in the unit. No man had talked that way to me in years, and my emotions were a mess. I was unhappy—and ashamed.

Keys clicked against the unit door, and it swung open. It was the relief officer. I smiled and said as casually as I could, "Thanks for talking to me, Mr. Adams. It was nice meeting you. See you around."

I walked down the corridor to my room, and the tears were already beginning to streak down my cheeks. Sitting on my bed, I watched from my window as Jack Adams walked away. I was confused and scared.

But I knew what I had to do. I closed my solid door for privacy and fell prostrate on the concrete floor, sobbing bitterly, my insides wrenching until I was afraid I would vomit. I could smell the dust on the floor and knew that I was nothing but a pile of dust, deserving of nothing but discarding.

"Jesus. Oh Jesus, please. I'm sorry. Please forgive me. I know I failed you the first time the going got tough. But I don't want to fail you, Jesus. I want to obey you. Please help me not to fail again. Please forgive me."

The tears and dust streaked the floor. The concrete became cool against my face and my arms stiffened in front of me. I lay unmoving for at least half an hour, perhaps more.

Slowly I lifted myself to my knees and threw the upper half of my body across the bed. I was conscious of calmness inching its way through my body. Quivering and nausea were replaced with stillness. God's peace was once again over me. I knew the presence of the Holy Spirit.

I got to my feet and prepared to face the remainder of the late afternoon and the evening. The pleading had gone from my voice as I said, "Jesus, I know my spirit was wounded today. Please heal that wound, Lord, and make that spot doubly strong so the enemy cannot hurt me there any more. And, Lord, please forgive Mr. Adams. Give me your kind of love for him. I don't like the other kind; it only hurts. Thank you, Jesus. Amen."

26

THE CALL

By June of 1975, the third member of the so-called Manson Family had been converted to faith in Jesus Christ. He was Charles Watson—Tex, although he had dropped all use of his nickname—also serving a life sentence in a California prison for murder. Very little news could have made me happier than the word about him, who I knew had suffered so much for his past.

More than a year after his conversion, I saw him interviewed on television by Chaplain Ray Hockstra of Dallas, Texas, and he was indeed a new creature in Christ. Charles was a new man, God's man. And his love penetrated to the marrow of my bones as I saw and heard him confirm what I had told Chaplain Ray when he visited me earlier—that, despite my lies and doubletalk, I had not actually taken anybody's life with my own hands. I had been unwilling to make such a statement publicly until I had heard my dear brother Charles volunteer that I had done no first-hand killing. I had known that there was no reason for anyone to believe me or for anyone to think I wasn't merely trying to dump everything onto Charles.

This, of course, is not in any way to attempt to deny my guilt in taking part in the 1969 rampage of murder. I deserved my conviction and my sentence. I am grateful to God beyond any ability for expression that he saw fit first to spare me and then to save me. And I am grateful beyond measure for my two brothers in the Lord, Bruce and Charles. It is my prayer each day that all of our colleagues from the past will come to know Jesus Christ as Lord and Savior.

One of my most fervent prayers after my conversion in September, 1974, was that the Lord would open the way for me to be transferred into the general prison population. I desperately wanted out of isolation to try once again to live with other people and to live my new life in Christ to the fullest.

I even went so far as to put the Lord on the spot, in a sense. I was well acquainted with the scripture that declared: ". . . whosoever . . . shall not doubt in his heart, but shall believe that those things which he *saith* shall come to pass; he shall have whatsoever he *saith*" (Mark 11:23). And I tried to adopt that attitude. I began to "confess with my mouth" that Jesus was going to get me out of SSU. My codefendants laughed at me. The staff said I was fanatical. Some said, "Sure, you'll get out one of these days, but it won't be Jesus. It will be simply a matter of time and politics."

But I held on—perhaps a little obnoxiously at times. I would go into my cell and get on my knees. "Jesus, I have been telling people that you are going to open those front doors for me to allow me into the general population. Please hurry up and do it!"

One day came the gentle reminder by the Holy Spirit that the Lord had a perfect time for everything and that I was getting a little too demanding.

But then, finally, came the word: The three of us were to be transferred out of SSU, after four and a half years, into a place called the Psychiatric Treatment Unit. The first stop for every woman from SSU on her way to the mainline campus is PTU. It has a population of about fifty women at a time and the tightest security of any unit short of SSU.

Pat and Leslie were eventually moved out into the regular prison life, but for reasons that were never fully clear to me, my integration into the general population was delayed. I was told, as were others who inquired, that there was widespread agreement that I was perfectly fit and reliable for life among the residents at large. Several members of the staff, when questioned, said without equivocation that they thought my conversion was genuine, that I was fully capable of life with others, that I was in fact the sort of person that they would like to have as a next-door neighbor. One highly placed prison official commented: "We see Susan twenty-four hours a day. She couldn't fake this new life every minute of the day. It has to be real."

But there were always suggestions that I was still a high security risk—a risk of someone doing harm to me perhaps more than my doing something wrong. There apparently was the fear that my reputation and unpopularity still prevailed to a dangerous extent. I was still Sadie Mae Glutz, the murderer of pregnant women, the one who talked to the grand jury. And there was always the question of public opinion generally. My notoriety was still rampant in many parts of the country.

Nevertheless, PTU was a giant step forward from the Special Security Unit, which was ultimately closed down after the infamous Manson women were moved out. There were other women of all kinds, an occupational therapy room directed by a Christian, a TV room and lounge area, a large yard with gardens. But most important were the other people—new faces, new personalities, new things to learn.

The rooms were the same as in SSU but our liberties with them were greater. I was given Room 63B. On the door a card said, "Atkins, Susan." Right beneath it I put a little sign: "Things go better with Jesus."

As in SSU, the room seemed very tiny—again, nine by eleven, but seemingly smaller because of all the things I steadily accumulated. One after another, all from the Lord's people since I had no money and wouldn't be allowed to keep it if I did have, I acquired tons of Christian books, a small battery-powered TV set, a wide variety of clothes (from long, flowing skirts and dresses to jeans and tank tops), two monstrous floppy hats that hang high on the walls, several artistic portrayals of Jesus, Christian banners and signs, and even some goodies to accommodate my unfortunate, but still prevalent sweet tooth. And, of course, there were the single bed, the toilet covered with a big wooden box, the wash basin, a desk with typewriter, and a tall wardrobe.

On those days when my battle against clutter faltered, I found it hard even to turn around in the little cell.

"Hello, Susan; I'm Maureen Rogers."

The tall, blonde staff woman stood at my door, smiling.

"Hi. It's nice to meet you."

"I'm glad you finally got out of SSU," she said, leaning her hand against the doorjamb. "This is going to be a lot better for you."

"I'm sure of it. It's better already."

Her expression turned serious for a moment, and her voice lowered. "I've heard about your finding the Lord."

My heart jumped. She sounded as though she knew what that meant. I could feel my face brightening. "Yes, I finally found him—or he found me, or however."

The woman hesitated. "I just wanted to tell you I'm a Christian, too, and I've really been pulling for you. It's great, what has happened to you."

She paused. "I can't talk too long right now, but I'd like to come back when things quiet down and maybe we can talk some—about the Lord, and things."

"Great! Praise the Lord. I'd like that."

That brief encounter set in motion a series of nightly conversations between Maureen and me that were significant in my young Christian life. Maureen would sit on a chair outside my door after lockup time, talking and listening through the slit. We talked about our own Christian experiences, about our hopes for the future, about our own families. Maureen's husband was paying no attention to the Lord at that time, which brought moments of distress for her.

We would pray for long periods each night, and I would play the autoharp and sing the songs the Lord had been giving to me in the last year.

These nightly times of sharing and growth continued for nine days. On the morning of September 9, I got out of bed and headed for the wash basin, only to notice a note lying in front of the door. It had been dropped through the slit during the night.

I picked it up and unfolded it. My eyes went to the bottom quickly. It was from Maureen.

Susan,

I feel that the Lord would have me share Isaiah

42:6-9 with you. I believe he is speaking to you in a special way (New American Standard Version):

"I am the Lord, I have called you in
righteousness,
I will also hold you by the hand and
watch over you,
And I will appoint you as a covenant
to the people,
As a light to the nations,
To open blind eyes,
To bring out prisoners from the dungeon,
And those who dwell in darkness from
the prison.
I am the Lord, that is My name;
I will not give My glory to another,
Nor My praise to graven images.
Behold, the former things have come
to pass,
Now I declare new things;
Before they spring forth I proclaim
them to you."

Praise God, Susan, He is declaring a new thing for you. You will be a light to the nations and open blind eyes—thus He has appointed us.

Love,
Maureen

"You've got to be kidding, Maureen," I said half-aloud. "*A light to the nations?* From prison? What can that mean?"

One day later I received a letter from Stan Atkinson, a well-known television newsman in California, anchorman on one of the news shows in San Francisco. He said he wanted to interview me about "the past, the present, and the future."

I was momentarily afraid. I quickly prayed, "Father, I don't know what to do about this. I know it may be from you. But you'll have to open the doors for him to get in if you want an interview done."

Such things were unheard of at CIW.

Four days later, Atkinson and his crew arrived for the taping, having been cleared by the prison. I was very nervous but managed to answer his questions about the past. Then came the present and the future, and I blurted it out: "I have accepted Jesus Christ as my Lord and Savior."

There it was! And Atkinson jumped on it, asking for details, kind but typically skeptical . . . for a while. I told him as much as I could in the few minutes we had, and I watched his open skepticism warm up to, if not belief, at least acceptance of what I had to say. We became friends immediately.

The showing of the interview in San Francisco was delayed until late in the month, but aroused enough interest to be syndicated and shown across the country in October. Quite naturally, although it caught me by surprise, a torrent of mail from all kinds of people was set off.

Meanwhile, right after the Atkinson taping, came three consecutive Sundays of extraordinary significance. First, Don Footitt, a lay minister from Faith Center in Palos Verdes, California, came to CIW to preach at one of our services. He didn't know me, and I didn't know him. But as I sat listening, the spiritual bells began ringing inside me and tears began flowing from my eyes. He preached from Isaiah 42:5-7, covering the same ground that Maureen had addressed: ". . . I the Lord have called thee in righteousness, and will hold thine hand, and will keep thee, and give thee for a covenant of the people, for a light of the gentiles. . . ."

The words were addressed specifically to me, and I knew it. I was new in the world of prophecy, confirmation, and miraculous signs, but I knew beyond question that the Lord was using Mr. Footitt to confirm Maureen's word to me.

The following Sunday he returned, but this time he spoke directly to me: "Susan, God is going to use you in a tremendous way to reach millions with the gospel." The directness of the remark frightened me at first. It didn't make much sense. I was in prison, with no prospects of that changing soon. But I determined to stay open to what the Lord was saying to me.

On the third Sunday, a man and a woman came to minister to our group. But nothing appeared to be directed at me particularly until the point where a fullness and a welling-up began to develop within me. A woman had just spoken to the group. In my spirit I knew she was deeply troubled and that the Lord was going to speak to her. I rose from my chair and, in a new experience for me, addressed the group in unknown tongues. I was trembling all over as I finished. Pausing for perhaps three seconds, I knew I was to bring the interpretation of the tongues and I began to speak. The words flowed smoothly and easily from my mouth and I knew the Holy Spirit was giving them to me. The woman immediately broke under the interpretation, weeping and confessing and calling upon Jesus to meet her need. In a few moments, she seemed to be a changed woman, ready to continue with her ministry.

When I sat down, the woman who had come to minister leaned over and placed a hand on my arm. We didn't know one another, but love and kindness were written all over her face. "God is going to use you to reach millions with the gospel."

There it was again!

In only a few days, I received a letter from a man named John Work of Charlotte, North Carolina. He said he had seen the Atkinson interview and that the Lord had spoken immediately to him to pray for me. Then, he said, came the scriptures Matthew 28:18-20. "They are for you, Susan," he wrote.

> And Jesus came and spake unto them, saying, All power is given unto me in heaven and in earth.
>
> Go ye therefore, and teach all nations, baptizing them in the name of the Father, and of the Son, and of the Holy Ghost:
>
> Teaching them to observe all things whatsoever I have commanded you: and, lo, I am with you always, even unto the end of the world. Amen.

A small group of us had been in a prayer meeting sponsored by Campus Crusade for Christ, which ministers regularly at CIW. We were standing near the control room when suddenly there was a loud commotion from the direction of the Quiet Room, a high security, scary section of PTU where women who lose control of themselves—who flip out—are placed. I went to the door and asked what was wrong.

"She's having a heart attack," a guard said.

I asked if I could go in, and rushed to the woman lying on the floor. I took her head in my lap and stroked it lightly. For reasons that eluded me at the moment, I was completely unafraid. I spoke softly, but audibly, "In the name of Jesus, be healed."

As I said the words, I felt evil all about me. I knew an evil spirit—a demon—was there. I had always felt the presence of demons in the Quiet Room. "You foul spirit," I said firmly, but still softly, "I command you in the name of Jesus to come out of her."

The woman, whose blue eyes had been watching me in terror, instantly collapsed and seemed dead. Someone else shouted, "Her heart's stopped!" I could see she had stopped breathing.

"Lord Jesus," I said louder than before, "she's not breathing!"

As clearly as though the speaker were kneeling right beside me, I heard the words, "Release your faith."

Without hesitating, I spoke again: "In the name of Jesus, be healed and breathe."

The woman gasped and opened her eyes. They were still filled with terror. But she was alive.

A doctor, a Jewish man, had arrived sometime during these tense moments. As he took charge, he looked quickly but intently into my face and said, "Keep praying, girl."

Several of us soon carried the woman to the hospital on a stretcher that had arrived from somewhere. I prayed silently all the way.

Back at the unit some time later, I was in my room praying for the stricken woman when the words came clearly into my mind: "Write to her. Tell her I've healed her."

Within three days, unknown to me, the woman was returned to PTU. I was still praying for her, when again, the words came clearly: "Brandy's down the hall. Go see her."

Sure enough, I found her down the hall. She was well. Even though the Lord had spoken to me, I still had trouble believing it. I'm sure my amazement showed as I went up to her.

"Hello; I'm Susan Atkins."

The pretty, blonde young woman smiled brightly. "I know you. You saved my life."

The smile began to fade as she looked at the floor. "Nobody has ever cared for me before."

"It was God who took care of you, Brandy, not me. He healed you. He loves you. I only prayed."

She was unable to reply for several seconds, but I still wasn't sure she understood. That night, the Lord directed me back to her room, and I talked to her into the night about Jesus and about his saving and healing power. Before I left her room, she had accepted Christ as her Lord and Savior.

Unhappily, Brandy eventually fell away from the Lord and back into her previous sins, although she remained healed of her physical affliction. This caused me great distress and turmoil until the Lord comforted me with the parable of the sower, in which some of the seed fell on rocky ground where there was little earth, springing up into growth only to wither under tribulation or persecution (Matt. 13:5-6, 20-21). "Your task is to sow, not fret over the growth," the Lord said to me.

Cathy was a homosexual and drug addict. Shortly after my arrival at PTU she made advances to me, but I immediately made clear that I was not a lesbian and did not believe in that way of life.

"Cathy," I said, "we cannot be lovers. Instead, let's be friends."

She agreed, and then asked if she could come to my room. As we sat there, I noticed that she never looked in the direction of a picture of Jesus hanging on the wall opposite her. But she expressed interest in the banners and the signs and especially in my books.

"You'll have to come and see my room," she said.

Later, I prayed, "Lord, cover me with your blood and give

me things to say," and I went to Cathy's room. Pictures of naked women covered the walls, and a red light burned.

As we talked, Cathy became very gentle and under urging by me, she began to talk about God. "I just don't feel he could love me," she said. But then she charged right onto the subject of homosexuality. "Is it wrong?" she asked, quite openly. "Is it a sin in the eyes of God?"

"Yes, Cathy," I said. "It is a sin. But it can be forgiven and you can be changed—stopped from sinning—if you want to. Jesus forgives you. He loves you."

She wept softly and put her arm around me. But I didn't feel threatened. It was not a lesbian advance, I was sure.

I began to talk softly. "Cathy, all you have to do is ask Jesus to forgive you. He'll forgive you for the drugs and for the lesbianism. He'll forgive you for all your sins. All you have to do is ask him, and ask him to come into your life. It's as simple as that. He loves you."

An awful sob was wrenched from her insides and she gasped loudly, "Lord, have mercy on my soul." We prayed for a minute or two, and she accepted Christ into her life. She was born again.

This small woman in her thirties, a Mexican-Indian with beautiful skin, who habitually wore tight blue jeans, tee-shirts, and boots, became a new woman. She began to soften, to use makeup modestly, and to enjoy her womanhood. And she pursued the Lord ardently, eventually receiving the baptism in the Holy Spirit alone in her room.

When she was released from prison, an entirely different person walked out the front gate, delivered from one of the most blatant sins found in a women's prison. Lesbianism is rampant, with sixty-five per cent of the women at least occasionally participating and forty-five per cent openly committed to it as a life style. Most of these become lesbians after entering prison, and prison officials seem unable or unwilling to do anything about it. They don't condone it, but they don't condemn it either.

On the main campus at CIW, women frequently manage to sleep together, and lesbian activity is often visible right on the lawns and other places.

Sharon Weston was a young black girl who had once known the Lord, but had slipped into the clutches of legalism and then into deep sin. She had no understanding of grace.

When I first met her, she was a frightful hypochondriac and depressive, who took awesome quantities of drugs each day, and she was even more foul-mouthed than I was in my SSU days. Having just given birth to a baby, she was carrying an enormous amount of fat—altogether, an unusually unlovable human being. But the Lord, after much prayer and waiting, finally gave me an opportunity to minister grace, peace, and joy to her, and her depression lifted. Her language cleared up almost immediately, and she began to care for herself physically, eventually returning to the size ten she had worn years earlier.

Jesus fully healed her, and even the staff had to acknowledge it. Furthermore, before she was released and restored to her family, she was given a beautiful ministry in song.

In my first two years as a Christian, the Lord enabled me to minister to more than one hundred women at CIW. Of these, fifteen prayed the sinner's prayer, accepting Jesus as the Lord of their lives. Of course, I have little knowledge about what ultimately happens to most of them. I can only trust that, having made such a step toward God, they will at least one day follow through on their commitment.

The Lord also gave me the opportunity to minister to members of the staff who had backslidden in their walk with the Lord. What a delight to see them walk away with their faces flooded by desire to return to Christ.

Up to this point, Jesus has given me no set pattern for ministry in prison. I do not preach, but often I'm given a chance to help someone with the Bible, to teach them how to pray, to counsel them about their lives. It's almost always one-on-one with somebody that the Lord places in my path.

And he has very specifically charged me to be aware of every Christian's ministry of love and edification on a day-to-day basis, encouraging women to do right and to see the wisdom of walking with God in love, peace, and joy, rather than battling the establishment in great agony and strife for a whole lifetime and then going to hell. This daily ministry must be one of trying to maintain a spiritually healthy environment and constantly pointing the way to Jesus. Every Christian has the responsibility to say, "Look, Jesus loves you. There are no sins too great to be forgiven. Look at me."

More indirect, but equally rewarding, is the opportunity the Lord has given me to minister to people outside prison. With the publicity regarding my conversion, I began to get mail from Christians and non-Christians alike, some merely in praise of the Lord for the miracle he had done in my life, others in search of help in some form. I carry on a ministry to about fifty people at any one time, and have mail contact with hundreds each year.

One of the most delicate, and often most gratifying, ministries I have been given has been to young people—ones just as I was, the alienated, the desperate, the lost. I receive an amazing amount of mail from youths who still believe that we in the Manson Family did nothing wrong. Despite all the horror that has been brought forth by us and about us, there are still angry, frustrated young people who would join up with a Manson Family in a minute if that were possible.

I respond to every such letter, praying with all my might that the Father will touch these broken, smashed souls and draw them to his Son as he did me. Oftentimes, I am able to develop a running discussion with these kids and have watched them go step by step to conversion. Shades of Bruce!

For now, God has me in this very dark place. He has allowed me to be a light. And I am willing to stay here as long as he wants me to. However, other Christians and I believe the Lord will one day release me from this place and give me a more direct ministry to people of all kinds, but especially to those who are as twisted and lost as I was from my earliest teen years. There are thousands upon thousands who are searching for, and at the same time rebelling against, authority and solidity in their lives. They, as I was, are looking for something that will hold still and be true. They are looking for a *real* family. And they are constantly running into counterfeits in gurus of one sort or another, in drugs, in sex, in mind control, in spiritualism. I ran into, and accepted, the worst counterfeits in modern history. But I also encountered, at long last, the one true, reliable, and unfailing being in the world—Jesus. He delivered me from all the counterfeits. And through him, I found the one true family I had so yearned for—the family of God.

My prayer is that Jesus will see fit to allow me to help in pointing the way from the counterfeits to the truth.

AN INVITATION
TO LIFE

Behold, I stand at the door, and knock: if any
man hear my voice, and open the door, I will come
in to him, and will sup with him, and he with me.

Revelation 3:20

The Bible says: ". . . if thou shalt confess with thy mouth
the Lord Jesus, and shalt believe in thine heart that God
hath raised him from the dead, thou shalt be saved" (Rom.
10:9). If you do not know Jesus as your personal savior but
want to know him and invite him into your heart, then pray
this simple prayer—a transaction between you and God,
who knows all your needs:

God, I'm a sinner. I need the forgiveness for my
sins that you promised in your Word. I believe that
Jesus Christ is your son, that he died for my sins,
that you raised him from the dead, and that he lives
today.

Lord Jesus, I open the door to my heart. Please
come in and forgive me my sins. Be the Lord of my
life.

Thank you, Jesus, for doing what you said you

would. I believe that I am born again, according to your Word. Thank you, Lord, for making the way for me to become a child of God.

Amen

Signed _____
Date _____

After praying this prayer with a sincere heart, please sign it and send it to the New Life Foundation, Cookville, Tennessee 28210.

This book is dedicated to Jesus Christ, without whom its message would have no meaning.

All royalties due to Susan Atkins will go directly to the non-profit Christian ministry, the New Life Foundation of Cookville, Tennessee, for the establishment of a community, known as the First Step, to minister to wayward women:

To open their eyes, and to turn them from darkness to light, and from the power of Satan unto God, that they may receive forgiveness of sins, and inheritance among them which are sanctified by faith that is in me.

Acts 26:18

For information on ministry to young women write:
New Life Foundation
P.O. Box 15291
Charlotte, North Carolina 28210